AUDIT, ACCOUNTABILITY AND GOVERNMENT

FIDELMA WHITE
and
KATHRYN HOLLINGSWORTH

CLARENDON PRESS · OXFORD
1999

Oxford University Press, Great Clarendon Street, Oxford OX2 6DP
Oxford New York
Athens Auckland Bangkok Bogotá Buenos Aires Calcutta
Cape Town Chennai Dar es Salaam Delhi Florence Hong Kong Istanbul
Karachi Kuala Lumpur Madrid Melbourne Mexico City Mumbai
Nairobi Paris São Paulo Singapore Taipei Tokyo Toronto Warsaw
and associated companies in Berlin Ibadan

Oxford is a registered trade mark of Oxford University Press

Published in the United States
by Oxford University Press Inc., New York

British Library Cataloguing in Publication Data
Data available

Library of Congress Cataloging in Publication Data
White, Fidelma.
Audit, accountability and government / Fidelma White and Kathryn
Hollingsworth.
p. cm.
Includes bibliographical references.
1. Administrative procedure—Great Britain. 2. Administrative
agencies—Great Britain—Auditing. I. Hollingsworth, Kathryn.
II. Title.
KD4882.W45 1999
342.41'064—dc21 98–30992
ISBN 0–19–826232–9

1 3 5 7 9 10 8 6 4 2

Typeset by Graphicraft Limited, Hong Kong
Printed in Great Britain
on acid-free paper by
Biddles Ltd., Guildford and King's Lynn

Foreword

The title of this publication, Audit, Accountability and Government, could not have been more apposite to the areas which the Committee on Standards in Public Life, studied in its first three years of business when I had the honour to be its Chairman. Issues of audit, accountability and governance (not to mention government) became a constant theme of our first three years' work.

I cannot claim a total ignorance of finance matters—until I became a judge, I spent my professional career at the tax bar and for some years was a member of an advisory committee run by successive Chairmen of the Board of the Inland Revenue; not to mention my membership of the Sandiland Committee on inflation accounting. However neither I, nor members of my Committee, were specialists on public finance.

The immediate impetus for setting up the Committee on Standards in Public Life, in October 1994, came from events connected with Parliament. But the Committee was not just asked to look at Parliament. It was set up as a standing committee, and was given very wide terms of reference,

to examine current concerns about standards of conduct of all holders of public office, including arrangements relating to financial and commercial activities, and make recommendations as to any changes in present arrangements which might be required to ensure the highest standards of propriety in public life.

Apart from MPs, holders of public office were defined to include Ministers, civil servants and people serving in Non-Departmental Public Bodies— NDPBs or 'Quangos' and local government, but also 'members and senior officers of other bodies discharging publicly funded functions.'

Because our task covered such a wide range of services and types of organization, going well beyond the traditional boundaries of the public sector, it seemed important to us to establish a general framework within which all these bodies could be considered. So the Committee operated from the start with the need for a common approach very much in mind. Moreover it rapidly became clear that this approach, initially suggested by our terms of reference, was of fundamental importance to meet the demands of what Kathryn Hollingsworth and Fidelma White refer to as the 'new public management'.

One of the key results of this new public management has been a steep change in the degree of diversity in our public services. Of course there has always been diversity, but not in recent memory to anything like the extent which exists today and which has largely been maintained with the 1997 Government. The unified public services of the late nineteenth and twentieth centuries have been restructured into forms of provision which are dictated principally by perceived management needs. As a result there is at national level a mixture of government departments, agencies, public boards and sometimes even voluntary organizations involved in service provision; at local level, too, people receive public services from bodies of widely varying structure and status, including once again government agencies as well as elected authorities, statutory boards, contractors, private companies with statutory functions, and voluntary organizations.

These bodies are accountable in a whole variety of ways, sometimes by local routes, and sometimes by national ones; sometimes through statutory obligations to consult and sometimes through informal arrangements; sometimes through local rights of appointment to boards and sometimes not. However efficient these bodies may be as vehicles for providing services, diverse routes towards accountability can create difficulties for the public, for Parliament and for local communities, and may reduce the effectiveness of that external scrutiny which is particularly necessary for appointed bodies. Accountability can be seriously weakened if people do not know who is responsible for the provision of particular services; if they do not know who is in a position to hold the service providers to account—who appoints them, who funds them, who has statutory responsibility for the service; and if they do not know who is empowered to investigate complaints about them or audit their accounts. Diversity in the manner in which services are provided does not necessarily mean that it is essential to have inconsistency in the manner in which service providers are held to account. In fact, the opposite is the case.

It is not just the diversity of mechanisms for providing services to the public that give rise to the need to have strong central frameworks. As well as a diversity of organizations, there is now a greater diversity of culture. People now come into these organizations, at all levels, from different backgrounds and with different ethical standpoints. Just as the organizations are no longer homogeneous, so their directors and employees are more varied. We cannot assume that everyone who joins an organization has assimilated the same moral or ethical code in the home, at school, or through one religion or another. The influences on young people, especially with the spread of the electronic media, have become diverse and international. We cannot assume either that senior managers and directors have been assimilating public service values throughout their careers. They may have values which are valid in one context, but do not transfer without amendment to another context. All these people, high or low, ought to be left in no doubt about the standards of conduct, governance and accountability which are expected of them.

In its first report, the Committee on Standards in Public Life touched on the issue of accountability as one of our seven key 'principles of public life'. The Committee felt that, with so many changes both in structure and in culture, it was important to restate the core values that governed the provision of public services and those who worked in them. We made Accountability one of these seven principles; the others being: Selflessness, Integrity, Objectivity, Openness, Honesty and Leadership. We spelt out the key to public sector accountability as: 'Holders of public office are accountable for their decisions and actions to the public and must submit themselves to whatever scrutiny is appropriate to their office.'

Not only was Accountability one of our seven key principles. Another one, Openness, was directly relevant to issues of Accountability. We explained Openness in the words: 'Holders of public office should be as open as possible about all the decisions and actions that they take. They should give reasons for their decisions and restrict information only when the wider public interest clearly demands.'

In the Committee's Second report, which was published in June 1996, the Committee specifically addressed the issue of accountability in local bodies and set out some overarching principles. First, we said that the elected body which provides the funds must retain responsibility for safeguarding the interests of both the user and the taxpayer regardless of the status of the service provider. We meant by that not just that value for money should be obtained, but that proper standards of conduct, and the type of fair dealing which is expected of public sector providers, must also be required of *all* providers, whether they are commercial bodies within the private sector or not-for-profit bodies.

Second, we believed that the first of these principles could be achieved without putting in place bureaucratic controls that second-guessed the day-to-day management of the bodies concerned. We said that central government should give local bodies which are centrally funded more freedom to respond to the needs of local communities, and instead of imposing bureaucratic central controls should require them to set up better mechanisms of local accountability. In making this recommendation we had very much in mind that a chain of accountability which runs from local bodies up to Parliament and back down again to local communities via their elected MPs is far too long and too easily broken.

Parliament cannot easily hold to account, in any degree of detail, thousands of local bodies which happen to be centrally funded. Nor should it be expected to do so. Effective accountability requires mechanisms appropriate to the bodies concerned, which bring into play those who have reason and incentive to exercise effective external scrutiny, namely the communities in which the bodies operate, and the people who need to use their services. As with conduct, so with accountability. It is important not only to recognize diversity, but also to ensure that there are strong central principles, which lead to consistent standards across the whole range of public services.

This brings me to the general question of Audit. In order for bodies to be properly accountable, clear, independent lines of audit must be established. I know, from comments at the time of publication of our various reports and from views that have been expressed subsequently, that this is an area that many would have wished the Committee on Standards in Public Life to have addressed in more detail. As Kathryn Hollingsworth and Fidelma White demonstrate, that would have taken us into an extremely complex field of study, which we had neither the time nor the expertise to explore.

I believe it is important that issues which go to the heart of the new public management are properly aired. One of the most fundamental amongst these is the question of the ability of the audit institutions to follow public money to its final recipient and to ensure that such money has been spent properly. It is clear from the discussion in this book that the limitation on the role of the National Audit Office in this respect continues to be a matter of lively debate. The debate will be advanced and stimulated by this admirable work.

Lord Nolan of Brasted
Chairman of Committee On Standards in Public Life 1994–1997

Preface

This book is the culmination of four years of research on the constitutional role of public sector audit. The book, and the underlying research on which the book is based, could not have been completed without the help of various people and bodies. The original research team comprised Professor Ian Harden, Fidelma White and Katy Donnelly, as research assistant. When Katy took up a research post with the Constitution Unit in 1995, she was replaced by Kathryn Hollingsworth. The research has benefited from a number of funding sources, namely Sheffield University Research Fund, the Law Department at Sheffield University, and, from September 1995 to March 1998, the Leverhulme Trust (grant reference F/118/AD).

The research was based, to a large extent, on interviews with members and officials from the relevant audit institutions and other interested bodies. We would like to take this opportunity to thank all those who gave freely of their time to agree to be interviewed, and to read and comment on draft chapters. Their input was invaluable.

The focus of the book is on the constitutional role of British central government audit, thereby excluding Northern Ireland. Chapter 7 concerns the Audit Commission's audit role in England and Wales. Local government audit in Scotland is also not considered in this book. These exclusions were based on practical issues such as the limitations of time and funding. There is an obvious need for further research in these areas, particularly as devolution takes shape.

The research has been disseminated in various forms to date. In particular, Chapters 7 and 8 of this book derive from earlier publications in Legal Studies and European Public Law respectively.

We are grateful to Lord Nolan for agreeing to write the Foreword to the book. We are indebted to our publishers and our indexer for their help in many ways. And finally, we must pay a special thanks to Ian Harden who diligently read numerous drafts of chapters and whose helpful criticisms and suggestions were invaluable in producing this book. The shortcomings, oversights and errors in the work are the authors alone.

The book purports to be up-to-date as of 30th June 1998.

Fidelma White &
Kathryn Hollingsworth

August 1998

Contents

List of Abbreviations

AC	Audit Commission
BCC	Budgetary Control Committee (of the European Parliament)
CR	Commission Regulation, 3418/93
C&AG	Comptroller and Auditor General
DA	District Audit
DG	Directorate General or Director General
ECA	European Court of Auditors
FR	Financial Regulation of 21 December 1977
INTOSAI	International Organization of Supreme Audit Institutions
NAI	national audit institution of an EU member state
NAO	National Audit Office
PAC	Public Accounts Committee
RA	Resource Accounting
RAB	Resource Accounting and Budgeting
RRV	Riksrevisionsverket
SAI	Supreme Audit Institution (as defined by INTOSAI)
TEU	Treaty on European Union
TOA	Treasury Officer of Accounts
vfm	value for money

1

Audit, Accountability and Government

In the British constitutional tradition, the 'power of the purse' is central to the ability of Parliament to call government to account. The power of the purse flows from the basic constitutional principle that government expenditure must be authorized by legislation. This forms the basis of requirements of financial control and accountability.

Government's accountability to Parliament for public expenditure is embodied in the Supply procedure. The annual public expenditure process in the United Kingdom can be analysed conceptually in terms of three different levels of decision. First, the total amount of expenditure that can be afforded must be decided. Then, within the ceiling set for total expenditure, choices have to be made between competing priorities. When the money finally comes to be spent, the question needs to be asked: 'Does this particular spending represent value for money in relation to the purpose for which Parliament has provided the money?'

In practice, these decisions are made through a process that has four successive stages:

(1) expenditure planning by the executive;
(2) Parliamentary debate and approval;
(3) spending of the money voted;
(4) accounting for the money spent.

In the first stage, the government determines the total of public expenditure and how the total is to be divided between different priorities. Decisions about total expenditure are made as part of the overall budget planning process within government. This includes longer term expenditure plans, which are rolled forward each year through the Public Expenditure Survey (PES)[1] and published as part of the annual budget documentation. The government's budget planning process also examines revenue and the difference between total expenditure and total revenue (the annual budget deficit or surplus). Increasingly, and despite the United Kingdom's opt-out from the Euro, the budget process has a European dimension, focused on the avoidance of 'excessive deficits'. As

---

[1] See, generally, Thain, C., and Wright, M., *The Treasury and Whitehall: The Planning and Control of Public Expenditure, 1976–1993*, (Oxford: Oxford University Press, 1995).

well as the obligation to endeavour to avoid such deficits, the United Kingdom must submit, and update annually, a convergence programme. The programme is examined, and its implementation monitored, in order to provide an early warning system for excessive deficits.[2]

The spending side of the annual budget is embodied in the Supply Estimates, which subsequently lead to the Appropriation Act. The tax side of the budget eventually leads to the Finance Act. In 1993, the government began to present to Parliament its expenditure decisions alongside its tax proposals in a 'unified Budget'.[3]

The government's expenditure decisions require the approval of Parliament. In practice, this means that they must be explained and debated, but they are rarely, if ever, amended.[4] Procedurally, it is not possible to propose an increase in an Estimate. This reflects the constitutional principle that it is 'the Executive which makes known to the Commons the financial requirement of the Government; the Commons in return grants such aids and supplies as are required to satisfy these demands'.[5] Amendments to reduce an Estimate are in order, but are normally treated as an issue of confidence by government. However, although Parliament does not alter the goverment's spending decisions, the requirement that expenditure must be authorized by law,[6] and the division of the total amount of expenditure into separate 'Votes',[7] are of great constitutional importance.

[2] See Articles 103 and 104c EC; Regulations 1466/97, (OJ 1997 L 209/1) and 1467/97 (OJ 1997 L 209/6). The Regulations are part of the 'Stability and Growth Pact'. See also Resolution of the European Council on the Stability and Growth Pact, OJ 1997 C 236/1. At a domestic level, the government announced in the March 1998 budget that a Code for Fiscal Stability will be given a statutory basis in the Finance Act 1998.

[3] *Budgetary Reform*, Cm. 1867 (1992); see, further, Procedure Committee, *The Unified Budget*, HC 727, 1992–93; Treasury and Civil Service Committee *The Government's Proposals for Budgetary Reform*, HC 583, 1992–93.

[4] Parliament has not rejected a single Estimate put before it since 1919 when the House reduced the Royal Palace's Vote to delete provision for an additional bathroom for the Lord Chancellor in the Houses of Parliament.

[5] *Erskine May's Treatise on the Law, Privileges, Proceedings and Usages of Parliament*, edited by Limon, D. W., and McKay, W. R., (London: Butterworths, 22nd edn., 1997), p. 973. See Standing Order No. 48: This House will receive no petition for any sum relating to public service or proceed upon any motion for a grant or charge upon the public revenue, whether payable out of the Consolidated Fund or the National Loans Fund or out of money to be provided by Parliament, or for releasing or compounding any sum of money away to the Crown, unless recommended from the Crown.

[6] According to *Erskine May*, the requirement of legal authorization of expenditure is 'based on ancient constitutional usage': ibid., p. 734.

[7] There is no specific statutory requirement that there should be separate Votes rather than just a global sum. The form of the Estimates is determined by the form of the Appropriation Accounts prescribed by the Treasury under the Exchequer and Audit Departments Act 1866 (*Erskine May*, ibid., p. 744). As a matter of constitutional convention, changes to the form of the Appropriation Accounts are made only after discussion with the Public Accounts Committee of the House of Commons.

According to Dicey's classical analysis, the 'power of the purse' provides the legal basis for the constitutional subordination of the executive to Parliament.[8] Beyond this fundamental point, however, there are two further constitutional purposes served by Parliamentary involvement in the public expenditure process. The first purpose is to require government to make promises about how the money provided by Parliament will be spent. The Votes represent the government's choice of priorities between competing claims on public resources. As the name implies, each is voted on separately by the House of Commons. The Votes are reproduced in the Appropriation Act and are legally binding. If government subsequently decides to alter the spending priorities embodied in the Votes, it must come back to Parliament for new legislation. The Votes are thus, in effect, a promise by government about how it will use the money provided by Parliament. This is not the only promise made about how money voted by Parliament will be used: our view is that there is also a constitutional convention that expenditure does not rest solely on the authority of the Appropriation Act.[9] While the Appropriation Act represents a *quantitative* allocation of money between priorities (the first promise), permanent legislation is used to provide a *qualitative* definition of the purposes for which government has requested the money from Parliament (the second promise). The second constitutional purpose served by Parliamentary involvement in the public expenditure process is to provide a framework of law which is the basis for financial control, reporting and accountability within government, using 'government' in the broad sense defined below.

These two constitutional purposes can only be achieved if there are appropriate mechanisms to ensure that money is spent in conformity both with the Appropriation Act and with the permanent legislation defining the conditions and purposes of expenditure. Such mechanisms exist at the third stage identified above, that is, when appropriated sums are spent, and at the fourth stage, when spending is accounted for. Once spending has taken place, the money must be accounted for by the department or other spending body and those accounts must be audited. The National Audit Office (NAO), headed by the Comptroller and Auditor General (C&AG), an officer of the House of Commons, reports to the House, normally to the Public Accounts Committee (PAC), on the accounts given by departments and other government bodies of what has been done with the money provided by Parliament.[10] As well as reporting on the accounts, the NAO may also

---

[8] Dicey, A. V., *Introduction to the Study of the Law of the Constitution*, 10th edn., (London: Macmillan, 1959), Ch. X.

[9] See Ch. 4, n. 31 and surrounding text.

[10] See generally, McEldowney, J. F., 'The Control of Public Expenditure', in Jowell, J., and Oliver, D., eds., *The Changing Constitution*, (Oxford: Clarendon Press, 3rd edn., 1995); and

make reports about value for money: that is, the 'economy, efficiency and effectiveness' of the expenditure.[11]

MINISTERIAL RESPONSIBILITY

In the constitutional textbooks, the financial procedures of the House of Commons and the role of the C&AG, the NAO and the PAC are normally subordinated to discussion (now more usually criticism) of ministerial responsibility as the dominant theory of the accountability of government to Parliament. Traditionally, ministerial responsibility for policy and administration encompassed both matters in which ministers were personally involved and those in which they were not. This doctrine enabled the ambiguity of the word 'government' to be ignored. 'Government' can have a narrow meaning in the sense of only elected politicians holding office, that is, ministers; or, it can have a broad sense and include not only ministers but also the whole range of public organizations, such as departments, agencies and non-departmental public bodies, along with the civil servants and other officials who staff them. An effective system of financial control, reporting and accountability is necessary to enable 'government' in this broad sense to deliver the promises for which 'government', in the narrow sense of ministers, especially the Cabinet and the Prime Minister, takes political responsibility.[12]

The traditional analysis tends to understate both the importance of government audit as a basis for ministerial responsibility in terms of substance and the extent to which it represents an exception to the doctrine in terms of procedure. As regards substance, the C&AG's reports examine the accounts of government departments and bodies and the expenditure which they represent, from the perspective of regularity, propriety and value

Harden, I., J., 'Money and the Constitution: Financial Control, Reporting and Audit', 13 (1993) *Legal Studies* 16.

[11] The National Audit Office describes these concepts in the following way. Economy is about minimizing the cost of resources acquired or used while having regard to appropriate quality. Efficiency is concerned with the relationship between the input of goods, services or other results and the resources used to produce the maximum output. How far is maximum output achieved for a given input, or minimum input used for a given output? Effectiveness is concerned with the relationship between the intended results and the actual results of projects, programmes or other activities. How successfully do outputs of goods, services or other activities achieve policy objectives, operational goals and other intended effects? See NAO, *A framework for value for money audits*, (undated); see, further, Ch. 4.

[12] For the distinction between different senses of the word 'government', see Harden, I., 'Regulating Government', 66 (1995) *Political Quarterly* 299; and White, F., Harden, I., and Donnelly, K., 'Audit and Government Accountability—a Framework for Comparative Analysis', Working Paper, No. 2, (University of Sheffield: Political Economy Research Centre and Department of Law), August 1994.

for money.[13] The application of these concepts involves establishing whether rules and principles laid down in advance have been complied with. Hence it has a strong 'legal' flavour. To the extent that the rules and principles are open-textured, their application involves professional judgment. Normally, however, it is the judgment of auditors applying professional audit standards and expertise, rather than that of lawyers applying legal norms and reasoning. From a constitutional perspective, the point is that accountability to Parliament through audit is structured in terms of rules, principles and professional expertise.

As regards procedure, it is the accounting officer rather than the minister who is subject to questioning at PAC hearings. An accounting officer is appointed by the Treasury for every Vote.[14] The long standing practice is that the permanent head of a department (that is, the top-ranking civil servant) is appointed as accounting officer. The chief executive of an agency is normally also appointed as an additional accounting officer. This accumulation of roles reflects the fact that the accounting officer has overall responsibility for the organization, management and staffing of the department as well as for financial procedures and control. The responsibilities of accounting officers are set out in the *Accounting Officer Memorandum*.[15] According to the *Memorandum*, an accounting officer's basic duty is to serve the minister, to whom he is responsible and from whom he derives his authority. The minister is responsible to Parliament for the policies, actions and conduct of the department. However, an accounting officer has a duty to ensure that the appropriate advice is tendered to the minister on all matters of financial propriety, regularity and value for money.[16] Furthermore, the accounting officer has the personal duty of signing the accounts of the department and by virtue of that duty, the further duty of being a witness before the PAC, following a report from the C&AG, on the department's accounts, or the value for money achieved by departmental expenditure.

ACCOUNTABILITY

Both the substantive and the procedural dimensions of audit are essential to effective accountability of government for expenditure. 'Accountability'

---

[13] On value for money see, *supra*, n. 11. The terms 'regularity' and 'propriety' include such matters as whether money is spent for the purposes for which it was authorized by the legislature; whether expenditure conforms with relevant legislation; and whether appropriate administrative procedures have been followed: see, further, Ch. 4.

[14] Exchequer and Audit Departments Act 1866, s. 22; and Government Trading Fund Act 1973, s. 4(6).

[15] See *Government Accounting: a guide on accounting and financial procedures for the use of government departments*, (2 vols., loose leaf) (London: HMSO, 1989 and seven amendments 1989–97), the text of the *Memorandum* follows 6.1.7.

[16] See Ch. 4 on the duty of accounting officers and the Pergau Dam case.

is a notoriously elusive idea, involving different, often overlapping, processes.[17] The first part of this section outlines our concept of accountability. In the next two parts the basic concept is developed into notions of democratic and managerial accountability. In the final part of this section, we argue that an important constitutional feature of government audit is that it provides an organic link between democratic and managerial accountability.

The Fundamental Concept

The concept of accountability implies the existence of at least two actors; a person (A) giving an account and another person (B) who receives it. Accountability consists of two elements:

(1) A's *duty* to render an account to B which discloses, explains and justifies A's conduct; and
(2) *liability* of A to subsequent action by B, in the event that B disapproves of A's conduct. This can also be expressed as B's *power* in relation to A.[18]

The second element is always present in the sense that, at a minimum, B has the power to express criticism of A. However, it is not essential to the concept of accountability that B should have any other power, such as, the power to dismiss A, to impose fines or other sanctions on A, or to direct A to act in a particular way.

Processes of accountability may operate before A acts (*ex ante*) or after the action has been completed (*ex post*). However, the duty to give an account *ex post* will normally have an effect *ex ante* on what A decides to do. This is likely to be the case even if B's power is limited to the expression of criticism, provided that there is a long-term relationship between A and B which A values, or there is the possibility that B's criticisms may influence others with whom A has such a relationship.

So far, we have considered accountability as a two-party relationship. However, third and fourth actors may enter the play:

(1) Where, for example, B lacks the capacity to receive, or to understand, A's account, or to exercise a power in relation to A, it may be that a surrogate (C) acts on B's behalf; and/or

---

[17] See Klein, R., and Day, P., *Accountabilities: five public services*, (London: Tavistock, 1987).
[18] 'Duty', 'liability' and 'power' are here used in the senses defined by Hohfeld, W. N. in Cook, W., ed., *Fundamental Legal Conceptions Applied in Judicial Reasoning and Other Essays*, (New Haven: Yale University Press, 1923). A can be considered 'accountable' for good or satisfactory performance, as well as bad. However, as satisfactory performance is considered the norm, the second element of accountability—A's liability to subsequent action by B—is generally thought of in terms of A's actions being unsatisfactory to B.

(2) B may obtain, from an expert (D), an independent evaluation of the accuracy and adequacy of A's account and/or performance.

Democratic Accountability

Democratic governments claim to be representative of the people they govern and are ultimately accountable to them for their actions. In terms of the categories above, the government, as A, is accountable to the electorate, as B. Democratic accountability acts as both a check on the abuse of the power voters place at the disposal of a government and as a safeguard against bad or ineffective government. Government's liability to render an account of its actions allows the electorate to exercise its power in relation to the government.

The extent to which the electorate can directly exercise power is limited. It can do so through periodic elections (and this also has an *ex ante* influence). Between elections, the electorate has to rely on surrogates to act on its behalf and hold government to account. In the British constitutional tradition, the most significant surrogate is Parliament. Hence, democratic accountability can be seen to embrace both periodic elections in which the electorate, as B, holds government, as A, to account directly, *and* government accountability to Parliament, as C, between elections.

One of the weaknesses of this approach is that it tends to view government as a unitary actor. However, as noted above, government can have at least two different meanings. Government, in the narrow sense described above, consists of ministers who, individually or collectively, may be thought to exercise a form of managerial accountability, as B, over government in the wider sense, as A. Government in this wide sense comprises the variety of bodies of civil servants and other public employees which, in France, is called 'the administration'. It is clear that government in the narrow sense cannot have absolute control over every detail of activities conducted by government in the broader sense. The extent of public activity necessitates the use of delegation and discretion. We will return to this point below. Moreover, government in the broader sense is not really a unitary actor at all but comprises a plethora of bodies including central government departments, non-departmental public bodies, NHS bodies, and local authorities.

Managerial Accountability

Forms of accountability that are internal to organizations constitute managerial accountability. Confusion often results from a failure to understand the relationship between: accountability as a general concept (above);

managerial *control* in organizations; and managerial forms of *accountability*. To avoid such confusion it is helpful to begin with a model in which those at the top of a hierarchical organization give orders controlling the behaviour of those below.

Complete managerial control, in which every aspect of A's behaviour is subordinated to B's direction, would require (i) full *ex ante* accountability of A to B, and (ii) B's unlimited power to intervene to alter what A proposes to do. Whilst this is conceptually possible, neither (i) nor (ii) is feasible in practice. There are very few activities where such detailed monitoring and control would be practical, or possible, and in any case it would be extremely inefficient. In order for an organization to function at all, some *delegation* from B to A must occur.

One form of delegation which has had a disproportionate influence on thinking about accountability is delegation through rules. Here, B ceases to examine A's actions *ex ante* and instead aims to control A's behaviour through making rules and monitoring A's compliance with them *ex post*. In practice, managerial forms of accountability necessarily move away from detailed control and involve the delegation of some discretionary decision-making authority from B to A. Legal theory provides useful insights into understanding the nature of discretion in relationships involving delegation. A basic contrast is that between 'strong' and 'weak' discretion.[19] 'Weak' discretion exists where there are rules and standards which govern A's behaviour, but they cannot be applied mechanically. Instead, they require some exercise of judgment by A. 'Strong' discretion exists where A is entitled to choose which rules or standards to apply.

This approach makes clear that the model of complete managerial control is located at one end of a continuum, the other end of which is the situation in which A enjoys complete 'strong' discretion. In practice, neither of these extremes is often found. For A to have complete strong discretion is rare; there are usually at least some standards that are objectively given. Correspondingly, it is rare for A not to have at least some weak discretion.[20] Real world situations are usually found in the rest of the continuum, which consists of rules that become progressively less complete and precise, shading into standards which become more abstract and vague.

This theory of discretion can be applied to an understanding of accountability. At one end of the continuum, A is bound to apply precise rules and is accountable in terms of such rules. At the other end of

---

[19] Dworkin, R., *Taking Rights Seriously*, (London: Duckworth, 1978), pp. 31–3.

[20] Even where A has strong discretion at the outset, he can be made accountable by requiring him to give reasons for decisions, develop policies, or make rules to govern himself. What K. C. Davis calls 'structuring' discretion: Davis, K. C., *Discretionary Justice: a preliminary inquiry*, (Urbana: University of Chicago Press, 1971).

the continuum, A has discretionary power and is accountable for how that discretion is exercised. Introducing discretion into an understanding of accountability is necessary to produce a useful theory, but it does not simplify matters. Precise rules provide objective norms against which an account given by A can be measured and establish the terms, or language, in which that account should be rendered. The introduction of discretion makes less rigid norms necessary and changes the terms, or language, in which an account is rendered. Correspondingly, once discretion is conferred on A, B's power over A is weakened. B may seek to structure or influence the way in which A exercises discretion, but can no longer require A to comply with a rigid set of requirements.

Audit and Accountability

In terms of democratic accountability, audit provides professionally structured and independent information to a variety of actors in the accountability process. The basic model is: government, A, has a duty to render an account to the electorate, B. Audit fits into this model as D, providing an independent evaluation of the accuracy and adequacy of A's account and performance. However, although the audit institution's findings may be generally available to the electorate, as B, B may not have the capacity or willingness to receive A's account or have only limited means of exercising a power in relation to A. As a result, B may rely on a surrogate, C, to act on its behalf and call A to account. The most obvious example of a surrogate is Parliament calling government to account. Other examples are the courts, the media and interest groups.

However, almost all public sector audit work is concerned with the decisions and activities of government in the broad sense, rather than the narrow sense. The work of public sector audit institutions is therefore also relevant to the internal managerial accountability of government. That is to say, audit is relevant to the process through which government in the narrow sense as B, calls government in the broad sense, as A, to account. Public sector audit therefore potentially straddles the area in which democratic and managerial accountability meet.

One of the key constitutional features of the system of central government audit in Britain is that this potential is realized. When the C&AG and the NAO audit the accounts of central government bodies, they report on the observance of rules: rules which are not so much imposed on government from outside but which government uses to control itself. The system of audit uses *democratic accountability* to Parliament to reinforce self-regulation within government; in particular to enable the Treasury to control departments and to reinforce *managerial accountability* within departments. At the same time, democratic accountability is given real bite; audit allows Parliament to draw aside, at least partly, the veil of min-isterial responsibility and to participate in the process by which govern-ment controls itself.

The same is true of value for money (*vfm*) reports. The NAO provides an independent external evaluation to Parliament of the *vfm* achieved by government. At the same time, *vfm* is a criterion government increasingly uses to evaluate itself. In particular, the pursuit of *vfm* has been a driv-ing force behind the 'new public management'.[21]

THE CHANGING SHAPE OF THE PUBLIC SECTOR

During the past two decades or so, quite fundamental changes have occurred in the public sector and its institutions. These changes reflect a set of ideas which have been labelled the 'new public management' (NPM). Hood identifies seven overlapping aspects of NPM:[22]

(1) an emphasis on management;
(2) explicit standards and measures of performance;
(3) greater emphasis on output controls;
(4) disaggregation of units in the public sector (such as, splitting depart-ments into agencies);
(5) greater competition;
(6) stress on private-sector styles of management practice; and
(7) stress on greater discipline and parsimony in the use of resources.

A number of these aspects of NPM involve the greater use of audit and auditing as a management tool. This involves both an increase in the quan-tity of audit activity and qualitative changes.

In terms of quantity, the creation of executive agencies, for example, has caused an increase in the volume of routine audit work.[23] Each agency is required to submit separate accounts which have to be indi-vidually audited each year, whereas previously there would have been just one set of accounts for the parent department. Furthermore, the NAO, though not in a position to tell the agencies what accounting systems to adopt, has invested a lot of time and resources into communicating to agencies what the NAO's requirements as auditors are.[24]

In qualitative terms, the implications of NPM for public sector audit flow mainly from the introduction of private sector concepts and practices

---

[21] Hood, C., 'A public management for all seasons?', 69 (1991) *Public Administration* 3.
[22] *Ibid.*
[23] See PAC Tenth Report, *National Audit Office Estimate*, HC 207, 1991–92.
[24] NAO, *Annual Report 1992*.

into public sector management. This has led to the widespread use of more commercial style accounts, alongside or sometimes replacing traditional accounts. The culmination of this process is the introduction of Resource Accounting and Budgeting into British central government.[25] Changes to accounting have knock-on effects for audit, as will be explained in detail in Chapters 2, 4 and 6.

However, the most important implications of NPM for audit result from the increase in the number of separate organizational units within the public sector; for example, the setting up of executive agencies. The creation of separate units in the public sector is an explicit recognition that the model of complete managerial control, explained above, does not exist. Equally however, the purpose of NPM is not to weaken the possibility of centralized direction of the public sector, but to shift its focus away from implementation and towards the policy level. Put crudely, the idea is that by stepping back from the details of the day-to-day activity of government (in the broad sense), government (in the narrow sense) can focus on strategic management to achieve its objectives. It is here that audit plays an expanded role. Strategic control is exercised through, for example, setting explicit targets and standards and then monitoring their achievement through performance indicators. Such monitoring of performance is, essentially, audit.

We have already stated our view that a key constitutional feature of the audit of central government in Britain is that it allows democratic and managerial accountability to be mutually reinforcing. At first sight, therefore, the fact that NPM increases the reliance on audit as a managerial tool should not prove disruptive; on the contrary, it goes with the grain of the present system and could enhance its operation. However, by increasing the number and visibility of separate organizational units in the public sector, NPM also makes it more obvious that government in the narrow sense and government in the broad sense are different things. This puts the traditional doctrine of ministerial responsibility under increasing pressure, although—or perhaps because—official acknowledgement that NPM has implications for constitutional accountability has been very limited.[26]

From the perspective of the traditional theory of ministerial responsibility, ministers speak for government as a whole. In terms of the theory of accountability developed earlier in this Chapter, the auditor (D) provides information which Parliament (C) can use to call government (A)

[25] See, further, Ch. 2.

[26] For instance: 'The Government does not envisage that setting up Executive Agencies within Departments will result in any changes to the existing constitutional arrangements . . .'; the Government reply to the Eighth Report of the Treasury and Civil Service Committee, Cm. 524 (1987–88).

to account on behalf of the electorate (B). From a managerial perspective, audit (D) provides information to government (narrow sense) as B, which it can use to call government (broad sense) to account as A. This leads to awkward questions about the relationship between the two perspectives. The delegation of responsibility to separate organizational units and the identification of named officials with specific decisions and activities may result in Parliament calling civil servants directly to account, even though the formal mechanism of accountability remains ministerial responsibility.[27] In terms of public sector audit, the risk is that processes of democratic and managerial accountability might come into conflict, or at least cease to be mutually reinforcing.

A similar risk is presented by the fact that NPM is intended to involve clearer lines of responsibility not just for those implementing policy but for policy-makers themselves. A discerning Parliamentary 'client' for *vfm* audit would want information not only about whether policies have been properly implemented, but also about whether the framework for strategic control is adequate. In making such an assessment the auditor may need to tread carefully to avoid appearing to make judgments about the performance of ministers. In the case of executive agencies, blurred lines of accountability between the parent department and the agency, especially in financial terms, have caused difficulties for the NAO.[28]

CONCLUSION

Constitutional analysis, especially by lawyers, has tended to underplay the significance of audit, especially the role of the C&AG and NAO, in the accountability of government. Our analysis in this book seeks to remedy that. At the same time, it is necessary to examine whether and how audit can continue to play that role following the changes, outlined above, in the operation of the public sector and the structure of its institutions.

As well as recognizing the multi-organizational characteristics of the public sector, analysis of the constitutional role of audit must also take into account that processes of governance are multi-layered. In particular, public money is spent and processes of accounting and audit take place at the level of local government and at the level of the European Union,

---

[27] For example, Ros Hepplewhite, the Chief Executive of the Child Support Agency, became a household name during an inquiry into the CSA by the Social Security Committee and as the result of extensive media attention. It has also become the practice that agency chief executives answer questions from MPs on the operational activities of their agencies.

[28] See Baines, P., 'Financial Accountability: agencies and audit', in Giddings, P., ed., *Parliamentary Accountability: a Study of Parliament and Executive Agencies*, (London: Macmillan, 1995).

dealt with in Chapters 7 and 8 below, respectively. Devolution will add a further layer.

The next chapter lays the groundwork for understanding both the traditional constitutional role of audit and its adaptation to a multi-organization and multi-layered framework of governance by looking, in some detail, at the basic concepts of accounting and audit.

2

Accounting and Audit

INTRODUCTION

We have seen in Chapter 1 how the public expenditure process operates. Once money voted by Parliament has been spent, it must be accounted for and those accounts must be audited. These are two separate processes, and so, in order to understand the constitutional role of audit it is essential that the concepts of accounting and audit are differentiated and examined.[1] This chapter will, therefore, look at the processes of accounting and audit, in the private and public sectors, though the focus is on the public sector. We will consider the different methods of accounting, comparing cash based accounting with accruals accounting, and in particular examine the recent introduction of accruals accounting techniques to British central government. In relation to audit, a number of 'types' of audit are explored, in general terms. The distinctions between: internal and external audit; transactions and systems audit; and financial, value for money, and newer types of audit will be considered.

ACCOUNTING

Accounting traditionally involved recording the financial transactions of an organization in the books of account. The accounting process normally culminates in a financial statement or report. Additionally, non-financial reporting methods are becoming more common. Like audit, accounting methods differ between the public and private sectors. The two sectors will, therefore, be considered separately. But first, it is necessary to look at the accounting techniques which can be adopted, some of which are used in both the public and private sectors. These different techniques determine the way in which income and expenditure is recorded, and at what point in time that information is recorded. They also provide different types of information on capital, assets and liabilities, and budget, for instance. The two accounting techniques with which we are most

---

[1] See section on 'Accountability' in Ch. 1, where the accounting process is represented by A's duty to render an account; and where the audit process is represented by D who provides an independent evaluation of the accuracy and adequacy of A's account and/or performance.

concerned, and which are currently at the centre of a reform process within central government, are cash accounting and accruals accounting.[2] We will consider the differences between these two techniques before looking at private and public sector accounting more generally.

Cash v. Accruals Accounting Techniques

Under cash based accounting, items are brought into account at the time when payments are made or received. Further, there is no accounting for assets and liabilities. Accruals accounting differs from cash accounting in three respects:

(1) it records expenditure and income in the period to which they relate (that is, when costs or revenues are incurred or earned, not when they are paid or received);

(2) it spreads the cost of capital across its lifetime; and

(3) it includes a balance sheet, showing assets and liabilities.

So, for example, assume that a company agrees to buy a computer and that, under the contract, payment is due when the computer is delivered. Under a cash-based system, expenditure on the computer would be recorded when the payment was actually made to the supplier, even if the payment were delayed. The accounts would record the cash flow from the company and nothing more. The computer would not be recorded as an asset: it would effectively disappear from the accounts. In contrast, under an accruals system, the purchase would give rise to an accounting entry when the payment became due.[3] Moreover, the cost of the computer would be spread over its lifetime (for example, three years) using depreciation techniques.[4] In addition, an accruals accounting system involves accounting for physical and financial assets and liabilities, as well as transactions.[5] In particular, these accounts will show depreciation costs and will reflect the cost of capital. Cash accounting, on the other hand, does not provide any information concerning changing asset values or the cost of capital.

Accruals accounting, it is argued, presents a *truer* picture of the cost of activities. It takes into account all economic costs of a particular activity or service, and relates them more directly to any revenues generated by those activities. Moreover, it is stated that the discipline of accruals

---

[2] Other financial accounting techniques include budgetary accounting, commitment accounting and fund accounting: see Jones, R., and Pendlebury, M., *Public Sector Accounting*, (London: Pitman, 4th edn., 1996), Ch. 8.

[3] For accounting purposes, payment normally becomes due when the goods are received: this may differ in time from when the sum becomes legally due, for example.

[4] This corresponds more closely to the approach of economic theory which views the object of the purchase as being not the computer itself but the continuing flow of services it provides.

[5] Note actual cash flows are still recorded in accruals accounts: see below.

accounting encourages good stewardship of assets and liabilities. In contrast, although cash accounting does not provide such information it does have a number of advantages over accruals accounting. First of all, cash accounting is cheaper because it requires less accounting and administrative expertise. Secondly, the accounting statements which it produces are more transparent because they show the movement of cash, making them easier to understand for non-experts. Thirdly, cash accounting is less subjective when compared with accruals accounting which involves judgments being made concerning depreciation costs and the valuation of assets and liabilities.

Generally speaking, private sector accounts are drawn up on an accruals basis. Accruals accounting has been adopted in many parts of the United Kingdom public service, including the NHS, nationalized industries and local authorities, for some time. Executive agencies in central government and most executive non-departmental public bodies also produce accounts on an accruals basis. At central government department level though, cash accounting was the norm until recently. But, accruals accounting has now also been introduced into central government, as part of the 1992–97 Conservative Government's proposals to implement Resource Accounting and Budgeting (RAB).[6] Some central government departments previously produced informal and unaudited 'memorandum trading accounts' to show the true costs of many activities. With Resource Accounting (RA), this information is more systematically and readily available. RA therefore sought to bring central government departments in line with other areas of the public service and with practices in states such as New Zealand,[7] Australia, Spain, Finland, Sweden, Iceland, Canada and the United States where accruals accounting techniques are being developed for use in the public sector.[8] RA will be analysed below and the implication of RA on

[6] *Better Accounting for the Taxpayer's Money: Resource Accounting and Budgeting in Government*, Cm. 2626 (1994) (the Green Paper); and *Better Accounting for the Taxpayer's Money: the government's proposals: Resource Accounting and Budgeting in Government*, Cm. 2929 (1995) (the White Paper). Resource budgeting (RB) involves the extension of accruals techniques to the processes by which public expenditure is planned and controlled (PES) and by which money is voted by Parliament. In this way the Parliamentary system for voting expenditure will be closely aligned with the Executive's own system for control and accounting. The first resource based PES is scheduled for 2000, and subject to Parliamentary approval, the first fully resource based Estimates will be presented for 2001–02. See, further, White, F., and Hollingsworth, K., 'Resource Accounting and Budgeting: Constitutional Implications', [1997] *Public Law* 437; and Shand, D., 'Resource Accounting and Budgeting: The Policy Issues', paper presented to the Public Finance Foundation Conference, (London, 1994).

[7] See Scott, G., et al., 'Reform of the core public sector: New Zealand experience', 3 (1990) *Governance* 138; Boston, J., 'The theoretical underpinnings of public sector re-structuring in New Zealand', in Boston et al., eds., *Reshaping the State: New Zealand's bureaucratic revolution*, (Auckland: Oxford University Press, 1991); and Pallot, J., and Ball, I., 'Resource Accounting and Budgeting: the New Zealand Experience', 74 (1996) *Public Administration* 527.

[8] OECD, *Accounting for What?* (1993).

the audit arrangements in British central government will be considered further in Chapters 4 and 6.

Private Sector Accounting

Accounting in the private sector can be one of two types: management accounting or financial accounting. Management accounting is the activity of providing information to enable management to make efficient decisions as regards the use and allocation of resources.[9] It is not subject to any form of external review, and is directed towards the needs of management. Financial accounting, on the other hand, traditionally emphasized the stewardship function.[10] This reassures the providers of financial resources—the shareholders—that their funds have been spent, by the manager, in accordance with the law and for the purposes intended. Furthermore, managers are expected to be concerned with profit. Hence, the accountability process is also concerned with whether the manager has achieved the objective for the lowest cost possible.[11] A distinctive feature of the private sector, when compared with the public sector, is that in the private sector the bottom line is profit. Accounting and audit in the private sector are both focused on this bottom line.[12] Accordingly, accounts need to be objective in order to provide a reliable check on managers.[13] This objectivity is secured, in part, by requiring financial accounting to comply with a series of legal rules and accounting practices.

The Governance of Private Sector Accounting

The legal basis for financial accounting is contained in the Companies Acts. Prior to the Companies Act 1981, the legal requirements for accounting were restricted to laying down the general rules on the scope of accounts, the requirement to give a 'true and fair' view, and a range of disclosure requirements. The 1981 and 1989 Companies Acts incorporated the fourth and seventh EC Directives which specify the format of the accounts to be presented and the accounting rules to be followed. The 1989 Act also requires a company to state in the notes to the accounts 'whether the accounts have been prepared in accordance with accounting standards'.[14] Accounting standards in the United Kingdom are developed

---

[9] See, generally, Glautier, M. W. E., and Underdown, B., *Accounting Theory and Practice*, (London: Pitman, 6th edn., 1997).

[10] Jones and Pendlebury, *supra*, n. 2, p. 117.   [11] *Supra*, n. 9.

[12] Profit, however, is not a simple concept when, for example, it is taken into account over a period of time.

[13] In *Leech* v. *Stokes* [1937] IR 787, at 832, Meredith J advised that 'the business of an accountant and auditor is innately unsympathetic, and it is liable to suffer in efficiency when undertaken in a more or less obliging and friendly spirit.'!

[14] Companies Act 1989, Sch. 4, para. 36A.

by the Accounting Standards Board and are referred to as Statements of Standard Accounting Practice (SSAPs). The Accounting Standards Board, established in 1990, has its origins in the Accounting Standards Steering Committee (later the Accounting Standards Committee), established in 1970 by the Institute of Chartered Accountants of England and Wales. Before 1970, there were no mandatory requirements, outside of company law, governing the presentation of financial statements. Today, compliance with SSAPs, as set by the Accounting Standards Board, is required for financial statements to give a 'true and fair' view.[15]

Both legal requirements (companies legislation and stock exchange rules) and accounting practices (SSAPs), are encompassed in UK Generally Accepted Accounting Practice (GAAP). GAAP also includes other acceptable principles not contained in the official literature. GAAP guides private sector accounting in the United Kingdom although it has no statutory or regulatory authority. It has been described as a 'dynamic concept which requires constant review, adaption and reaction to changing circumstances'.[16] Its application to central government will be considered below.

Other Accountabilities

The accounting function in the private sector has developed as the concept of accountability has grown. Reporting is now used to provide information to 'stakeholders', as well as showing the accountability and efficiency of the management of the organization to the shareholders. 'Stakeholders' can include employees; suppliers; consumers; local and central government; and the community at large. A result of this wider accountability has been the inclusion of non-financial information in reports in addition to the traditional 'bottom line profit' figures. Nonetheless, the primary duty of managers in the private sector is still seen as increasing profits on behalf of the shareholders. A distinction can therefore be made between accountability, which the manager owes to shareholders, and responsibility, which the manager owes to the stakeholders.[17]

Public Sector Accounting

It is not possible to talk about the public sector as a single entity. The public sector comprises a number of different parts including central

---

[15] Accounting Standards Board, *Foreword to Accounting Standards*, (1993), para. 16.

[16] Davies, M., and Paterson, R., and Wilson, A., *UK GAAP*, (London: Macmillan, 5th edn., 1997), p. 2.

[17] Our definitions of accountability and responsibility should not be confused with those used in relation to ministerial responsibility and accountability. The literature has sought to distinguish between ministerial responsibility and ministerial accountability. See for instance, Scott, R., 'Ministerial Accountability', [1996] *Public Law* 410.

government, the NHS, local government, and nationalized industries. Because of the variations in funding, functions and accountability, each of these parts has its own method of accounting. Further, as noted previously, unlike the private sector which is primarily driven by the profit-motive, there is no similar single objective in the public sector. Instead, there are a variety of objectives depending on the department, authority or body in question. The focus of this part of the chapter is on central government where Treasury rules on regularity, propriety and value for money dominate the nature of accounting.[18]

Resource Accounting in British Central Government

Section 23 of the Exchequer and Audit Departments Act 1866 governs the form of central government departmental accounts. This provision gives the Treasury the authority to 'prescribe the manner in which each department of the public service shall keep its accounts'. The manner prescribed until recently was cash accounting.[19] In 1995, the Conservative Government published a White Paper[20] which, among other things, set out proposals for changing the cash based accounting system, for central government departmental accounts, to a resource based system, which included using accruals accounting techniques similar to those already used in much of the private sector.[21] These proposals were adopted by the Labour administration when it was elected in May 1997. RA was to be implemented in all departments by 1 April 1998. The first year for which resource accounts are to be published and laid before Parliament is 1999–2000.[22] There is to be a two-year period where both appropriation and resource accounts will be run side-by-side and the intent is that appropriation accounts will be discontinued from 2001–02.[23]

RA has two basic components:

(1) accruals accounting techniques; and
(2) a framework for analysing expenditure by objectives, related to outputs.

There are a number of reasons why the Conservative Government wished to introduce RA in central government. First, it offers consistency across the public sector, since many parts of the public sector already accounted on an accruals basis. Consistency is particularly useful between departments

---

[18] For more detail on regularity, propriety and value for money, see Ch. 4.

[19] See *Government Accounting: a guide on accounting and financial procedures for the use of government departments*, (2 vols., loose leaf) (London: HMSO, 1989 and seven amendments 1989–97), 12.2 and 12.6.

[20] *Supra*, n. 6.

[21] A number of other accounts will continue, for the present, to be drawn up on a cash basis: for example, revenue accounts such as the consolidated fund account.

[22] This allows departments to produce resource accounts on a dry-run basis for the financial year 1998–99.

[23] Parliamentary approval will be needed for the discontinuance of appropriation accounts.

and their agencies, the latter having operated on an accruals basis for some time. The Government believed that the relationship between departments and their agencies would be improved if they both operated on the same accounting basis. More generally, the Conservative administration hoped that implementing RA (together with resource budgeting) would achieve improved management and increased value for money for the taxpayer because: it forces decision-makers to focus more on resources consumed and not just on cash spent; it treats capital and current expenditure in a way which better reflects their different economic significance; it encourages greater stewardship of assets and liabilities;[24] and it places a greater emphasis on outputs and the achievement of aims and objectives. In addition, the full cycle of planning, budgeting, monitoring and reporting would be better integrated under RAB.[25]

The departmental resource accounts will form the principal financial report of departments. It will be published annually. There will be one departmental resource account per department, replacing the one appropriation account per Vote, causing a reduction from 111 accounts to 59. The resource account consists of the following:

(1) an Operating Cost Statement, showing the administrative and programme costs of the department's operations;
(2) a Balance Sheet, showing the assets and liabilities;
(3) a Cash Flow Statement, analysing cash outflows by operating and investing activities;
(4) a Summary of Resource Outturn, comparing outturn with the amount voted; and
(5) a Statement of Resources, analysed by aims and objectives.

(1) to (3) correspond to the main financial statements in private sector accounts; (4) and (5) have no private sector parallel.[26] In addition, there will be a statement reporting on outputs and performance: an Output and Performance Analysis. This will accompany the Departmental Resource Account, but will not form part of it, and so will not be audited. This Analysis, and the Statement of Resources (which does form part of the account and so will be audited), are intended to generate information about

---

[24] The Government published the first ever National Assets Register in November 1997 which built upon the assets inventories that departments had been developing as part of RAB. Government departments had previously been required to maintain inventories of assets though these were not valued. Since 1993, the Treasury has encouraged departments to publish information on the value and make-up of their assets holdings, though few did so. The PAC has also called for improved information on assets holdings: see their Eighth Report of 1986–87.

[25] *Supra*, n. 6.

[26] Likierman, A., 'Resource Accounting and Budgeting: Rationale and Background', 73 (1995) *Public Administration* 562, and 'Applying Accruals-Based Accounting and Budgeting to UK Central Government', 4 (1997) *Irish Accounting Review* 55.

value for money. It is notoriously difficult, however, to encompass many public service activities within quantifiable performance measures—that is often why they are in the public sector.[27] On a positive note, the NAO has stated that the integration of performance information with financial statements would help standardize their presentation and assist Parliament to focus on costs and achievements.[28] However, the PAC noted that there was no authoritative body of standards and best practice and so stressed the desirability of ground rules on the admissibility of performance data.[29] For example, there should be consistency in the use of performance indicators so that public bodies cannot pick and choose between different indicators from year to year.[30]

The Governance of Public Sector Accounting

The highest level of guidance is the law. For central government, this is found mainly in rather old primary legislation, namely the 1866 and 1921 Exchequer and Audit Departments Acts. This legislation provides that accounts shall be prepared by those departments which the Treasury directs, and in a manner which the Treasury directs.

In addition to the law, accounting standards and other forms of guidance may apply to central government accounts.[31] Under RA, the rules governing the accounts are based on UK GAAP, the private sector standards, adapted where appropriate to take account of the public sector context, and that of central government in particular.[32] The question of a fundamental difference between private and public sector accounting, and between private and public sector audit remains though. Public sector accounting and audit continue to be distinct from private sector accounting and audit largely because of the requirements of regularity, propriety and value for money, in relation to public expenditure. These terms, which are instruments of both Treasury financial control and Parliamentary accountability, have no private sector equivalent.[33]

---

[27] See Carter, N., and Greer, P., 'Evaluating Agencies: Next Steps and Performance Indicators', 71 (1993) *Public Administration* 407.

[28] NAO, *Resource Accounting and Budgeting in Government*, HC 123, 1994–95, para. 18.

[29] PAC, Fifteenth Report, *Resource Accounting and Budgeting*, 1994–95, para. 2 (xv).

[30] The Treasury has published guidance in this regard: see *Output and Performance Analysis Guidance* (December 1997).

[31] See Henley et al., *Public Sector Accounting and Financial Control*, (London: Chapman & Hall, 4th edn., 1992), Ch. 2.

[32] See p. 17 of the White Paper on RAB, *supra*, n. 6.

[33] The technical difficulties which arise in incorporating private sector accounting techniques into the public sector may reflect a more fundamental incompatibility. An example of a technical difficulty arose regarding the C&AG's opinion on the accounts. Where an account is drawn up on a cash basis, the C&AG is required to certify that he has examined the accounts and to state his opinion whether the account 'properly presents' the expenditure and receipts of a particular Vote. The White Paper on RAB proposed that the C&AG should audit Resource Accounts on a 'presents fairly' basis (also used for local authority audit)

As well as GAAP, there are specific publications which relate solely to central government and the application of RA. Most importantly, there is a Summary of Accounting Policies, accompanied by a more detailed Code of Practice. Both types of guidance are encompassed in the Resource Accounting Reference Manual, issued by the Treasury to all departments. The Conservative Government established a Financial Reporting Advisory Board (FRAB) to advise the Treasury on the application of accounting principles and standards to RA.[34] The Board comprises an independent chairman and eight board members, four of whom are from outside government, thus giving an independent flavour to the work of the Board. Although the Treasury has statutory responsibility for directing the form of accounts, there is a convention that important changes in their form and content are made only with the approval of Parliament, through the PAC. The PAC have made it clear that any proposals for change should first be considered by FRAB. However, FRAB, though independent, has only an advisory role. This may be contrasted with the position in New Zealand, where an independent Accounting Standards Review Board—common to the public and private sectors—exists under the Financial Reporting Act 1993. Similar boards also exist in Canada, the US and Australia.[35] The Treasury stated that once the work on the Referencing Manual was complete, it would review the remit of FRAB and consider whether the review and reporting arrangements provide for sufficient independence. While it is understandable that a government may be reluctant to divest itself of the power to set its own accounting rules, the advantages in terms of greater legitimacy and transparency of an independent body to set accounting standards should not be underestimated.[36]

with an additional reference to the 'propriety and regularity' of the spending. The NAO, the PAC and the Treasury and Civil Service Committee, all favoured the 'true and fair' opinion which is the normal opinion for accounts following GAAP. The Treasury subsequently agreed to this recommendation, thereby avoiding the danger that the NAO might appear to operate below the normal professional standard. See Treasury Minute to the Ninth Report of the PAC, 1996–97, para. 12.

[34] See p. 17 of the White Paper on RAB, *supra*, n. 6. FRAB does not replace the Accounting Standards Board (ASB) Public Sector and Not-for-Profit Committee. Indeed, ASB is represented on FRAB. The Committee oversees the application of ASB principles to the public sector generally. In contrast with FRAB, which was established with a specific remit to advise the Treasury on RA, its role is largely reactionary.

[35] In the USA, for instance, the General Accounting Office, which is responsible for the audit of all levels of government, is also responsible for prescribing the accounting standards and principles for the executive branch, and for setting the auditing standards to evaluate government programs, organizations, activities and functions. This body reports to Congress and is independent from the executive branch. See Government Auditing Standards produced by the US General Accounting Office.

[36] The Treasury has stated that FRAB will continue to keep the Manual under review: see *Resource Accounting and Budgeting: A Short Guide to the Financial Reforms*, (January 1998).

In addition to the external rules of law and external accounting standards there are also internal rules set by the Treasury. Probably the most important source of these rules is *Government Accounting*.[37] It lays down the principles of central government accounting which have been developed over a number of years.[38] It includes a wide range of advice, from important constitutional principles (such as the 1932 PAC Concordat),[39] to what might simply be referred to as 'best practice' for the good administration of government accounting. Explanations of the different types of accounts, the expenditure process, the role of accounting officers and other matters dealing with government accounts, are given. It also defines 'regularity' and 'propriety', the standards against which public expenditure is judged as part of the accounting and audit process.[40] *Government Accounting* is kept under regular review by the Treasury and is subject to amendments: the latest being the seventh in 1997. The exact legal status of the directions and advice given in *Government Accounting* is not clear. It is provided for by the 1866 Act which states that the Treasury can prescribe the form of the accounts. This seems to suggest that it is in fact delegated legislation.

Non Financial Reports

In the public sector generally the use of non financial reports is becoming more common. These reports act as a supplement to financial reports, and provide information concerning the wider impact of a particular scheme or policy. It is important that this kind of information is provided because, unlike the private sector which has a single objective (bottom-line profit), the public sector has a number of objectives, many of which cannot be measured in financial terms. Non financial reporting can include reporting on the social or the environmental impact of an organization, for instance, and the use of performance indicators. Performance indicators in the public sector were largely the product of the Thatcher administrations, although attempts had been made to measure performance for many years before 1979.[41] They were introduced as part of a package of measures designed to increase efficiency in the public sector. Performance indicators were initially used in the nationalized industries which remained after the programme of privatization, where it was seen as desirable to introduce specific targets to compensate for the lack of market forces.[42]

---

[37] *Government Accounting: a guide on accounting and financial procedures for the use of government departments*, (2 vols., loose leaf) (London: HMSO, 1989 and seven amendments 1989–97).

[38] See Foreword to *Government Accounting*.

[39] This records an agreement between the PAC and the Treasury which requires departments to have specific statutory authority for continuing functions in addition to the authority provided by the Appropriation Act: see, further, Ch. 4.

[40] See, further, Ch. 4.   [41] Particularly in the NHS and local government.

[42] See, further, Jowett, J., and Rothwell, M., *Performance Indicators in the Public Sector*, (London: Macmillan, 1988).

The monitoring of performance of organizations has spread from the nation-alized industries to the rest of the public sector—to health, education and local government, for instance. The Audit Commission, the body re-sponsible for the external audit of local government and NHS bodies in England and Wales, has a duty to direct local authorities to publish com-parative indicators of performance on an annual basis.[43] The *Citizen's Char-ter* (1991) brought the concept of performance measurement more firmly into the minds of those in central government. Most departmental and agency annual reports will include non financial information.[44] Agency annual reports, for example, will include information on how well the agency has met the targets which are set in consultation with the minis-ter of the sponsoring department. The Output and Performance Analysis, which is to accompany the new resource accounts, is a further extension of this form of non financial reporting. The validation or audit of this type of information is considered in Chapter 4.

AUDIT

When the accounting process has been completed, an external audit evalu-ates and reports on the accuracy of the account. This is the second stage, and a separate stage, in the process to hold to account those responsible for the management of an organization's finances.

In the private sector, there is a legal requirement, under the Companies Acts, for the accounts of most companies to be audited by an independ-ent auditor.[45] The content of the auditor's report is provided for in sections 235–7 of the Companies Act 1985.[46] Under these sections, the aud-itor must report to members his opinion as to whether proper books of account have been kept by the company and whether the company's bal-ance sheet and profit and loss account are in agreement with the books of account. The auditor must also consider whether the information given in the director's report is consistent with the accounts. If the aud-itor is not satisfied that the accounts comply with the Companies Acts or show a true and fair view of the state of affairs of a company then the auditor has a number of options. If appropriate amendments are not made to the accounts, or if certain information is not available, the auditor

---

[43] See, further, Ch. 7.

[44] For example, the Prison Service Annual Report and Accounts for 1996–97 includes in-formation on the population in the prisons, the number of escapes, the conditions for prisoners, health care and education provided for prisoners and information on returns to the community: HC 274.

[45] Companies Act 1985, s. 384(1).

[46] See Boyle, A. J., and Birds, J., *Boyle and Birds' Company Law*, (London: Jordan, 3rd edn., 1995), p. 404.

may give a qualified opinion on the accounts; as well as qualifying the opinion in his report to members, he may also report to a regulator; or he may be required to report to a regulator whether he qualifies his opinion or not.

In the public sector, the legal basis for central government audit is found in the Exchequer and Audit Departments Acts 1866 and 1921, and the National Audit Act 1983. For local government and the NHS, the relevant legislation is the Audit Commission Act 1998.[47] The detail of this legislation is analysed in Chapters 3–7. But as a preliminary to this analysis certain basic distinctions, often shared by the public and private sectors, need to be made. These distinctions are between internal and external audit; transactions and systems audit; and financial and value for money (or performance) audit. In conclusion, a brief look will be taken at one of the 'newer' types of audit: environmental.

Internal and External Audit[48]

Audit is used to serve two purposes in both the public and private sectors. First, it can act as a tool of management: this is *internal* audit. Internal audit has been described as:

. . . an independent appraisal function within an organization for the review of activities as a service to all levels of management. It is a control which measures, evaluates and reports upon the effectiveness of internal controls, financial and other, as a contribution to the efficient use of resources within an organisation.[49]

Secondly, audit can be used as a form of external review, conducted by an independent auditor in order to hold the organization and its management to account. This is *external* audit. Although the two types of audit serve different purposes and different audiences, they are linked. The purpose of internal audit is to improve value for money, avoid and detect fraud, and check and improve the financial systems. These are not dissimilar from the functions of external auditors, and clearly there is a degree of overlap. This allows the external auditor to rely on the work of the internal auditor if he is satisfied that the internal audit findings are accurate. Therefore, the closer the fit between the internal and external processes the more efficient and effective the latter is likely to be. The independence of audit is explored in Chapter 5 and, as will be demonstrated in that Chapter, both internal and external audit, to be effective, must benefit

---

[47] See, further, Ch. 7.
[48] The internal/external distinction is comparable to the distinction between managerial and democratic accountability analysed in Ch. 1.
[49] See CIPFA, *Statements on Internal Audit Practice—Public Sector*, (1979).

from some degree of independence from the subject of the audit: the auditee. One of the areas where these two types of audit diverge is with regard to their respective audiences. With internal audit, the audience is internal to the auditee; with external audit there is commonly an independent outside audience. However, as will be seen from Chapter 6 (and Chapters 7 and 8, in relation to the Audit Commission and the European Court of Auditors, respectively) the identification of the audience for audit, while vital, is not always a simple task.

In central government, internal audit has become increasingly important. Every government department is now required to have some system of internal audit. Its role is to give assurance to the accounting officer on the adequacy and effectiveness of the internal control systems and the extent to which they can be relied on.[50] External audit of central government is the responsibility of the NAO, headed by the C&AG. The PAC, probably the most powerful of the backbench committees of the House of Commons, also plays an important role in the external audit process. The PAC conducts hearings based on the NAO reports, where it holds those responsible for financial control to account. The accountability is therefore, parliamentary. This is unlike local government, where, for example, legal rules on surcharge, prohibition orders, and judicial review can be used as a means of holding officers accountable.[51]

Transactions and Systems Audit

This distinction is easiest to explain in an historical context. When the position of C&AG was first created under the Exchequer and Audit Departments Act 1866, the number of financial accounts which the C&AG was responsible for auditing was quite small. Therefore, the C&AG was able to undertake what is known as a transactions based audit. Accordingly, *every* item or transaction was checked to ensure that it complied with the relevant governing rules so that the auditor could draw the necessary conclusions and give an opinion on the account. This involved the auditor obtaining high quality direct substantive evidence in order to conduct the audit.

This kind of audit is now virtually impossible in any large organization, such as central government. Instead, today, private and public sector auditors undertake what is called systems based audit. This involves

[50] See, further, Ch. 3.

[51] In the Third Nolan Report, it is recommended that the power of surcharge be abolished and replaced by the criminal offence of misuse of public office: see *Standards of Conduct in Local Government in England, Scotland and Wales*, Cm. 3702 (1997). The DETR, at the time of writing, has published a consultation document which invites views on, amongst other things, Nolan's recommendations to create a misuse of public office offence. See 'Modernising Local Government: A New Ethical Framework', pp. 34–5. See, further, Chs. 6 and 7.

reaching an assurance on the reliability of the internal controls or systems within an organization which have been set up to control the processing of individual transactions. As well as testing the systems, individual transactions are tested and, through using particular sampling techniques, conclusions as to the reliability, or otherwise, of the internal controls and the validity of the underlying transactions can be drawn.

Financial and *VFM* Audit

Financial audit in the private and public sectors are similar, to a degree. External financial audit has been defined as an 'independent examination of, and expression of opinion on, the financial statements of an enterprise'.[52] This is sometimes referred to, in the public sector, as 'certification audit' because it involves the auditor giving a certified opinion on the state of the account. However, public sector financial audit goes further than in the private sector to examine whether money has been spent for the purposes intended by Parliament and whether the expenditure conforms with the authority governing it (the requirements of regularity and propriety).[53]

Value for money (*vfm*) audit is unique to the public sector in the sense that it is an essential part of the C&AG's statutory responsibility. Although similar work can be, and often is, commissioned by an organization in the private sector, this sort of management consultancy work forms no part of the private sector auditor's statutory duties. The C&AG has only had statutory responsibility for *vfm* audit since the 1983 National Audit Act,[54] but, it is clear that these types of studies were conducted prior to 1983.[55] Prior to the 1970s, *vfm* was regarded as the prevention of wastefulness. Canada was the first country to introduce *vfm* reports in 1973, although it is the United States General Accounting Office which is credited with separating *vfm* into its component parts of the '3Es': economy, efficiency, and effectiveness. The 3Es have various definitions depending upon who is using them. In the context of United Kingdom central government, they are normally defined as follows. Economy is concerned with minimizing the cost of resources acquired or used, having regard to the appropriate quality (spending less); efficiency is about the relationship between the output of goods, services or other results and

[52] Councils of the Institute of Chartered Accountants of England and Wales, the Institute of Chartered Accountants of Scotland, the Institute of Chartered Accountants of Ireland, and the Chartered Association of Certified Accountants, *Explanatory Foreword*, (1980). See, further, Jones and Pendlebury, *supra*, n. 2, p. 205.

[53] For the meaning of these terms, see further Ch. 4.

[54] National Audit Act 1983, s. 6.

[55] One author, a former Assistant C&AG until 1994, claims that the principle of *vfm* can be traced back 800 years: see Dewar, D., 'Value For money audit: the first 800 years', (1985) *Public Finance and Accountancy* 10.

the resources used to produce them (spending well); and effectiveness involves the relationship between the intended results and the actual results of projects, programmes or other activities (spending wisely).[56] Alternatively, economy is concerned with reducing the input; efficiency is concerned with output divided by input (the greater the ratio then the more efficient the policy is) and effectiveness is concerned only with outputs and looks at the success or otherwise of achieving an objective, regardless of how much it cost.[57]

Efficiency, as stated above, is the primary measure in the private sector, and is sufficient to show that the aims of the organization, such as to increase profit, have been achieved. But in the public sector where there are a number of objectives, some of which cannot be measured in monetary terms, it is necessary to look also at economy and effectiveness to determine how well a particular aim has been achieved.

To some extent, the 3Es are mutually supporting. But in certain situations, they may point in different directions. Effectiveness is a particularly sensitive matter because it has the potential to bring matters of policy into account. Assessing effectiveness means asking whether policy objectives are being achieved. Ministers assert that they alone are accountable for policy and hence that auditors should not stray into the policy arena. The 3Es also depend on the existence of clearly defined and coherent objectives. If the objectives of a policy are vague, self-contradictory or unidentifiable, a *vfm* examination can hardly avoid pointing this out. Those with political responsibility for policy matters are unlikely to welcome such criticism. Accusations of trespass into politics are thus a constant risk for public sector auditors who bring *vfm* issues into account.

The National Audit Act 1983 prohibits the questioning of policy objectives by auditors when conducting *vfm* studies.[58] This can cause difficulty when looking at 'effectiveness', in particular. For example, looking at whether a particular course of action was more effective than another, can often be confused with questioning the policy underlying that course of action, rather than the method used to implement the policy. Sir Douglas Henley, a former C&AG (1976–81), pinpoints five possible courses of action which an auditor can take in conducting a *vfm* study:

(1) to question whether the goals which the policy decision are meant to serve have been established;
(2) to examine whether management have themselves established adequate procedures and criteria to assess the effectiveness of their policies;
(3) to quantify the costs of the decision taken;

[56] NAO, *A Framework for Value for Money Audits*, (undated).
[57] *Supra*, n. 2, pp. 222–33.   [58] 1983 Act, s. 6.

(4) to report on whether the goals have in fact been achieved; and
(5) to suggest alternative ways in which the goals might have been more effectively met.

Henley has stated that, in principle, the C&AG's remit would include (1)–(4) of these possible courses of action, but not (5).[59] Accordingly, the C&AG cannot risk being seen to be critical of policy-makers by suggesting alternative ways in which the goals might have been achieved more effectively. It is not clear on what basis the above distinction is made, nor is it certain that this distinction reflects current understanding and practice at the NAO.[60] Nevertheless, the distinction between 'policy' and 'the means of implementing policy', the former being outside the C&AG's remit, the latter being inside the C&AG's remit, remains obscure. It may simply be a matter of presentation. This distinction is addressed further in Chapter 5.

'Performance audit', sometimes used to mean *vfm* audit, can also be used in a more particular sense. In Canada, performance audit is seen to be part of *effectiveness* audit. But, a distinction is made between a systems audit, that is where the systems in place within a department for assessing effectiveness are checked, and actually assessing the effectiveness of a department at achieving its objectives. This latter type of effectiveness audit can be referred to as 'performance audit'. In this sense it may be said that the NAO conducts 'performance audit' since *vfm* audit can encompass both a systems audit and looking at actual effectiveness itself. In the United States General Accounting Office, performance audit includes *vfm* but, in this context, the objectives in performance audits are more comprehensive than those in *vfm* audits.[61] For example, what is called program audit, which along with economy and efficiency audits makes up a performance audit, can in itself include an assessment of whether the objectives of a proposed, new, or ongoing program are proper, suitable or relevant.[62]

The Governance of Auditing in the Private and Public Sectors

Arguably all audit is about making judgments. Today, however, auditors are guided in their work by a series of professional standards, principally Statements of Auditing Standards (SASs), published by the Auditing

---

[59] Henley et al., *supra*, n. 31, p. 259.

[60] It is not uncommon for NAO reports to suggest alternatives to the course of action taken by the government, for instance, see the NAO report *Privatisation of Rolling Stock Leasing Companies*: HC 576, 1997–98.

[61] See General Accounting Office, *Government Auditing Standards*, (1988), pp. 2–3.

[62] Ibid., pp. 2–4.

Practice Board (APB).[63] These standards apply to the private and public sectors where a 'true and fair' opinion is required and they are stated to be mandatory in application. Around 1994, the Central Government Auditing Standards Advisory Panel was established. This is not a subsidiary of the APB, though the APB is represented on the Panel. In February 1996, following a project led by the NAO, the Northern Ireland Audit Office, the Accounts[64] and Audit Commissions, and the Treasury, the Panel published a *Central Government Sector Practice Note—Practice Note 10*, covering the application of individual SASs to government departments, including agencies, trading funds and executive non-departmental public bodies.[65] The Practice Note, which is about 200 pages long, is described as 'persuasive and not prescriptive', and 'is indicative of good practice'.[66] It is supplemental to the relevant SASs. The practice at the NAO is to comply with the Note. The Panel has more recently published a consultation practice note on 'regularity'.[67] *Practice Note 10* is supplemented by a Financial Audit Manual (September 1995) and a number of Field Manuals, and a Value for Money Handbook and Guides (Spring 1997) which are pitched at a lower level of abstraction.

These standards which apply to central government do not apply equally throughout the public sector. Instead, there is considerable divergence between audit frameworks in the United Kingdom in terms of audit scope, appointment of auditors and audit techniques. The Conservative Government's Green Paper, *Governance and Audit*, advocated having different audit frameworks to suit the different constitutional frameworks of, for example, central government, the NHS and local government.[68] In their White Paper, *The Governance of Public Bodies: A Progress Report*,[69] it was proposed that a National Consultative Forum, or Public Audit Forum, would be established to oversee these different frameworks and to bring together the key issues in public sector audit. At the time of writing there was no published remit for the Forum, though there are a number of areas

[63] The APB was established in 1991 by the Consultative Committee of the Accountancy Bodies (CCAB) to advance standards of auditing and associated review activities in the UK and Ireland. The CCAB comprises the six principal accountancy bodies in the UK and Ireland, including the Institute of Chartered Accountants in England and Wales, and the Chartered Institute of Public Finance and Accountancy (CIPFA).

[64] The body responsible for the audit of local and health authorities in Scotland.

[65] *Practice Note 10* does not apply to health authorities or NHS trusts, nor does it apply to local authorities, public corporations or the nationalized industries.

[66] See *Practice Note 10*, (1996).

[67] APB, *Practice Note: The Audit of Regularity in the Central Government Sector*, a consultation draft, (December 1997).

[68] *Spending Public Money: Governance and Audit Issues*, Cm. 3179 (1996).

[69] *The Governance of Public Bodies: A Progress Report*, Cm. 3557 (1997). This was the government's stated response to the *Second Report of the Committee on Standards in Public Life: Local Public Spending Bodies*, Cm. 3270 (1996).

to which it is likely to address itself. In particular, the nature of public sector audit and its distinguishing features, and the meaning of 'propriety',[70] seem two likely candidates. According to Lord Nolan,[71] the Forum will not have statutory powers, but it will have responsibility for establishing some kind of central audit framework, within which the different operational arrangements must work. This would still recognize and allow for the diversity between the different bodies. An alternative approach, would be to have a set of guiding principles and audit standards intended to apply to *all* public sector bodies.[72] Both these approaches share the same, basic, dilemma. Where common standards are stated, they may need to be stated at such a level of abstraction that they have little meaning. Against this, where separate frameworks are allowed to exist, maintaining any essential core of public sector audit becomes very difficult.

Other Types of Audit

Power has described an 'audit explosion' occurring in recent years.[73] He states that we now live in an 'audit society' which is exemplified by the establishment of the NAO and the Audit Commission, as well as the growth in the major accounting firms. The word audit is no longer solely associated with checking the finances of an organization, but is used in a much wider sense to include a general checking of assurances. There are many types of audit: environmental audit; educational audit;[74] and clinical audit,[75] to name but a few examples. It is beyond the scope of this book

[70] See, further, Ch. 4. It may be that the Forum will replace the Central Government Auditing Standards Advisory Panel, in due course.

[71] See Lord Nolan's speech given to the Chartered Institute of Public Finance and Accountancy on 24 February 1997, entitled 'Governance and Audit Matters'.

[72] The USA, for instance, has a set of government auditing standards for all auditors of federal, state or local government organizations, programs, activities and functions. The standards put considerable emphasis on the comprehensive nature of government audit and on co-operation between different sets of auditors and encourages them to rely on each others work to satisfy some of their requirements: see the Single Audit Act 1984.

[73] Power, M., *The Audit Explosion*, (London: Demos, 1995).

[74] Education provides a number of examples of audit, in this wider sense. The teaching and research assessment exercises conducted by the funding councils can be considered examples of audit of the quality of teaching and research output within institutions of higher education. In addition, the Department of Education and Employment has established what it calls a 'Skills Audit'. This was commissioned in the second competitiveness White Paper: *Competitiveness: Forging Ahead*, Cm. 2867 (1994–95) and involves comparing the UK with four other countries at four different levels of skills and education, ranging from basic numeracy and literacy skills, to degree and postgraduate level. See web site: http://www.open.gov.uk/dfee/skills/skills.htm

[75] See, for example, NAO, *Clinical Audit in England*, HC 27, 1995–96; PAC, *National Health Service Executive Clinical Audit in England*, HC 304, 1995–96; Department of Health, *Working for Patients: Medical Audit: Working Paper 6* (1989); and the White Paper, *Working for Patients*, Cm. 555 (1989).

to consider these other types of audit, but one in particular, environmental audit, is relevant because of the establishment of a House of Commons Select Committee on Environmental Audit.

Environmental Audit

In their manifesto, the Labour party proposed that every department should be a 'green' department and that Parliament should have an environmental audit committee. Subsequently, in 1997, the Environmental Audit Select Committee was established with 15 members.[76] It is chaired by an Opposition member and, in addition to the 14 backbench members, the Minister for the Environment has ex officio membership on the Committee.[77] While the Committee can receive written evidence from interested parties as part of its investigation,[78] it does not have a body like the NAO to provide it with expert information. This could hinder the Committee's effectiveness and longer-term success.

Lessons may be drawn from the Canadian experience of environmental audit. In 1992, the Canadian Government produced an environmental strategy for the Office of Auditor General. The Auditor General's 'vision' was that the Office would ensure that, in carrying out its audit responsibilities, it would make a positive contribution to the protection and improvement of the national and global environment. At that time, it was stated that it was unnecessary to introduce an Environmental Auditor General. However, since then, there have been changes to the Auditor General Act 1976–77, and in 1996 a new position of Commissioner of the Environment and Sustainable Development was created.[79] Although the Auditor General had performed over 40 audits, in the previous decade, which had a largely environmental component, it was felt that a Commissioner for the Environment was necessary to encourage stronger performance by the federal government in the areas of environment and sustainable development. The Commissioner's role is to provide Parliament with independent information which enable it to hold the federal government to account for its performance in protecting the environment. The Commissioner also assists the Auditor General with his audit duties in the field of environment and sustainable development.

In addressing the provision of expert information for the House of Commons Select Committee on Environmental Audit, there are at least

[76] See generally, Ross, A., 'Monitoring Environmental Performance in Government: the role of the new Environmental Audit Committee of the House of Commons', [1998] *Public Law* 190.

[77] This is a position similar to that of the Financial Secretary on the PAC. See further Chs. 3, 5 and 6.

[78] See, for example, the Committee's First Report, *Pre-Budget Report*, HC 547, 1997–98.

[79] See s. 15.1(1) and (2), Auditor General Act 1976–77: see, further, web site: http:// www.oag-bvg/coe/html/env_e/menu_e.html

three possible alternative institutional structures from which to choose. First, the C&AG, in addition to his current audit functions, could provide this information to Parliament, through the Audit Committee.[80] This was in effect the original position in Canada, as described above. An alternative would be to establish a separate office of environmental audit, headed by a commissioner with his own staff. A third option would involve a hybrid of the above along the lines of the current Canadian arrangements, whereby a commissioner for the environment could be established to work within the C&AG's Office to assist the C&AG with his audit functions where they relate to the environment. Whether any of these models would prove acceptable to the Government remains to be seen. There is, of course, a fourth alternative. The Environmental Audit Committee may continue to find itself without any dedicated source of expert information.

A recognition of the extent to which audit permeates throughout current society is necessary in order to provide a backdrop for the constitutional role of public sector audit. However, the remainder of the book will draw the focus back to financial and *vfm* audit. The next four chapters concentrate on central government audit, while Chapters 6 and 7 deal with audit at local and European levels, respectively.

---

[80] In the Memorandum submitted by the C&AG to the PAC on the NAO Estimate for 1998–99, it is stated that the NAO plans, for 1998–99 to 2002–03, include some introductory work for the Select Committee on Environmental Audit, though the Estimate does not include provision for any significant increase in the volume of work in this area: see Minutes of Evidence before the PAC, *NAO Estimate*, HC 383, 1997–98.

3

The Framework of Central Government Audit

THE ORIGINS OF AUDIT[1]

The origins of public sector audit in Britain date to the fourteenth century. Until 1866, two separate offices existed—the Audit Office and the Exchequer Office. The Audit Office had its origins in the Auditors of the Imprest Office which was created in 1559 and abolished in 1785 when it was replaced by the Office for Auditing the Public Accounts. The Audit Office comprised a number of Commissioners. During the nineteenth century the size of this Office increased as it took over responsibility for other Commissioners, including the Commissioner for Auditing the Accounts of Ireland. From 1832 onwards, a system developed whereby the Commissioners reported to the House of Commons on the appropriation accounts (those departmental accounts which recorded the expenditure of voted monies) which they audited and compared with the estimates. The Office of Auditor of the Exchequer can be traced back to 1314. In 1834, the duties of this Office were abolished and a new department, called the Office of Comptroller General of the Exchequer, or more simply, the Exchequer Office, was created. The Head of this Office was the Comptroller General of the Exchequer. The Comptroller General had responsibility for authorizing the issue of public money requested by the government.

GLADSTONE'S REFORMS

During his time as Chancellor of the Exchequer, Gladstone recognized the need to transform the system of control of public expenditure in Britain. His primary concern was to save, and account for, every penny of public money. At the same time, Gladstone wanted to improve the material conditions of the country. He aimed to avoid excessive public expenditure, to reduce the level of taxation as much as possible, and to remove all restrictions on trade. He sought to achieve these aims through a series

[1] See generally, Normanton, E. L., *Accountability and Audit in Governments*, (Manchester: Manchester University Press, 1966), p. 14; Garrett, J., and Sheldon, R., *Administrative Reform, the Next Steps*. Fabian Tract 426 (London: 1973); and Garrett, J., *Westminster, Does Parliament Work?*, (London: Gollancz, 1992), Ch. 6.

of reforms, between 1859 and 1866, designed to create an independent and controlling Treasury, represented at Cabinet level by a powerful 'minister of finance'.[2] Statistics show that Gladstone's plans to reduce public expenditure and taxation were successful. This was accompanied by an increase in national income between 1853 and 1861 of 20 per cent.[3] Gladstone also wanted to ensure that Parliamentary control of public expenditure was real.[4] One of the ways in which Gladstone set about achieving this was the establishment in 1861 of the PAC.[5] The setting up of the PAC followed the recommendation of the Select Committee on Public Monies, which considered the appropriate role of such a body to be the examination, on behalf of Parliament, of annually audited accounts.[6] Five years after the establishment of the PAC, the Exchequer and Audit Department was created.[7] This was an amalgamation of the Exchequer Office and the Office for Auditing the Public Accounts. The Head of this new Department was the C&AG. The establishment of the PAC, and the Exchequer and Audit Department, headed by the C&AG, was the first step towards achieving the financial accountability of modern government.

The full title of the C&AG is the Comptroller General of the Receipt and Issue of Her Majesty's Exchequer and Auditor General of the Public Accounts. As *Comptroller General*, the C&AG authorizes the issue of public money to government departments and other public sector bodies.[8] As *Auditor General*, his statutory duties are to examine and certify the accounts of all government departments and a number of other public sector bodies; and to report the results of his examination to Parliament. Since the National Audit Act 1983, the C&AG has also had statutory powers to conduct value for money (*vfm*) investigations. The office of C&AG as we know it today, and the duties and powers of that office, derive from a number of statutes and reforms dating back to 1866. The most important of these are the Exchequer and Audit Departments Acts 1866 and 1921, and the National Audit Act 1983.[9]

---

[2] See Matthew, H. C. G., *Gladstone 1809–1875*, (Oxford: Oxford University Press, 1988).

[3] Magnus, P., and Murray, J., *Gladstone: A Biography*, (London: John Murray, 1954).

[4] See Mobeley, *Life of W. E. Gladstone, Vol. 1*, (New York: Macmillan, 1905).

[5] The Committee of Public Accounts (PAC) was established under Standing Order 122, now Standing Order 148. This states: 'There shall be a select committee to be called the Committee of Public Accounts for the examination of the accounts showing appropriation of the sums granted by Parliament to meet the public expenditure, and of such other accounts laid before Parliament as the committee may think fit, to consist of not more than 15 members, of whom four shall be a quorum'.

[6] See Wilding, N., and Laundy, P., *An Encyclopaedia of Parliament*, 3rd edn., (London: Cassell, 1968), p. 148.

[7] See the Exchequer and Audit Departments Act 1866.   [8] See, further, Ch. 4.

[9] The substance, but not the precise wording, of the main statutory provisions currently governing audit can be found in the Appendix to *Government Accounting: a guide on accounting and financial procedures for the use of government departments*, (2 vols., loose leaf) (London: HMSO, 1989 and seven amendments 1989–97).

THE EXCHEQUER AND AUDIT DEPARTMENTS ACT 1866

The Exchequer and Audit Departments Act 1866 (hereinafter the 1866 Act) created the office of C&AG to head the newly established Exchequer and Audit Department. The 1866 Act provided for the appointment of the C&AG by the monarch, by convention, on the advice of the Prime Minister.[10] The Exchequer and Audit Department, as a government department, was staffed by civil servants. The Treasury appointed the staff and regulated their number and salaries.[11] In terms of appointment and remuneration therefore, under the 1866 Act, the C&AG and the staff of the Exchequer and Audit Department, were not independent of the executive.

The duties of the C&AG are set out in section 5. This states that the C&AG shall have and perform all the powers and duties conferred or imposed on the Comptroller General of the Exchequer and the Commissioners for Auditing the Public Accounts. Section 22 provided for the examination of all appropriation accounts and set out the annual timetable for their preparation and laying before Parliament. The Treasury was to determine which departments would prepare and render accounts to the C&AG. The C&AG would certify and report upon such accounts and the reports thereon would be signed by the C&AG. Section 27 gave the C&AG the power to examine every appropriation account and ascertain first, whether the payments which the department had charged to the grant were supported by vouchers, or proofs of payment, and secondly, whether the money expended had been applied for the purpose or purposes for which such grant was intended to provide. In theory, the 1866 Act required that *all* transactions should be audited, rather than the systems audit which exists today.[12] The C&AG was given free access, at all convenient times, to the books of account and other documents relating to the accounts of such departments.[13] The Act also provided for the C&AG to report to Parliament on any appropriation account if the Treasury had not done so by the required date. Although the C&AG was to report to Parliament, and the intention was for him to work on behalf of Parliament, he was not an Officer of the House of Commons. Indeed, the Treasury retained many powers of direction over the C&AG and his staff.

THE EXCHEQUER AND AUDIT DEPARTMENTS ACT 1921

The 1866 Act was a vast improvement to the system of audit which had existed previously in Britain. But by 1921, the 1866 Act was considered

---

[10] 1866 Act, ss. 3 and 6.   [11] 1866 Act, s. 8.
[12] See Ch. 2.   [13] 1866 Act, s. 28.

to be out of date. The Exchequer and Audit Departments Act 1921
(hereinafter the 1921 Act) followed a Report of a Committee appointed
to consider the provisions of the 1866 Act.[14] The 1921 Act was intended
to modernize the statutory provisions and to bring them in line with changes
in government. It did not make any radical changes, however.

During the Second Reading of the Bill in the House of Commons it was
stated that the growth of government expenditure since 1866 meant that
the 1866 Act needed to be brought up to date to cope with the then current conditions.[15] Expenditure had increased from £39 million in 1866 to
£669 million in 1921.[16] It was stated, again during the Second Reading,
that the general trend of the changes in the Bill was to give the C&AG
greater discretion in conducting the audit. In particular, it was felt that
the requirement under the 1866 Act to audit every transaction was no longer
necessary.[17] This was because the increase in expenditure made the
checking of every account a more onerous task, and because, it was claimed,
improvements in accounting techniques and the quality of staff resulted
in less mistakes being made in the accounts. In fact, around the beginning of the twentieth century, the C&AG ceased to carry out a 100 per
cent transactions audit of all accounts. Instead, audit staff checked that
each department effectively carried out a detailed audit of vouchers (basically, a type of systems audit). This was supplemented by testing particular
transactions to ensure the effectiveness of the departmental checks. In
addition, the 1866 Act was considered to be out of date because it did
not provide for the audit of new types of accounts which had grown up
since its enactment. Particularly, since the First World War, a number of
new accounts, such as trading accounts, had emerged. New legislation
was therefore necessary to provide the statutory authority to audit these
accounts. Another relatively important change, in constitutional terms,
which needed statutory authority, was the abolition of the post of
Assistant Comptroller and Auditor General.[18] This post was no longer seen
as useful. It was considered more appropriate for the C&AG to be solely
responsible for his department. By abolishing this post the government
also saved a massive £1,600 per annum![19]

Looking more specifically at the 1921 Act, it repealed and amended a
number of the provisions of the 1866 Act. Most importantly, section 1,
which set out the duties of the C&AG, replaced section 27 of the 1866
Act. Section 1(1) states that every appropriation account shall be examined by the C&AG on behalf of the House of Commons, and in the examination of such accounts the C&AG shall satisfy himself that the money
expended has been applied to the purpose or purposes for which the grants
made by Parliament were intended to provide and that the expenditure

---

[14] Cm. 1383 (1921).   [15] *Hansard*, Vol. 145: cols. 1883–1890, 5 August 1921.
[16] Ibid., col. 1883.   [17] Ibid., col. 1884.
[18] 1921 Act, s. 8(4).   [19] *Supra*, n. 15, col. 1887.

conforms to the authority which governs it. This is the C&AG's *regularity* role. Section 1(2) deals with the accuracy of the appropriation accounts. This section allows the C&AG, having satisfied himself that the vouchers have been examined and certified as correct by the accounting department, to rely on the individual department's checking system, without further evidence of payment in support of the charges to which the sums relate. However, if the Treasury required the C&AG to consider the vouchers in greater detail he was required to do so. Together, sections 1(1) and 1(2) constitute what used to be known as certification audit. Section 3 of the 1921 Act required the C&AG to audit certain other cash accounts by direction of the Treasury though the order by the Treasury had to be approved by a resolution of the House of Commons.[20] Section 4 provides for the examination of stock and store accounts and section 5 for the examination of trading, and other accounts, thus providing the statutory authority needed by the C&AG to audit these newer types of accounts. Section 8 of the 1921 Act repealed section 8 of the 1866 Act, which gave the Treasury power to appoint the Exchequer and Audit Department staff. Instead, the 1921 Act allowed the C&AG to appoint his own staff, with the approval of the Treasury. This, in effect, gave the Treasury a veto over the appointment of staff. The Treasury also continued to determine the salaries of the staff.[21]

The 1921 Act went some way to ensure that the audit arrangements in Britain were brought up to date. However, it failed to address the key issue of the independence of the C&AG and his staff. The Act also retained a number of provisions—and created some new ones—which gave the Treasury powers of direction over the C&AG. It is interesting to note that although the C&AG was referred to as a servant of the House of Commons during the debates on the Bill, no reference was made to the subservient position of the C&AG to the Treasury. This was precisely the type of criticism which arose later in the century when, again, the appropriateness of the then existing audit arrangements were brought into question.

THE ORIGINS OF THE 1983 NATIONAL AUDIT ACT

'Big Government'

The Exchequer and Audit Departments Acts 1866 and 1921 dominated central government audit for a large part of the twentieth century. From the 1960s onwards, it became apparent that the existing system was not

---

[20] Subsections 3(3) and 3(4) of the 1921 Act were repealed by s. 14 of the National Audit Act 1983.

[21] 1921 Act, s. 8(2). Subsections 8(1) and 8(2) were, in turn, repealed by s. 14 of the National Audit Act 1983.

meeting the needs of accountable government. During the 1960s, when
the civil service was under examination by the Fulton Committee,[22] criticisms of the role of public sector audit in the British constitution were
raised by Normanton in his 1966 book, *Accountability and Audit in
Governments*.[23] Normanton highlighted many shortcomings in the audit
arrangements of Britain. He argued that the system established by
Gladstone's reforms, to cope with a government which was concerned
with minimizing expenditure and, which spent money primarily on
defence and servicing the public debt, could not cope with 'big government'.[24] 'Big government' arose during the course of the twentieth century when government spending increased and the state became more
involved with public welfare and economic control.[25] Where public
money was spent by a central government department, and thus fitted
within the traditional system of accountability, there were few problems.
However, where public money was spent by other bodies, such as a nationalized industry, which did not match this traditional accountability
model, difficulties arose. This created what Normanton termed a 'crisis
of accountability', which together with a 'crisis of planning', led to a 'crisis of the whole system of financial controls'.[26]

In particular, Normanton pinpointed two aspects of the audit arrangements which needed most attention: the scope of audit; and the quality
of audit. Regarding the scope of audit, Normanton felt that, where public services did not fit neatly within the traditional model of expenditure
and accounting, they tended to escape accountability.[27] Thus, the scope
of the C&AG's audit needed to be widened to capture those other public services and to ensure some degree of accountability. The quality of
audit was also lacking in Normanton's view. Normanton recognized that
'certification audit' was essential to ensure that there was no irregular or
improper spending, though this on its own was too narrow. Normanton
felt that, in addition, audit investigations concerned with the economy,
efficiency and effectiveness of activities should be conducted. If public auditors were concerned only with certification audit then, it was argued,
they were doing little more than the auditors of private companies. Public
audit and accountability should involve more than this. These reforms,
Normanton believed, would result in a massive improvement in the
quality of information provided and an increase in the quality of
accountability achieved.[28] The C&AG had actually conducted investigations concerned with economy and efficiency, particularly during the twentieth century, though during that time they were regarded as a means to
prevent wastefulness, rather than the economy, efficiency and effective-

---

[22] See the Fulton Report, Cm. 3638 (1968).   [23] See, *supra*, n. 1.
[24] *Supra*, n. 1, p. 9.   [25] Ibid., p. 8.   [26] Ibid., p. 10.
[27] Ibid., p. 20.   [28] Ibid., p. 22.

ness audit that we know today.[29] During the period leading up to the 1983 reforms, the C&AG carried out investigations which were actually referred to as value for money studies. However, Normanton felt that it was necessary that this part of the C&AG's functions should be put on a statutory basis along with the certification role.

Additionally, Normanton focused on the constitutional status of the C&AG and his staff, in particular the relationship with the executive, and more specifically, the Treasury. He detailed the ways in which the Treasury could control the C&AG's actions, and showed how, rather than being a servant of the legislature, the C&AG audited on behalf of the legislature *and* the executive. As stated above, the Treasury had powers to define the limits of audit and the form of the accounts on which the audit was based, as well as having responsibility for the staffing of the Exchequer and Audit Department. Normanton saw independence of the state audit institution from the executive as essential. It was the auditor's duty to assess the conduct of financial administration by the executive and accordingly, the executive should not be able to weaken its main critic. The independence of the auditor was seen by Normanton to be akin to the protection of independence which should be afforded to the judiciary. He pointed out that many countries had legislated to ensure the independence of the state auditor from the executive.[30]

Parliamentary Calls for Reform

During the 1970s and 1980s, Normanton's criticisms and concerns were adopted by a number of MPs and Parliamentary committees. Similar complaints to those which were made against the 1866 Act in 1921—that the system was inappropriate for modern day government—were again raised. A number of Parliamentary committees reported on the audit arrangements and made recommendations for change. These included the Expenditure Committee,[31] the Select Committee on Procedure,[32] and, of course, the Public Accounts Committee.[33] Some of these recommendations were addressed in a Green Paper,[34] and later, in a White Paper.[35] Eventually, reforms were implemented in the 1983 National Audit Act.

[29] Dewar, D., 'Value for money audit: the first 800 years', (August 1985) *Public Finance and Accountancy* 10.

[30] For example, the Budget and Accounting Act 1921, ss. 301–314 which secured the independence of the auditor in the USA.

[31] Eleventh Report of the Expenditure Committee, HC 535, 1976–77; and Twelfth Report of the Expenditure Committee, HC 576, 1977–78.

[32] First Report of the Select Committee on Procedure, HC 588, 1977–78.

[33] First Special Report of the Committee of Public Accounts, HC 115, 1980–81; see, further, Treasury and Civil Service Committee Report, HC 236, 1982.

[34] *The Role of the Comptroller and Auditor General*, Cm. 7845 (1979–80).

[35] *The Role of the Comptroller and Auditor General*, Cm. 8323 (1980–81).

Before looking at the 1983 Act, it is useful to consider the debates surrounding the reform proposals. The Committees' concerns were very similar to those which were voiced by Normanton and can be looked at under two main heads: the status of the C&AG and his staff; and the scope of audit. The latter category involves both a consideration of the bodies which should be subject to audit by the C&AG, and the type of audit, that is whether it should include *vfm* investigations.

The Status of the C&AG

Evidence from the then C&AG before the Expenditure Committee stated that the C&AG was not constitutionally a servant of Parliament, though he operated in effect on Parliament's behalf. Despite being seen to operate on behalf of Parliament, a number of concerns were raised about the apparent lack of independence of the C&AG from the executive, in particular the Treasury. In response to this, in the Minutes of Evidence taken before the Expenditure Committee, the C&AG said that the powers of direction which the Treasury had under section 3 of the 1921 Act provided a 'long stop', which would not actually be used to prevent the C&AG from auditing a particular account.[36] However, if a particular body could request the C&AG to look at specific accounts (rather than directing him not to look at specific accounts) this could, in itself, have an adverse affect on his independence. The C&AG would not have complete control over the distribution of audit resources and a consequence of this might be that he would be unable to audit other accounts of his choice. John Garrett MP, in evidence to the Expenditure Committee, said that the C&AG, and the Exchequer and Audit Department, were too close to the executive to act effectively as an independent and authoritative auditor, particularly if there was a move to *vfm* audits.[37] Both the Expenditure Committee and the Select Committee on Procedure[38] recommended that the then existing statutes needed to be amended to provide safeguards against executive control. In particular, Recommendation 49 of the Expenditure Committee stated that the relevant Select Committee of the House of Commons (that is, the PAC) should be consulted about the appointment of the C&AG and suggested that the previous practice whereby a new C&AG was selected from candidates from the Treasury should not be continued.

In their response to the Expenditure Committee's report,[39] the Government said that it would take account of Recommendation 49 and, in future,

---

[36] Minutes of Evidence taken before the Expenditure Committee (General Sub Committee), HC 661, 1977–78, para. 112.

[37] Ibid., para. 127. Presumably there is more concern for the independence of the auditor conducting *vfm* studies because of the greater degree of judgment involved.

[38] *Supra*, nn. 31 and 32.   [39] Cm. 7117.

would consult with the Chair of the PAC before appointing a C&AG. The Government did not accept Recommendation 51 which stated that the C&AG and his staff should be placed under the House of Commons Commission and thus be Parliamentary staff. The Procedure Committee had agreed with the Expenditure Committee that Exchequer and Audit Department staff should be regarded as servants of the House and that the House should be able to request the C&AG to undertake enquiries. The Committees also suggested that Exchequer and Audit Department staff should be available for secondment to help select committees other than the PAC. The Government White Paper of 1981 did not accept that the C&AG should be subject to direction from the PAC, or any other select committee. The Government view was that the C&AG should be independent of any form of external influence or direction. In line with this statement, the Government stated the power under section 3 of the 1921 Act, which gives the Treasury the power to issue directions, should be removed.[40] In addition, the Government said that they would be prepared to consider some form of control by the House of Commons Commission over staffing. The Government also stated that the C&AG's independence would be best safeguarded if he remained an office holder under the Crown rather than becoming a servant of the House.

It was not until the PAC's Special Report in 1980 that the suggestion of establishing a National Audit Office was made by a Parliamentary committee. This was a much more radical suggestion than had been previously put forward in any of the other committees. The PAC recommended that this newly established Office should have responsibility for the audit of all government, local authority and health authority accounts, and that the Office should be financed by a separate vote, thus guaranteeing its financial independence. In addition, the PAC recommended that a Public Accounts Commission be established to appoint staff; to prepare the annual estimate of expenses; to appoint an accounting officer; and to appoint an auditor for the Office. They also recommended that the C&AG should be an officer of the House of Commons. The PAC's recommendations were the closest of any of the committees to what was actually implemented.[41]

The Scope of the Audit

Recommendation 45 of the Eleventh Report of the Expenditure Committee stated:

... the current system of audit is out of date and the Exchequer and Audit Departments Acts should be amended and should state as a principle that the Exchequer and Audit Department may audit any accounts into which public money

---

[40] *Supra*, n. 34.   [41] See below.

goes even if such public money is not the bulk of the receipts into such accounts. Where public money is the bulk of receipts into an account, the Exchequer and Audit Department should always audit them, subject only to such specific exceptions as are made in the amended Act.[42]

The Procedure Committee agreed that the C&AG should be able to examine all bodies in receipt of funds voted by Parliament. However, the Government did not accept this recommendation, because it would mean that the remit of the C&AG's examination rights would be extended to include nationalized industries, local authorities and health authorities.[43] The Government did not think that the cost in setting up this extended system was justified. It also believed that it would not be possible to define in advance those circumstances in which the C&AG should have specific rights of access, and that it was more desirable that this be judged on the merits of each individual case. This was confirmed in the later Green Paper. In the PAC's First Special Report, the question of what accounts the C&AG could examine was again considered.[44] The PAC recommended that, whenever an account is mainly supported from public funds, the C&AG should have the right to audit that body and its accounts should be laid before Parliament. Despite these continuous calls for the extension of the C&AG's remit, the White Paper maintained that the Government did not believe that the C&AG should be able to audit nationalized industries, water authorities or public corporations.

Both the Expenditure Committee and the Procedure Committee further recommended that either the C&AG take over responsibility for the audit of local authorities from the District Audit Service, the body which at the time was responsible for providing auditors to local authorities, or that the Exchequer and Audit Department and the District Audit Service should be amalgamated. The Government disagreed because, it claimed, there was no evidence that the independence of the District Audit Service was not secured under the current system. Also, there would be difficulties in reconciling the constitutional arrangements if the two were amalgamated. Local authorities are not accountable to Parliament, but to the local elector, and so being held to account before the PAC would not have been appropriate. There were also calls for the C&AG to audit the NHS, but again these were rejected by the Government.

The other aspect of the scope of audit is what types of audit should be included in the C&AG's remit.[45] In evidence given to the Expenditure Committee, the C&AG explained that for many years he had in fact conducted *vfm* audits, though he drew a distinction between 'efficiency' audit, which he did conduct, and 'effectiveness' audit, which he did not conduct.[46]

---

[42] *Supra*, n, 31.   [43] *Supra*, n. 39.   [44] *Supra*, n. 33.   [45] See, generally, Ch. 2.

[46] *Supra*, n. 31. In the context of central government, efficiency is concerned with achieving the best outputs for the cost and effectiveness deals with whether the outcomes obtained meet the intended goals.

Recommendation 47 of the Expenditure Committee suggested that the C&AG be empowered to conduct audits of management efficiency and effectiveness of all the bodies which he audits financially. The Government in its response to the Committee's Report welcomed the intention of the C&AG to develop *vfm* audit further. It stated, however, that there was no need for new legislation because the Exchequer and Audit Departments Acts did not prevent such a development.[47] However, the Committees, including the PAC, agreed with Normanton's comments in the 1960s that *vfm* audit should be on a statutory basis and that it should include all the 3Es of economy, efficiency *and* effectiveness (though questioning the merits of policy objectives would not be allowed). A related issue was raised by the Expenditure Committee which felt that the Exchequer and Audit Department should change its recruitment policy to provide staff capable of carrying out this type of extended audit. The Government responded by saying that the recruitment policy would be kept under continuous review.

During the late 1970s and early 1980s the issue of reform of the audit arrangements was therefore very much in the public arena and had received a lot of attention from various Committees and the Government itself. However, in line with many of their responses to the recommendation put forward by the Committees, the Government, in its White Paper, stated that it did not see any pressing need for statutory changes to the existing arrangements for audit.

In the 1982–83 Parliamentary session, a private member's bill, the Parliamentary Control of Expenditure (Reform) Bill, was introduced by Norman St John Stevas MP. He stated that the Bill had three purposes:

(1) to establish that the appointment of the C&AG should be made by Her Majesty on behalf of the House and not the government, making the C&AG what he had long been in practice—an officer of the House of Commons;

(2) to recognize the principle that Parliament has a right to follow public money wherever it goes; and

(3) to set up a National Audit Office.

The Bill proposed that the C&AG should have the power to carry out *vfm* examinations of the use of resources by public departments and all other bodies of which he is the appointed auditor or to which he has statutory or other inspection rights.[48] The Bill also provided for the C&AG to have inspection rights to carry out *vfm* examinations of the use of resources by nationalized industries, publicly owned corporations and any company

---

[47] *Supra*, n. 34.

[48] Inspection rights refer to the C&AG's power to have access to bodies which are not subject to a full audit by the C&AG, but because they spend public money some assurance is needed that they are spending that money correctly: see, further, Ch. 4.

where more than 50 per cent of shares are publicly owned. In addition, the Bill provided for the C&AG to have the power to audit and certify the accounts of health authorities. These provisions thus satisfied the second of St John Stevas's stated aims. Part II of the Bill provided for the establishment of a National Audit Office and sought to establish a Public Accounts Commission to have the power to examine the annual estimate of the NAO, to appoint and determine the duties of an accounting officer, and to appoint an auditor for the NAO. Clause 11 of the Bill stated that the C&AG should be an officer of the House of Commons and that he should be appointed by the House of Commons. Finally, the Bill stated that the C&AG may conduct *vfm* audits when requested to do so by the PAC.

The Government took over the Bill from Norman St John Stevas. When the National Audit Act was finally passed in 1983 it included quite a number of changes from the original Bill introduced by Norman St John Stevas. The Act came into force on 1 January 1984.

THE NATIONAL AUDIT ACT 1983

The National Audit Act 1983 (hereinafter the 1983 Act) established the NAO which replaced the Exchequer and Audit Department and is headed by the C&AG. This followed the recommendations of the PAC, and remained in keeping with the original Bill. As well as establishing the NAO, the Act deals with two broad areas, which are those highlighted in the preceding debate: the status and independence of the C&AG; and the scope of the audit.

The Status of the C&AG

The Act was quite rigorous with regard to the status and independence of the C&AG and his staff. It reinforced the C&AG's financial and operational independence from government. A number of changes were made to ensure this. Most importantly, the establishment of the NAO, replacing the Exchequer and Audit Department, formally removed the staff of the C&AG from the civil service, and from any attachment to a government department. Instead, the C&AG was empowered to appoint, and remunerate, his own staff.[49] The C&AG, in line with the recommendations made by the various Committees, was made an officer of the House of Commons[50] and statutory provision was made for the promise made

---

[49] 1983 Act, s. 3.　　　[50] 1983 Act, s. 1(2).

by the Government in the Green Paper that the Chairman of the PAC would be consulted in the appointment of the C&AG.[51] However, this differed from the original Bill which provided that the House of Commons would be responsible for the appointment of the C&AG and not the executive. The inclusion of the Chairman of the PAC in the process provides some protection against abuse of power by the executive since the Chairman of the PAC, by convention, is a member of the Opposition. Had the House of Commons had the power of appointment this would have helped secure independence from the executive but not from the legislature. Independence from Parliament and the executive was additionally secured by giving the C&AG complete discretion in the discharge of his functions, particularly under Part II of the Act, concerning *vfm* studies.[52] There was no provision for the PAC or any other select committee of the House to be able to direct the C&AG to conduct an audit into a particular area. Financial independence was secured by the establishment of a Public Accounts Commission which has responsibility for approving the estimates of the NAO, and also for appointing an accounting officer for, and an independent auditor to audit the accounts of, the NAO.[53] This was in line with the recommendations made by the PAC and the proposals in the original Bill.

The Scope of the Audit

The NAO took over the financial audit functions of the Exchequer and Audit Department, as set out in the 1866 and 1921 Acts. More importantly however, Part II of the 1983 Act gives formal recognition to the practice of *vfm* audit, by authorizing the C&AG to consider the economy, efficiency and effectiveness with which departments, authorities, and other bodies have used public resources in discharging their functions.[54] The Act also gives the C&AG authority to carry out a *vfm* examination into any body which receives half its income from public funds.[55] However, section 6(2) states that the C&AG cannot question the merits of the policy objectives in respect of which a *vfm* examination is carried out. Under section 8, a right of access to such documents and persons as the C&AG may reasonably require for the purpose of such examination is guaranteed. And, section 9 provides that the C&AG can report to the House of Commons the results of any *vfm* examination. Although the Act increased the scope of the C&AG's responsibilities in *vfm* terms, it did not go as far as Norman St John Stevas had proposed, that is, to allow Parliament to follow public money wherever it goes. There were still no

---

[51] 1983 Act, s. 1(1).　　[52] 1983 Act, s. 1(3).　　[53] 1983 Act, s. 2 and Sch. 1.
[54] 1983 Act, s. 6.　　[55] 1983 Act, s. 7.

provisions to allow the C&AG to audit nationalized industries, health authorities or local authorities.[56]

The National Audit Office

The C&AG is given a wide discretion regarding the staffing of the NAO. Subsections 3(2) and 3(3) of the 1983 Act, give the C&AG the authority to appoint such staff as he considers necessary for assisting him in the discharge of his functions, on such remuneration and other terms as he may determine. Though section 3(4) does provide that when setting salary levels, the C&AG should bear in mind the desirability of keeping them in line with remuneration paid to civil servants. The C&AG's own salary has been linked by statute to that of senior civil servants.[57] Next to the C&AG, the Deputy C&AG is the most senior officer of the NAO.

The Office's audit staff are recruited as university graduates and trained as professional accountants. The Office employs around 750 staff of which some 600 are professionally qualified accountants, technicians, or trainees. Other specialists, for instance, economists or statisticians, are generally employed on short-term contracts, particularly for *vfm* studies. In contrast, the US General Accounting Office, is staffed by a wider variety of graduates including political scientists, engineers, and lawyers. This could be taken to indicate more of an interest on behalf of the GAO in *vfm* audit rather than systems based financial audit. The NAO also subcontracts financial audit work and some *vfm* work to the private sector. The use of specialists and private firms is said to allow the NAO to draw on best practice in the private sector.

Today, the NAO is divided into six units. A central unit offers administrative support to the other five audit units. These remaining units are responsible for both the financial and *vfm* audit within particular areas of government: Unit B, for instance, covers environment, home affairs, agriculture, inland revenue, customs and excise, transport and finance. Each unit is headed by an Assistant Auditor General appointed by the C&AG. The head of the central unit is in charge of policy advice.

---

[56] See 1983 Act, Schedule 4. The matter of the audit of local authorities had been dealt with in the 1982 Local Government Finance Act which had established the Audit Commission to be responsible for the appointment of auditors to local authorities. Therefore, by the time the 1983 National Audit Act reached the House of Commons the audit of local authorities was no longer an issue. And in 1990 the National Health Service and Community Care Act provided for the Audit Commission to take over responsibility for the appointment and oversight of auditors to the health authorities: see, further, Ch. 7.

[57] See Exchequer and Audit Departments Act 1957, s. 1, as amended by the Parliamentary and other Pensions and Salaries Act 1976, and a Parliamentary Resolution: *Hansard*, Vol. 878: col. 745, 3 July 1974.

The Public Accounts Committee (PAC)

The constitutional status and functions of the PAC are based on statute and long-standing convention. As was stated earlier, the PAC was established in 1861 by Standing Order 122, now Standing Order 148.[58] Little has changed in its operation since. The PAC is still regarded as the most senior House of Commons committee. It is the primary audience for NAO reports, financial and *vfm*. Through hearings, based on NAO reports, the PAC holds those responsible for public spending to account. For present purposes, there follows an outline of the role of the PAC. A more detailed description and analysis is provided in Chapter 6.

The 1983 Act did not alter the close relationship between the C&AG and the PAC. Indeed, the role of the Chair of the PAC in appointing the C&AG has probably brought these two institutions closer together. Also, the 1983 Act gave the PAC an overt role in the selection of topics for *vfm* studies. Section 1(3) of the 1983 Act provides that in determining whether or not to carry out a *vfm* study, the C&AG must take into account any proposals made by the PAC.

The PAC usually has 15 members,[59] and by convention is chaired by an experienced member of the Opposition. The Financial Secretary of the Treasury sits as a member in an ex officio capacity. In practice, this means that the Financial Secretary has access to the PAC's papers but the Financial Secretary does not usually attend hearings. While the role and composition of the PAC was not directly affected by the establishment of the NAO, the quality of information which the PAC receives as a result of the establishment of the NAO has probably improved.

The Standing Order 148 distinguishes the PAC from the departmental committees in two main regards. First, the PAC cannot meet in recess—this has practical implications for its timetable—and secondly, it cannot appoint specialist advisors. The NAO acts as the PAC's specialist adviser.

The PAC meets twice a week when Parliament is sitting, about 45 times a year in all. The hearings are normally based on a NAO report, either on the accounts of a department or public body or more commonly on a *vfm* study. When looking at *vfm* reports, it operates under the restriction that it does not consider the merits of the policy objectives underlying the programme or activity under examination. The average hearing on a *vfm* report lasts about two and a half hours. Hearings are usually in public unless the matters under review concern national security or are commercially sensitive. The PAC is able to call anyone as a witness. However, the main

---

[58] House of Commons Public Business Standing Orders were renumbered in 1997.
[59] The current PAC actually has 16 members, including the Financial Secretary.

witness is the accounting officer of the department or body concerned. The C&AG or his deputy is present at each hearing to answer any questions arising. The Treasury Officer of Accounts[60] or his deputy also attend. The PAC is supported by a small secretariat, including a Clerk. Following the PAC hearing, the minutes of evidence are drawn up and circulated to witnesses for amendment. Drafting the PAC report is the responsibility of the Chair of the PAC, though he is assisted by the NAO. The practice is that there must be unanimous support within the PAC for a report before it can be published. The government responds to the PAC report in the form of a Treasury Minute issued as a White Paper.

The Treasury

The institution with primary overall responsibility for supervision of the spending of public monies is the Treasury.[61] It has to combine its role as a government department with responsibility for the management of the economy, with its role as overseer of the internal financial control of other government departments. In performing this latter role, the Treasury has both *ex ante* and *ex post* financial control functions. Even when money has been voted by Parliament and included in the Appropriation Act, no expenditure or commitment can, in principle, be undertaken without Treasury approval.[62] The Treasury does not in practice exercise detailed control of most individual items of expenditure *ex ante*. It delegates to departments the authority to spend within defined limits. However, spending proposals that fall within certain defined categories must be referred to the Treasury for approval.[63]

Traditionally, although the sub-heads of a Vote were not legally binding, the Treasury required departments to obtain its permission before transferring money from one sub-head to another (a process known as *virement*). Simplification of the estimates from 1996–97 onwards means that the Treasury approval will be required only for virement between Expenditure lines (similar to sections in old estimates) of which there will be about 550, rather than between pre-simplification sub-heads, of which there were about 2,000.[64] This is likely to result in a 'downward' shift of power within the executive, from the Treasury to departments.

    [60] See below.
    [61] See Harden, I., 'Money and the Constitution: Financial Control, Reporting and Audit', 13 (1993) *Legal Studies* 16.
    [62] HM Treasury, *Government Accounting: a guide on accounting and financial procedures for the use of government departments*, (2 vols., loose leaf) (London: HMSO, 1989 and seven amendments 1989–97), 2.3.4.
    [63] Ibid., 2.4.9, 2.4.10.
    [64] See *Report on the Fundamental Expenditure Review of Running Costs: Improving the Treasury* (internal document, undated); and Treasury and Civil Service Committee Fourth Report, *Simplified Estimates and Resource Accounting*, HC 212, 1994–95.

Furthermore, the Treasury appoints accounting officers and, in a document of fundamental constitutional importance, the *Accounting Officer Memorandum*, defines and promulgates their responsibilities.[65] A departmental accounting officer is also normally the permanent secretary of the department.[66] This accumulation of roles reflects the fact that the accounting officer has responsibility for the overall organization, management and staffing of the department and for department wide procedures in financial and other matters. The accounting officer must ensure that there is a high standard of financial management in the department as a whole; that financial systems and procedures promote the efficient and economical conduct of business and safeguard financial propriety and regularity throughout the department; and that financial considerations are taken fully into account in decisions on policy proposals. The accounting officer's internal role is therefore similar to the external function which the C&AG carries out.[67] More specifically, the accounting officer signs the accounts of the department and, as mentioned above, is the principle witness before the PAC. Within a department, there will also be a Principle Finance Officer. The Principle Finance Officer is responsible for the financial systems, rules and procedures of the department.[68]

The link between financial and other management functions, embodied in the role of the accounting officer, is a fundamental characteristic of the British system of government. It involves a largely decentralized system of financial control as noted above. The position in Britain may be contrasted with the system of financial control that exists in the European Communities and in many continental European states that have followed the French model.[69] In Italy, for example, the *Ragioneria Generale dello Stato* ('General Accounting Office') is the most powerful part of the Treasury. As its name suggests, the basic mission of the Ragioneria concerns the system of state accounting. This embodies an extremely detailed system of regulation, dating back to decrees of 1923 and 1924, through which the Ragioneria exercises *ex ante* control of all commitments and payments. Its control is exercised through a network of outposts (*centrali*) in each of the ministries, regions and provinces.[70] Similarly, under the system of financial control and management that currently operates

[65] For the *Accounting Officer Memorandum* see *Government Accounting, supra,* n. 62, 6.1.5.
[66] In an executive agency, it is the chief executive.
[67] See McEldowney, J., *Public Law*, (London: Sweet & Maxwell, 1994), p. 305.
[68] *Supra*, n. 62.
[69] On which see, e.g., Loïc Philip, *Dictionnaire Enyclopédique des Finances Publiques*, (Paris: Economica, 1991).
[70] See, generally, Cassese, S., 'Special Problems of Budgetary Decision-Making in Italy', in Coombes, D., *The Power of the Purse*, (London: Allen and Unwin, 1976); Gaetano d'Auria, 'La fonction législative de l'administration en Italie', Table Ronde des Sciences Administratives, Aix-en-Provence 22–23 October 1994. Until recently, this *ex ante* control was duplicated by the *Corte dei conti*.

in the European Communities, all commitments of expenditure and payments need the *visa* or prior approval of the relevant institution's financial controller.[71]

The Treasury is divided into a number of directorates, including the
Finance Management, Reporting and Audit Directorate headed by the Chief
Accountancy Officer and including the Treasury Officer of Accounts. Also,
within this Directorate are the Treasury Internal Audit Unit and the
Audit and Policy Advice Unit.

The Treasury Officer of Accounts

The job of the Treasury Officer of Accounts (TOA) is to promote a high
standard of propriety, regularity and effective accountability. Value for
money is more the concern of the spending directorate within the
Treasury, though the TOA is concerned with *vfm* in the sense that most
NAO reports, considered by the PAC, are *vfm* reports. The TOA, or his
delegate, attends all PAC hearings as a witness and can be questioned by
the members of the committee to explain the Treasury's position on
financial matters within the department or other body. In advance of the
PAC hearing, the TOA will meet with the relevant accounting officer to
assist with the preparation for the hearing. Also, the TOA assists departments or other bodies in producing the Treasury Minute in response to
the PAC's report.

The other important function of the TOA is giving advice on financial
management procedures. In particular, the TOA is responsible for updat-
ing *Government Accounting*, the Treasury's internal rules on accounting and
financial procedures, and for making it more user-friendly.

The Audit Policy and Advice Unit

Responsibility for internal audit in United Kingdom central government
straddles the Treasury and the individual departments and bodies. Within
the Treasury a unit called 'Audit Policy and Advice' has existed since
the early 1980s. Its original role included the setting and monitoring of
standards. Today, its monitoring role has diminished and its emphasis is
on maintaining standards and establishing best practice through the
publication of a *Government Internal Audit Manual*.[72] Internal audit is used
to support the accounting officer who, as part of his responsibilities, must
have some form of internal audit service provided within the department.[73]
Further, audit committees exist in many departments (they are mandatory for non-departmental public bodies) to advise and report on matters
of audit and internal control and to link internal and external audit.

---

[71] See, further, Ch. 8.
[72] See HM Treasury, *Government Internal Audit Manual*, (London, 3rd edn., 1996).
[73] *Supra*, n. 62, 6.4.

Within a department, the internal audit function can be provided by an internal unit or the work or part thereof can be contracted out. Where internal audit units exist within a department they are not arms of the Treasury but part of the department. The independence of the internal auditor is just one aspect covered in the *Government Internal Audit Manual*.[74] While internal auditors *operate* independently of those responsible for spending decisions, their existence as separate entities and their independence are not legally defined or guaranteed. The main audience for the work and findings of the internal auditor is the department itself, of which an internal audit unit is often a part.[75] From a lawyer's perspective, it seems that our understanding of the unwritten British constitution should include some recognition of the role of internal audit. British lawyers tend to think of 'independence' either as an aspect of the traditional principle of the separation of powers between the executive, the legislature and the judiciary, or as a status specifically conferred by public law (as, for example, in the case of an independent central bank). Internal audit units are clearly within the executive branch of government and are invisible to both statute and the common law. However, their 'withindependence' is clearly an important aspect of the process of ensuring that money is spent as intended by Parliament.[76]

Other Public Sector Auditors in the United Kingdom

The C&AG is one of a number of public sector auditors in the United Kingdom, though it is the NAO which is recognized by the International Organization of Supreme Audit Institutions (INTOSAI) as the United Kingdom Supreme Audit Institution.[77] It is important to be aware of the geographical limitations of the C&AG's jurisdiction. The C&AG is responsible for the audit of central government departments and bodies in England, Wales and Scotland.[78] Devolution, it appears, will alter this jurisdiction.[79] Northern Ireland has its own Comptroller and Auditor General established under the Government of Ireland Act 1920. The functions of the Northern Ireland C&AG are provided for in the Exchequer and Audit (Northern Ireland) Act 1921, and these functions correspond to those which the C&AG

[74] The independence of the external auditor is considered in Ch. 5.

[75] The department is not necessarily the only audience: NAO auditors may rely on internal audit in performing their function.

[76] Harden, I., Hollingsworth, K., White, F., 'The Control and Audit of European Community Spending', 23 (1996) *Auditorium* 8.

[77] Supreme Audit Institution is defined in the INTOSAI *Auditing Standards*, as 'The public body of a State which, however designated, constituted or organised, exercise by virtue of law, the highest public auditing function of that State'.

[78] See, further, Ch. 4.   [79] On devolution generally, see Ch. 9.

has, but in relation to the government in Northern Ireland. The Northern Ireland C&AG is assisted in his work by the Northern Ireland Audit Office, established under the Audit (Northern Ireland) Order 1987, supported by some 100 staff. Again, the work of the Northern Ireland Audit Office corresponds to that of the NAO. Although the two offices are completely separate, the NAO and Northern Ireland Audit Office work closely together. Audit reports are submitted to Parliament and considered by the PAC. The Northern Ireland Office is different from the NAO, in that, since 1 April 1997, it has assumed responsibility for the audit of local government and NHS bodies in Northern Ireland. Previously, these audits were undertaken by government departments.[80]

For local government and health authorities elsewhere, the responsibility for audit lies with the Audit Commission (for England and Wales) and the Accounts Commission (for Scotland). The Audit Commission was established by the Local Government Finance Act 1982, and is responsible for the audit arrangements for local authorities in England and Wales. Since the 1990 National Health Service and Community Care Act the Audit Commission has also taken over responsibility for the audit of health authorities in England and Wales.[81] In Scotland, the Accounts Commission has had responsibility for the audit arrangements for local government since 1974,[82] and again since the National Health Service and Community Care Act 1990 has had responsibility for health authorities in Scotland.

CONCLUSION

The 1983 Act was the first legislation to address the constitutional role of central government audit in over 100 years but was far from a thorough reappraisal of the role of state audit in modern Britain. This was in contrast with the reorganization of local government audit in 1982 when the Audit Commission was established.[83] Although the 1983 Act was successful at securing the independent status of the C&AG and his staff, the same criticisms which were aimed at public sector audit in Britain in the 1960s by Normanton regarding the scope of audit need to be addressed again today. As the nature of government continues to change in Britain, so too does the scope of audit need to change. With more and more public money being spent outside government departments, by non-departmental

---

[80] See the Conservative Government's Green Paper *Spending Public Money: Governance and Audit Issues*, March 1996, para. 66.

[81] The governing legislation has been consolidated in the Audit Commission Act 1998: see, further, Ch. 7.

[82] The Local Government (Scotland) Act 1973, Part 7.   [83] See, further, Ch. 7.

public bodies and by private companies carrying out public functions, for instance, it is vital that these bodies are held financially accountable for their activities. The NAO will provide the focus for the next three chapters of this book. In particular, we will consider the ways in which it has adapted to the changing public sector. Finally, we will discuss the NAO's ability to provide accountability within this altered state.

4

The Jurisdictions of the C&AG

As noted in Chapter 3, following the amalgamation of the Exchequer Office and the Audit Office in 1866, the C&AG's full title is the *Comptroller General of the Receipt and Issue of Her Majesty's Exchequer and Auditor General of the Public Accounts*. The focus of these next three chapters is central government audit: the latter aspect of this title. Indeed, the bulk of the work conducted by the NAO, involves the audit function. Nevertheless, the C&AG's Comptroller function is of constitutional significance, in its own right, and, in its relationship with the audit function.[1]

As *Comptroller General*, the C&AG authorizes the issue of public monies to government departments and other public sector bodies. The Comptroller function is performed in the Exchequer Section of the NAO. The day-to-day work of the Section is done by a small number of staff, though 'credits' (expenditure) are formally authorized by a member of a panel of about twelve directors drawn from throughout the NAO.[2]

Numerous functions are performed by the Exchequer Section, but one of the main functions involves the granting of credits to allow monies to be released from the Consolidated Fund and the National Loans Fund.[3] The Consolidated Fund was first established in 1787 as the fund into which all public revenues (taxes, duties, etc.) flow and all monies for the supply of public services are taken. The legislation supporting the Comptroller function today is the Exchequer and Audit Departments Act 1866, and the National Loans Act 1968. The 1968 Act established the National Loans Fund as the fund for all government borrowing and lending. Both Funds are kept and operated by the Treasury and the Bank of England.[4]

---

[1] Internal reviews of the Comptroller function have resulted in it remaining largely unchanged. It is worth noting that this function costs relatively little to perform.

[2] See the Exchequer and Audit Departments Act 1957, s. 2(2).

[3] See *Government Accounting: a guide on accounting and financial procedures for the use of government departments*, (2 vols., loose leaf) (London: HMSO, 1989 and seven amendments 1989–97), Ch. 3.

[4] The National Loans Act 1968, s. 21 requires the Treasury to prepare annual accounts for these Funds, and to forward these accounts to the C&AG who must examine, certify and report on them to Parliament. This audit is the responsibility of the Exchequer Section.

However, only the C&AG (as *Comptroller General of the Receipts and Issues of Her Majesty's Exchequer . . .*) can authorize issues from these Funds,[5] the exception being transfers between the two Funds.

Issues are first requested by the Treasury. When issues are sought for Supply purposes, the requisition for credit from the Treasury is for total amounts. It does not specify the individual services for which the money is required. This procedure is followed because the originating legislation, the Appropriation and Consolidating Fund Acts, provides for an overall sum voted by Parliament. Accordingly, requisitions for credit for Supply purposes are made in amounts of £20,000,000,000 about every 3–4 weeks. In general, when the C&AG informs the Bank of England that he grants the necessary credit, the Treasury directs the Bank to make the required daily issue to the Paymaster General. Only at this stage, does each issue specify the Vote to which it relates.

Requisitions for credit come in daily to the Exchequer Section from the Treasury around 12 noon and are dealt with within the day to ensure that signed credits can be hand delivered to the Bank of England early the following morning, thereby authorizing the release of funds. At the same time, the Bank of England supplies the Exchequer Section with the bank statements of the Consolidated and the National Loans Funds for the previous day for checking.[6]

When the Treasury requisitions an amount of money it quotes the relevant legislation. Requests for issues for Supply purposes tend not to cause the Exchequer Section concern, as long as they are within the limits approved by Parliament through the Appropriation and Consolidated Fund Acts. Other requisitions,[7] such as judicial pensions, can involve more checking. Each requisition must be signed by two authorized Treasury signatories. The amount sought is checked to ensure that it comes within the total voted, and it may be necessary to refer to the legislation. Other checks might involve ensuring that the person to whom the pension is being paid is still alive! Most requests follow a standard pattern and legal advice is rarely required. There is a close working relationship between the Exchequer Section and the Treasury. Provided the above criteria are complied with, credits are rarely refused. An agreed adjustment will usually be implemented by the Treasury, if needed. A credit might be refused because the request accidentally exceeded the monies voted by

---

[5] 1866 Act, ss. 13 and 15.   [6] 1866 Act, s. 10.

[7] Charges on public revenue are divided into two categories: charges payable out of monies voted annually by Parliament through the Supply procedure; and charges payable directly out of the Funds under statute. The latter category exists independently of the annual authorization by Parliament of Supply expenditure. Items in this latter category include: payments to service the national debt; payments to Northern Ireland for its share of taxes; payments to the EC; civil list salaries, salaries and pension of judges and other individuals, including the C&AG.

Parliament, or there could be an error concerning the authorizing legislation quoted.

The Comptroller function is essentially a high level, *ex ante* checking, or financial control, function. In a separate exercise, an auditor is responsible for checking the regularity, propriety and value for money of the spending *ex post*. The relationship between the *Comptroller* and *Auditor* functions is considered further in Chapter 5 on 'Independence'.

THE AUDITOR GENERAL'S JURISDICTION

The term 'jurisdiction' is used here to refer to two distinct, though closely related, areas of the C&AG's competence.[8] In its first sense, jurisdiction refers to the *types of audit* (for example, financial or *vfm*) which the C&AG is empowered by legislation or agreement to conduct—this we will refer to as the C&AG's *material audit jurisdiction*. In its second sense, jurisdiction refers to the *bodies*, public or otherwise, over which the C&AG has authority, derived largely from legislation or agreement, to conduct some form of audit or inspection—this we will refer to as the C&AG's *institutional audit jurisdiction*. In general, the scope and terms of the C&AG's, and hence the NAO's, material and institutional audit jurisdictions are set out in the 1866 and 1921 Acts for financial audit purposes; and in the 1983 Act for *vfm* purposes. However, it is necessary to go beyond the legislation and to examine the other sources of authority under which the NAO operates to appreciate more fully the nature and scope of the NAO's audit work.

The remainder of this chapter examines the nature and extent of the C&AG's material and institutional audit jurisdictions, and the different ways in which they are secured. The theory and practices of financial audit will be outlined and compared with those of *vfm* audit. We will argue that what might appear at first sight to be two separate disciplines of audit, in fact share more common ground than may be appreciated currently. In addition to its more traditional audit function, there is evidence of the NAO developing a wider role, as a sort of expert adviser to government. The implications of this wider role will be considered. Finally, the changing shape of the public sector has raised questions concerning the C&AG's *institutional audit jurisdiction*. Problem areas which have come to light more recently—quangos, local spending bodies,[9] and private

---

[8] The audit function is conferred on the C&AG by the legislation, though under the 1983 Act it is the staff of the NAO, and others, who conduct the audit.

[9] Within this phrase, the Nolan Committee included: further and higher education institutions, grant-maintained schools; registered social landlords in England and Wales (registered housing associations in Scotland); and Training and Enterprise Councils in England and Wales (Local Enterprise Companies in Scotland): see the Nolan Committee Second Report, *Standards in Public Life*, Cm. 3270 (May 1996).

contractors—will be considered in terms of the adequacy of the framework of central government audit.

There are two main schools of thought when it comes to improving the framework of central government audit. One favours uniformity as the best means of providing an effective system; the other prefers that the framework of audit should reflect the diversity in size, funding, activities and governance structures of the bodies funded by public monies. While there would appear to be no need for a single audit structure for all spending bodies, there is a need to ensure that audit arrangements are in place to follow all public money, regardless of the nature of the spending body. The C&AG and the Audit and Accounts Commissions, in their joint response to the Conservative Government's Green Paper, *Spending Public Money: Governance and Audit Issues*,[10] stated that 'the public have the right to expect that all bodies which rely on public money should be fully accountable for the use of that money'.[11] In particular, and since the publication of the Nolan Committee's First and Second Reports,[12] the issue of the NAO's ability to follow public money wherever it goes, including into private contractors' hands, has come under review and will be examined further below.

THE C&AG'S MATERIAL AUDIT JURISDICTION

As outlined in Chapter 2, there are two basic categories into which the audit work of the NAO can be divided:

(1) financial audit; and

(2) *vfm* audit.

A commonly held view is that financial audit and *vfm* work are, in essence, two separate disciplines within audit. For instance, separate theory and techniques underlie financial and *vfm* audit (see further below). Also, the staffing structure of the NAO reflects this perception. Generally, NAO audit staff can be divided into two groups: those who conduct financial audit and those who conduct *vfm* studies. In reality, an overlap between these two types of audit exists at a number of levels. On a day-to-day level, there is continuous communication between financial and *vfm* auditors at the NAO whereby, for example, information obtained in

---

[10] The Green Paper, (March 1996).

[11] *Spending Public Money: Governance and Audit Issues—A Joint Response by the Comptroller and Auditor General and the Controllers of Audit at the Audit and Accounts Commissions*, (June 1996) para. 2.

[12] Nolan Committee First Report, *Standards in Public Life*, Cm. 2850, (May 1995) paras. 104–109; Nolan Committee Second Report, *Standards in Public Life: Local Public Spending Bodies*, Cm. 3270, (May 1996) paras. 9–23, 260–265.

a financial audit may be relevant for *vfm* purposes, and vice versa. On a more theoretical level, it is arguable that some spending is such bad value for money that it is unlawful.[13] This proposition undermines the distinctiveness of these two disciplines. Support for this proposition can be found in recent case law and will be examined further below.

Financial Audit

Traditionally referred to as certification audit, financial audit includes and goes beyond certification audit to incorporate work under sections 2 and 4 of the Exchequer and Audit Departments Act 1921 and work to meet the wider responsibilities of the C&AG regarding regularity, propriety, probity and financial control.[14] An important example of this wider jurisdiction is the C&AG's exercise of inspection rights (see further below). Along with *vfm* work, this wider aspect of financial audit is largely what distinguishes public sector audit from private sector audit.

Hence, financial audit can be divided in two sets: certification audit and what can be referred to as 'risk audit'. Risk audit represents the residual of work done by the financial auditor beyond the minimal financial assurance. It involves identifying and addressing areas of risk where problems of financial control and accountability might arise. The auditor looks for specific risks to regularity and propriety, and if found, can report to the PAC and the auditee.[15] For example, where a contract to provide public services is awarded and money goes missing, this fact should be apparent from the certification audit of the funding body. However, where the contract is awarded to a brother-in-law of the minister say, this latter fact would not necessarily appear from a certification audit: this is a matter of propriety which could be examined under the heading of 'risk audit'.

Certification Audit

Certification audit is the work necessary to enable the C&AG to form an opinion on the annual accounts. Certification audit includes checking that:

(1) the figures in the account are properly stated;
(2) the money has been used for the purposes intended by Parliament; and
(3) the payments and receipts accord with the relevant legislation and other regulations.[16]

---

[13] See, further, Harden, I., White, F., and Hollingsworth, K., 'Value for Money and Administrative Law', [1996] *Public Law* 661.

[14] Section 2 deals with the examination of accounts of receipts of revenue, and section 4 the examination of stock and store accounts.

[15] See, further, Ch. 6.

[16] The Exchequer and Audit Departments Act 1921, s. 1: see generally Ch. 3.

Under the legislation governing the activities of the NAO,[17] the C&AG has a duty to 'examine, certify and report upon' the accounts of all government departments and a range of other public sector bodies (a total of 520 accounts in 1996–97).[18] The number of accounts increases with the creation of new executive agencies though, when Resource Accounting in central government has been fully implemented (in the year 1999–2000) this will cause the number of accounts to be audited to reduce somewhat.[19]

In theory, the C&AG is statutorily responsible for forming an opinion on the accounts. In fact, the work necessary to form that opinion is delegated to a team of auditors, usually comprising a director, an audit manager, and a principle auditor who might be assisted by more junior staff.[20] The size of the team varies depending on the size of the account. With large accounts, such as the Benefits Agency, there could be in excess of 20 auditors working on the account.[21] An audit team might work together for two to three years. Any changes in the membership would be incremental in the interests of consistency and expertise. There is no set maximum for the number of years which a person can audit the same body, but it would be unusual in the NAO to find a director on the same account for more than five years. The director is largely involved in the planning and later review of the audit work and it is on his recommendation that the C&AG either signs-off or qualifies the account.[22]

The Examination

The work of a financial auditor involves gathering information to form a body of evidence so that the C&AG can provide an assurance to Parliament that the monies voted have been spent for the proper purposes.

[17] Namely, the Exchequer and Audit Departments Acts 1866 and 1921, and the National Audit Act 1983.

[18] This figure includes 166 Departmental Appropriation Accounts (expenditure and revenue), and National Loans Fund Accounts (dealing with Government borrowing and lending); 93 Agency Accounts; 208 accounts of other public bodies, including quangos, and 53 international accounts: see NAO, *Annual Report 1997*.

[19] The number of accounts to be certified has risen by 8 per cent since 1993–94 and will continue to rise as a result of new executive agencies: NAO, *Annual Report 1997*. Prior to the introduction of resource accounting there were approximately 111 Appropriation Accounts. Under resource accounting there will be 59 accounts. Other accounts which make up the total include what are referred to as White Paper Accounts. The term 'White Paper' has no statutory significance. It is a convenient expression used to refer to the annual accounts, prepared by public sector bodies, which are separate from departmental appropriation/resource accounts but which are similarly presented to Parliament.

[20] The hierarchy of auditors at the NAO is as follows: directors; audit managers; principal auditors; senior auditors; auditors; assistant auditors; and trainees.

[21] In 1996–97, for example, the annual expenditure of the Department of Health was £43,000 million, while the annual expenditure of the Benefits Agency was £81,479 million: see NAO, *Annual Report 1997*.

[22] See, further, below.

To do this the financial auditor must be assured that the figures in the accounts can be supported. Because auditees are required to present their accounts in a particular form, prescribed by the Treasury under section 23 of the 1866 Act, extracting the necessary information is easier than, for example, with *vfm* audit where the relevant information, if kept at all, can be kept in whichever form the auditee chooses. In contrast, with financial audit, the 'audit trail' is usually already in place. As well as testing individual figures in the accounts, the auditor has other sources of assurance. The auditor can, for example, examine the accounts as a whole by looking at the relationship between debtors and income.[23] The auditor may also use internal audit material.

Different accounts have different year ends. For example, agencies operate with the same financial year end, that is 31 March. Draft accounts would be produced by an agency the following May. The period between May and July would be very busy for the auditors as they ensure that the accounts are audited and signed-off before the summer recess. To expedite this process auditors may conduct an interim audit. No interim accounts are produced. Instead, the auditor might audit the payroll or other systems and test transactions from the start of the financial year (1 April) to the date of the interim audit.

Before the annual audit commences, a planning process occurs. For an account with a year end of 31 March, this process occurs around October or November of the previous year. This process directs and sets the parameters of the audit. It is during this stage that 'materiality' is set. This involves the director setting a range of acceptable errors.[24] Where the total errors in the accounts fall within the range, which once set cannot be altered, the accounts will be judged to give an accurate view of the underlying transactions.[25] The range can be expressed in various ways, for instance, between 0.5 to 2.0 per cent of gross expenditure, or of gross assets. The ranges set by the NAO would be broadly similar to those used in the private sector, though they are not openly disclosed. The materiality figure is only a guide though. An auditor could decide to qualify an account even where there is no breach of the monetary figure for materiality: the overriding criterion is whether the accounts are accurate. Further,

[23] By using these figures an auditor can calculate how long it takes to collect debts: if the yearly income is £12 million and debtors are £1 million, it takes on average one month to collect debts—this might be reasonable. Where income is £12 million and debtors are £48 million this would suggest that it takes four years to collect debts. This would give rise to concern and would prompt a more detailed examination.

[24] The European Court of Auditor's Statement of Assurance (DAS) also recognizes a range of acceptable errors, though a different methodology is used in testing the accounts and the underlying transactions: see, further, Ch. 8.

[25] Accruals accounts are never, in a true sense, 'correct', because they are based on estimates: see Ch. 2.

during this planning stage, areas of risk may be identified, if any. With financial audit, this planning stage involves less dialogue with the auditee than with a *vfm* study. The plan will be discussed with the auditee but only when the NAO have settled on the parameters of the audit first.

The Certificate

The standard form of the C&AG's certificate comprises a 'scope paragraph', for example:

I certify that I have examined the above financial statements in accordance with the Exchequer and Audit Departments Acts 1866 and 1921.

and an 'opinion paragraph', for example:

In my opinion:

- the appropriation account *properly presents* the expenditure and receipts of Class . . . Vote . . . for the year ended 31 March 1998; and
- in all material respects the expenditure and receipts have been applied to the purposes intended by Parliament and conform to the authorities which govern them.[26]

Certification is not simply a matter of the accuracy of the accounts. It is also concerned with the activities that underlie the accounts. The C&AG's opinion relates to 'the proper conduct of public business, including issues of legality, regularity, propriety and probity'.[27] Where an auditor comes across an error in the draft accounts, such as an incorrect date or an incorrect amount or total, the accounts can sometimes be adjusted by the auditee. Other errors however cannot be 'corrected'. Where, for example, amounts have been spent without proper statutory authority it is often impossible to reclaim the expenditure. If the auditor is unable to give a clear opinion, as quoted above, because of doubts either about the accuracy of the accounts because the amount of uncorrected errors is material, or about the activities to which they relate, the C&AG can qualify his opinion on the accounts in question.[28] The C&AG might qualify an account where, for instance, the money expended exceeded the funds voted by Parliament; or where there were issues of regularity; or omissions; or inaccuracies; or limitations on the scope of the audit (e.g., if key documentation were missing). The C&AG has qualified the Lord Chancellor's departmental account (Class IX, Vote 1) each year since 1990–91, for example, because of the limited evidence available to demonstrate full

---

[26] The phrase *'properly presents'* is used when the accounts are drawn up on a cash basis. With RA, this will change to a *'true and fair view'*.

[27] NAO, *Annual Report 1993*, p. 6.

[28] In 1994–95, the C&AG qualified 24 of the 542 accounts; in 1995–96 he qualified 20 out of 575 accounts; and in 1996–97 he qualified 18 out of 520 accounts: NAO, *Annual Reports 1995, 1996* and *1997*, respectively.

compliance with statutory regulations relating to the award of criminal legal aid and the determination of contribution orders in magistrates' courts. Where a limitation on scope is so material or pervasive that the auditor cannot express an opinion on the account, a disclaimer of opinion can be issued.[29]

Regularity, Propriety and Probity

These are the standards against which the auditor judges expenditure and receipts, as represented in the financial accounts. To assist those with an interest in the use of public money, *Government Accounting* offers a definition of two of the three.[30] Accordingly, regularity 'is the requirement for all items of expenditure and receipts to be dealt with in accordance with legislation authorising them, including any applicable delegated authority and the rules of Government Accounting'. So, for expenditure and receipts to be regular, they must be authorized by Parliament in the first place, and secondly, they must comply with Treasury rules, as set out in *Government Accounting*. The Exchequer and Audit Departments Act 1921, section 1(1) provides:

Every appropriation account shall be examined by the [C&AG] on behalf of the House, and in examination of such accounts the [C&AG] shall satisfy himself that *the money expended has been applied to the purpose and purposes for which the grants made by Parliament were intended to provide and that the expenditure conforms to the authority which governs it.* (authors' emphasis)

There are two elements to Parliamentary control. First, as noted in Chapter 1, expenditure must conform with the ambit of the relevant Vote, which is reproduced in the Appropriation Act and is legally binding. The Votes represent the government's choice of priorities between competing claims on public resources. As the name implies, each is voted on separately by the House of Commons. If government subsequently decides to alter the spending priorities embodied in the Votes, it must come back to Parliament for new legislation. The ambit records Parliament's intention as to the purpose of the expenditure. The Votes are thus, in effect, a promise by government about how it will use the money provided by Parliament. However, this is not the only promise made about how money voted by Parliament will be used: our view is that there is also a constitutional convention that expenditure does not rest solely on the authority of the

---

[29] See, generally, SAS 600 *Auditors' Reports*; see, for example of disclaimer, the C&AG's certificate regarding the Child Support Agency, 28 June 1996.

[30] See *Government Accounting*, *supra*, n. 3, 6.2.14. These definitions are elaborated upon in *Regularity and Propriety—A Handbook*, HM Treasury (July 1997). Also, the Central Government Auditing Standards Advisory Panel has produced a consultation practice note on regularity (December 1997).

Appropriation Act.[31] While the Appropriation Act represents a *quantitative* allocation of money between priorities (one promise), permanent legislation is used to provide a *qualitative* definition of the purposes for which government has requested the money from Parliament (a second promise).

Furthermore, expenditure must be authorized by the Treasury. As noted in Chapter 3, even when money has been voted by Parliament and included in the Appropriation Act, no expenditure or commitment can, in principle, be undertaken without Treasury approval.[32] In practice, the Treasury delegates to departments the authority to spend within defined limits.[33] Also, the Treasury requires departments to obtain its permission before transferring money from one subhead to another (a process known as *virement*).[34] Section 1(3) of the 1921 Act provides:

If in examining the appropriation account it appears to the [C&AG] that the account includes any material expenditure requiring the authority of the Treasury which has been incurred without such authority he shall report that fact to the Treasury, and *any such unauthorised expenditure shall, unless sanctioned by the Treasury, be regarded as not being properly chargeable to a Parliament grant, and shall be so reported to the House of Commons.* (authors' emphasis)

Accordingly, where a department or other body acts outside the authority delegated to it or without the necessary Treasury approval, such expenditure is 'irregular'.

There is no separate requirement of 'legality', because, it is understood to be subsumed within regularity. Legality would include matters governed by the criminal law, such as fraud and corruption, as well as the requirements of constitutional law and the principles of judicial review of administrative action which, over the past 30 years or so, have developed considerably and are still developing. All unlawful expenditure is irregular, but not all irregular expenditure is unlawful. In practice, neither the Treasury, nor the NAO, have sought to establish clear boundaries between matters of legality and regularity.[35]

---

[31] In 1932, the Public Accounts Committee considered whether the Appropriation Act provided sufficient authority for expenditure or whether further statutory authority was needed. In the PAC Concordat (1932) it was accepted by the Treasury that, whilst the Appropriation Act is sometimes sufficient, the practice should normally be that where it is desired that continuing functions should be exercised by a government department it is proper that the powers and duties to be exercised should be defined by specific statute. See *Government Accounting, supra,* n. 3, Ch. 2, Annex 2.1. We understand that the Treasury now views the PAC concordat as merely an understanding rather than a constitutional convention and that a considerable number of continuing services rest on the sole authority of the Appropriation Act.

[32] *Government Accounting, supra,* n. 3, 2.4.

[33] *Government Accounting, supra,* n. 3, 2.4.9, 2.4.10.

[34] Treasury and Civil Service Committee Fourth Report, *Simplified Estimates and Resource Accounting,* HC 212, 1994–95. See, further, *Government Accounting, supra,* n. 3, 11.7.

[35] For auditing practice generally on this issue, see *Practice Note 10,* issued by the Auditing Practice Board (February 1996); see, further, Ch. 2.

Government Accounting defines propriety as 'the further requirement that expenditure and receipts should be dealt with in accordance with Parliament's intentions and the principles of Parliamentary control, including the conventions agreed with Parliament (and in particular the PAC)'.[36] This is similar to the definition of regularity above and seems to add little in itself. The PAC has offered some clarification when, in its Report, *The Proper Conduct of Public Business*,[37] it spoke in terms of 'the standards of public conduct', 'care for the honest handling of public money' and 'traditional public sector values'.[38] Most useful in defining this concept is the Auditing Practice Board's *Practice Note 10, Audit of Central Government Financial Statements in the United Kingdom*,[39] which provides:

Propriety is concerned with Parliament's intentions as to the way in which public business should be conducted, including the conventions agreed with Parliament and in particular, the Committee of Public Accounts.

Whereas regularity is concerned with compliance with appropriate authorities, propriety goes wider than this and is concerned more with the standards of conduct, behaviour and corporate governance. It is concerned with fairness and integrity and would include matters such as the avoidance of personal profit from public business, even-handedness in the appointment of staff, open competition in the letting of contracts and the avoidance of waste and extravagance.[40]

'Probity', in turn, appears to go beyond regularity and to overlap with notions of propriety to include a standard of honesty and integrity. It is not defined in *Government Accounting*. These questions of terminology are not merely of academic interest. They have a very practical bearing on how ministers and officials behave, as can be seen from the Pergau Dam case.

The Pergau Dam Case

On 26 February 1991, the Secretary of State for Foreign Affairs decided to fund the Pergau Dam project in Malaysia.[41] This decision was taken despite advice from the Overseas Development Administration (ODA),

---

[36] See *Government Accounting, supra,* n. 3, 6.2.14.

[37] Eighth Report, HC 154, 1993–94.

[38] See also the Nolan Committee's First Report, *supra,* n. 12, which states at para. 73: 'We take propriety to encompass not only financial rectitude, but a sense of the values and behaviour appropriate to the public sector'.

[39] *Supra,* n. 35.

[40] On the overlap between financial and *vfm* audit: see, further, below.

[41] The project was to be funded by Britain up to the sum of £234 million. The total cost of the project was originally estimated at £316 million. This estimate was subsequently increased twice and in March 1995 the British consortium building the project was reported to have asked the Malaysian authorities for up to £40 million more: *Guardian,* 6 March 1995. The £234 million British contribution was the largest sum ever provided under Aid and Trade Provision (ATP) for an individual scheme. The next most expensive scheme cost £59 million and at the time Pergau was approved, the total cost of the 66 projects supported by ATP was £576 million.

that the project was 'unequivocally bad ... in economic terms' and 'a very bad buy'.[42] The ODA's accounting officer also communicated his reservations. He made clear that it was his responsibility 'to ensure that aid funds were administered in a prudent and economical manner'[43] and that funding the Pergau project would not be consistent with this. In a minute of 7 February he stated that he would require a ministerial direction before any expenditure could be incurred. On 4 July 1991, the Secretary of State gave the accounting officer written instructions to proceed.[44] The Secretary of State's decision was said to be taken from a 'wider perspective', taking into account a number of political and economic factors.[45]

These events gave rise to criticism from the PAC,[46] based on an NAO *vfm* report on the administration of the project.[47] Throughout the NAO investigation, and the subsequent PAC hearing, however, it was assumed that the relevant issue was *vfm* and that no question arose relating to matters of 'regularity and propriety' or, indeed, 'legality'. This assumption was identified as incorrect in *R* v. *Secretary of State for Foreign and Commonwealth Affairs, ex parte The World Development Movement Ltd.*, where a successful application was brought for judicial review of the funding decision.[48] The Pergau Dam case is of constitutional significance for a number of reasons, not least because the court recognized the standing of the World Development Movement, a pressure group, to make the application for judicial review.[49] The main issue of concern for us is a proposition put forward by Rose LJ:[50]

... where, as here, the contemplated development is, on the evidence, so economically unsound that there is no economic argument in favour of the case, it is not, in my judgment, possible to draw any material distinction between questions of propriety and regularity on the one hand and questions of economy and efficiency of public expenditure on the other.[51]

The Pergau project was funded under the Overseas Development and Co-operation Act 1980, section 1 of which provides:

---

[42] Evidence to the Committee of Public Accounts, HC 155, 1993–94, pp. 5, 8.

[43] Seventeenth Report of the Public Accounts Committee, *Pergau Hydro-Electric Project*, HC 155, 1993–94, p. xii.

[44] See *Government Accounting*, supra, n. 3, 6.1.5 and the *Accounting Officer Memorandum*, which follows 6.1.

[45] See the Evidence to the Foreign Affairs Committee from the Foreign Secretary, HC 271, 1993–94, p. 32.

[46] *Supra*, n. 43.   [47] See NAO, *Pergau Hydro-Electric Project*, HC 908, 1992–93.

[48] [1995] 1 All ER 611. The Secretary of State announced on 13 December 1994 that he would not appeal the decision.

[49] On the *locus standi* issue see Cane, P., 'Standing up for the Public', [1995] *Public Law* 276; and Hare, I., 'Judicial Review and the Pergau Dam', 54 (1995) *Cambridge Law Journal* 227.

[50] At p. 627: Rose LJ gave the leading judgment; Scott Baker J concurred.

[51] The words 'economy' and 'efficiency' are used in s. 6 of the National Audit Act 1983 which empowers the C&AG to carry out *vfm* examinations. Rose LJ, however, did not make a direct reference to this statutory provision in his judgment.

The Secretary of State shall have power, for the purposes of promoting the development or maintaining the economy of a country . . . or the welfare of its people, to furnish any person or body with assistance, whether financial, technical or of any other nature.

The applicant argued, and the court agreed, that aid must be for *sound* development purposes, though the word *sound* is not used in the legislation. Rose LJ referred to ministerial statements, guidelines, and white papers, over the years and without exception, as having construed the above ministerial power as relating to economically *sound* development. The court stated that if the power had been exercised for sound developmental purposes, the Foreign Secretary would be entitled to take other factors, such as political and economic considerations, into account. However, the court held that the project was so economically unsound that there was no economic argument in its favour. In these circumstances, it was not possible to draw any material distinction between matters of propriety and regularity, and questions of economy and efficiency, of public expenditure. Hence, the decision was unlawful.

The Pergau Dam case has resulted in two different levels of response from government. The first has been to adjust the balance of the Victorian machinery of expenditure control, in the light of general lessons drawn from the affair. Following a recommendation from the PAC, the Treasury issued an amendment to the *Accounting Officer Memorandum*. It supplements the provision that already existed under the *Memorandum* prescribing what should be done in cases where an accounting officer considers that a course of action proposed by a minister would infringe the requirements of 'regularity or propriety'. In such a situation, the accounting officer should set out in writing, to the minister, his objection to the proposal, the reasons for his objection, and, his duty to inform the C&AG should his advice be overruled. If the minister decides to proceed with the expenditure, the accounting officer must seek a written instruction to take the action in question. Having received such instruction the accounting officer must comply with it, but should then inform the Treasury of what has occurred and should also communicate the papers to the C&AG without undue delay.[52] The post-Pergau amendment of the *Memorandum* now requires an accounting officer to inform the Treasury, and to communicate to the C&AG without undue delay the papers relating to all cases, where ministers issue instructions on matters involving 'economy, efficiency and effectiveness' also.[53]

---

[52] *Government Accounting, supra*, n. 3, 6.1.5 and para. 13 of the *Accounting Officer Memorandum*.

[53] Treasury Minute on the Seventeenth to Twenty-First Report from the Committee of Public Accounts, Cm. 2602 (1993–94); and see *Government Accounting, supra*, n. 3, 6.1.5 and para. 14 of the *Accounting Officer Memorandum*.

The second level of response has been to what have been perceived to be the legal implications of the judgment. Here, the response has been much more restricted. Both government and the NAO assumed that the decision in the Pergau Dam case was dependent on the particular statutory context of the Overseas Development and Co-operation Act and, that there are no more general legal implications of the judgment. In our view, this analysis is wrong. The Pergau Dam case represents the application of a general principle of public law, applicable across the whole range of government spending.

The view that the Pergau decision is dependent on the particular statutory context appears to be based on the fact that the words 'economic development' appear in the statute and that the plaintiff argued successfully that this should be read as meaning *sound* economic development. However, the word 'sound' is no more than a dead metaphor. If its significance is unpacked—by asking what are the different ways in which economic development might be 'unsound'—we come back to the 3Es: economy, efficiency and effectiveness. In other words, 'sound economic development' is just another way of saying 'economic development that passes a value for money test'. The principle that spending should represent value for money is of general application, as Parliament recognized when it passed the National Audit Act 1983. This principle has been emphasized in successive waves of reforms of the public sector, beginning with the *Financial Management Initiative* in the early 1980s, continuing through the *Next Steps* and *Citizen's Charter* programmes and, more recently, with the introduction of Resource Accounting and Budgeting.

It cannot be supposed, however, that public law principles require every spending decision to represent the *best possible* value for money. This would be simply unachievable. Value for money is a matter of degree and the Pergau principle can do no more than require a minimum acceptable standard. The obvious way to express this, in terms of the familiar categories of judicial review of administrative action, is as an aspect of the *Wednesbury* test:[54] that is, *proposed expenditure by the Executive of money voted by Parliament is unlawful if, in relation to the object for which the money has been provided, no reasonable minister could think that it represented value for money. Mutatis mutandis,* the same principle should apply to all public bodies, including local government (the Pergau principle represents the core of good sense in the notion of fiduciary duty).[55]

Where doubts are raised about the value for money represented by proposed spending, the Pergau principle means that accounting officers should advise ministers that a question of 'legality' is potentially involved.

---

[54] *Associated Provincial Picture Houses Ltd.* v. *Wednesbury Corporation* [1948] 1 KB 223.
[55] See *Bromley London Borough Council* v. *Greater London Council* [1983] 1 AC 768.

Accounting officers need also to ensure, in fulfilment of their own responsibilities both to the minister and to Parliament, that legal advice is sought in cases of serious doubt about whether a reasonable minister could think that proposed spending represented value for money in relation to the object for which the money has been provided by Parliament.

Following the judicial review of the Pergau Dam decision, the C&AG qualified his opinion on the External Assistance Vote of the Foreign and Commonwealth Office for 1993–94. The qualification was made on the basis that the expenditure of £14.65 million in that year by the ODA on the Pergau project was 'irregular', because it was not a proper charge to Class II, Vote 5, that is, the Vote for expenditure under the Overseas Development and Co-operation Act 1980.[56] It could be argued that it was right to express the qualification in terms of regularity rather than legality because there was no doubt that permanent legislation existed under which expenditure on the Pergau project could lawfully have been incurred. The problem was that the expenditure had been charged to the wrong account (that for the Overseas Development and Co-operation Act 1980) rather than the right account (that for the Export and Investment Guarantees Act 1991). It needs to be recognized, however, that the requirement that spending be authorized by legislation, although 'based on ancient constitutional usage' is a legal requirement.[57] Any other view is unacceptable because it would throw into doubt the whole basis of constitutional government. Ministers may do many things without any specific statutory authorization, including making contracts.[58] The one thing they cannot do, however, is actually pay any money out of public funds.

Auditing Performance Data

Under RA, as well as the more usual financial type of reports, the department or other body must produce a Statement of Resources, analysed by aims and objectives, as part of the annual accounts. And, accompanying these accounts, must be an Output and Performance Analysis.[59] These are intended to generate information about value for money. The Green Paper left open the audit status of both these reports.[60] The NAO and PAC

---

[56] With regard to the Comptroller function, note that only the relevant Class and Vote under the Appropriation Act would have been checked by the Exchequer Section of the NAO before granting the credit, and not the Overseas Development Act 1980.

[57] See *Erskine May's Treatise on the Law, Privileges, Proceedings and Usages of Parliament*, edited by Limon, D. W., and McKay, W. R., (London: Butterworths, 22nd edn., 1997), p. 734.

[58] See Daintith, T., 'The Techniques of Government', in Jowell, J., and Oliver, D., eds., *The Changing Constitution*, (Oxford: Clarendon Press, 3rd edn., 1995); Harris, B. V., 'The "third source" of authority for government action', 109 (1992) *Law Quarterly Review* 626; and see also *Government Accounting, supra*, n. 3, 2.2.

[59] See Ch. 2.

[60] *Better Accounting for the Taxpayer's Money: Resource Accounting and Budgeting in Government*, Cm. 2626 (1994).

were of the view that the analysis of departmental expenditure by objectives was critical to a full understanding of performance and stewardship.
This analysis also provides a direct link to the purpose of expenditure—
the basis on which Parliament votes funds. The NAO argued that this analysis should be audited so that Parliament could have an independent
assurance that departments have used the monies voted to them for the
purposes intended. The Treasury was agreeable.[61]

The Output and Performance Analysis, however, is to remain outside
the C&AG's audit remit, for the present. The NAO, supported by the PAC
and the Treasury and Civil Service Committee, suggested that, as the quality of the data improves, performance measures should become of a
sufficiently high standard to make a formal audit opinion achievable. The
Treasury response was that they would work with departments to
improve their performance data and accordingly, the Treasury has produced a document, *Output and Performance Analysis Guidance*, for departments.[62] However, the Treasury did not address directly the question of
the audit of performance data. In their response to the White Paper, the
NAO pursued the matter further and questioned the publication of performance data that cannot withstand external scrutiny, without a 'health
warning'. They suggested that the NAO should, at least, be assigned the
role of validating the performance data, if audit was not judged possible.
The PAC supported such a role for the NAO and recommended that, until
independent validation becomes practicable, performance data should be
reviewed by the C&AG to ensure that it is not inconsistent with the resource
accounts or otherwise misleading.[63]

The NAO's role in relation to the Output and Performance Analysis is
of particular importance because of the NAO's own *vfm* studies. Value
for money is a distinctive criterion of public sector audit. One of the main
achievements of the National Audit Act 1983 was to confirm the C&AG's
authority to undertake *vfm* work and report on it to Parliament.
Departments' Output and Performance Analyses will be, in effect, their
own *vfm* analysis of themselves. It is important to maintain the principle
that the NAO has professional responsibility for the *vfm* information
that is provided to Parliament, either directly through its own *vfm* audits
or indirectly through the audit of departments' own analyses. This is the

[61] *Better Accounting for the Taxpayer's Money: the government's proposals—resource accounting and budgeting,* Cm. 2929 (1995).
[62] December 1997.
[63] In the Memorandum submitted by the C&AG to the PAC on the NAO Estimate for
1998–99, it is stated that the NAO plans, for 1998–99 to 2002–03, include some development work on performance validation, though the Estimate does not include provision for
any significant increase in the volume of work in this area: see Minutes of Evidence before
the PAC, *NAO Estimate,* HC 383, 1997–98.

position in Sweden where a similar performance analysis is attached to the annual accounts and audited by the *Riksrevisionverket*, the state audit institution.

The C&AG's Report

As noted previously, departments and public bodies must present their accounts in a form prescribed by the Treasury, following a Treasury direction.[64] Taking the Royal Parks Agency as an example, an annual report is presented to Parliament around July each year for the previous financial year (1 April–31 March). The annual report will usually contain 'glossy' material at the start which is not audited by the NAO. According to the Treasury direction, the accounts must have a 'Foreword', which must cover certain points. The Foreword is not audited but it is reviewed for consistency with the accounts. For companies preparing accounts under the Companies Acts, the equivalent of the Foreword is the 'director's report'. Next comes a statement of the agency's, and the chief executive's, responsibilities. Following this is the C&AG's certificate and report on the accounts. The accounts themselves, and the notes thereon, are reproduced next. Where the C&AG has nothing, either positively or negatively, to report, the report merely consists of a sentence, such as: *I have no observations to make on these financial statements*. Where the C&AG has something to report, the reader will be referred to the full printed report, following the certificate.[65] A report does not necessarily mean that the accounts have been qualified. The fuller report is a means by which the C&AG can bring some matter, which has arisen in the course of the audit, to the attention of Parliament and into the public domain.[66]

There are, in fact, three options for the C&AG when it comes to certifying accounts and reporting thereon. The C&AG can give:

(1) a clear opinion; or
(2) a clear opinion and a report; or
(3) a qualified opinion and a report.

Because of time restrictions, the PAC do not consider every account. The PAC usually does take a close interest in a qualified account though, and will normally seek and act on the advice of the NAO as to whether a hearing is necessary. A report on an account can be used as a basis by the PAC in any hearing on that account.[67] In 1996–97, for instance, the C&AG

[64] The accounts direction from the Treasury remains in force, often for many years, until revised. It is reproduced with the accounts but is not audited.

[65] See, for example, the Defence Research Agency Annual Report 1994–95.

[66] As well as reporting in this public or democratic sense, the NAO also reports more privately to management in the form of management letters: see, further, Ch. 6.

[67] See, further, Ch. 6.

qualified, and issued reports on the accounts of 18 bodies.[68] The PAC took evidence on seven of those reports, including the resignation of the chief executive and accounting officer of the National Heritage Fund due to a conflict of interest that arose when her partner's firm tendered for a contract to be let by the Fund and was later awarded further contracts.[69]

Signing-off the Account

When the audit is completed and the account has been examined, certified and reported upon, the C&AG 'signs-off' the account. Whether the audit work has been conducted by NAO staff or by a private firm of accountants under contract, it is the C&AG, who normally 'signs-off' the account or, in appropriate circumstances, his delegate.[70] In deciding to 'sign-off' an account, the C&AG acts on the advice of the director of the audit. The effect of signing-off is to close the account to further audit. Once the account has been signed-off, it cannot be reopened. The indelible effect of signing-off was evidenced in the Pergau Dam case mentioned above. There, the C&AG qualified his opinion on the External Assistance Vote of the Foreign and Commonwealth Office for 1993–94, on the basis that the expenditure was 'irregular'. But, the C&AG had previously given a clear opinion on the 1992–93 accounts, before the Court's judgment that the expenditure was unlawful. This fact cannot be altered.

Value for Money Audit

The existing practice of *vfm* studies was formally sanctioned in the 1983 Act, Part II. Sections 6–9 represent a large part of the C&AG's material and institutional jurisdictions for *vfm* purposes.[71] Section 6 provides that the C&AG may carry out examinations into the economy, efficiency and effectiveness with which any department, authority or other body to which this section applies, has used its resources in discharging its functions. There is no statutory definition of the 3Es, but the NAO defines the 3Es, collectively referred to as *vfm*, in their publication *A Framework for VFM Studies*.[72] Accordingly, 'economy' is about minimizing the costs of resources

---

[68] An accumulation of the C&AG's reports on accounts are published in a separate volume, in addition to the Appropriation Accounts which are published in a series of volumes. Also, since 1994–95, the NAO has published an annual general report on financial auditing and reporting.

[69] See C&AG's Report, *National Heritage Memorial Fund and Lottery Distribution Accounts 1994–95*, HC 765, 1995–96; and the PAC's Twenty-Third Report, 1995–96.

[70] See Exchequer and Audit Departments Act 1957, s. 2 on delegation by the C&AG to a principal officer.

[71] See, further, Inspection Rights, below.

[72] NAO, *A framework for value for money audits*, (undated).

acquired or used, having regard to appropriate quality ('spending less'), 'efficiency' means achieving the maximum output from a given input, or achieving a given output for the minimum input ('spending well'), whilst 'effectiveness' is concerned with the extent to which outputs of goods, services or other results achieve policy objectives ('spending wisely').[73]

Effectiveness is a particularly sensitive matter because it has the potential to bring matters of policy into account. Ministers assert that they alone are accountable for policy. Effectiveness audit thus risks becoming an audit of how far ministers have been successful. Like judges, auditors need ways to avoid too many direct clashes with political power.[74] Subsection (2) therefore prohibits the C&AG from questioning the merits of the policy objectives of any department, authority or body in respect of which an examination is carried out. This prohibition is a common feature of public sector audit which, in the case of most *vfm* studies, does not cause problems. The theory is that it is the executive's job to decide policy and to allow another body, such as a state audit institution, or indeed the judiciary or some quasi-judicial body, to criticize those policy decisions, would somehow upset the balance and separation of constitutional powers. This prohibition and the question of what constitutes 'policy objectives' is discussed further in the next chapter.

The NAO's examination of the Pergau Dam project was a *vfm* examination and hence subject to the prohibition on questioning the merits of policy objectives. The NAO took the view that the ministerial direction to the ODA's accounting officer to incur the expenditure under the Aid and Trade Provision budget was a 'policy decision'. The NAO stated in the conclusions of its report that 'it is not for the National Audit Office to question the merits of this policy decision'.[75] Section 6(2) of the 1983 Act must now be applied in the light of the Pergau principle outlined above. Since breach of the principle makes the decision to incur expenditure unlawful, section 6(2) cannot constitute any bar to the NAO examining whether the principle has been breached or not. Such an examination is required as part of the C&AG's responsibility to satisfy itself that an unqualified certificate may be given on the relevant account. The fact that the NAO first learns of matters giving rise to doubts about the lawfulness of expenditure as part of what it classifies as a *vfm* examination is neither here nor there.

Section 7 extends the C&AG's *vfm* jurisdiction to other bodies which are mainly supported by public funds.[76] Section 8 gives the C&AG a right

[73] See, generally, Ch. 2.

[74] In particular, auditors like judges tend to focus on procedure rather than substance: see Power, M., *The Audit Explosion*, (London: Demos, 1994).

[75] *Supra*, n. 47, p. 11.   [76] See 'Institutional Audit Jurisdiction' below.

of access at all reasonable times to all documents in the custody or under the control of the department, authority, or other body being audited, as he may reasonably require to conduct a *vfm* study.[77] Finally, section 9 states that the C&AG may report to the House of Commons the results of any *vfm* investigation.

The VFM *Study Life Cycle*

Since 1992–93, the NAO has produced about 50 *vfm* reports each year. Although each study is unique, the following outlines the stages in the life cycle of a *vfm* study.[78] Some studies short-circuit this cycle.[79] It is also important to appreciate that the C&AG has complete discretion in the performance of his *vfm* duties, under s.1(3) of the 1983 Act, and accordingly, he can have an input at any of the stages described below.

The first stage involves research and study selection, referred to as 'marking'. A general survey, carried out by all audit staff on a day-to-day basis as well as part of an annual review, identifies areas of risk to *vfm*. A study can originate from this internal process but studies can also originate from other sources, including: MPs; the departments themselves; or the public. The PAC has a particular statutory role in relation to study selection. Section 1(3) of the 1983 Act provides that in determining whether or not to carry out a *vfm* study, the C&AG must take into account any proposals made by the PAC.

Strategic planning is next. The strategic plan sets out the proposal in broad terms, including the background, the potential risks to *vfm*, and likely findings. It also involves planning the study in resource terms—staffing, costs and timetable. Following approval from the C&AG, the study moves to the next stage.

Stage three is the preliminary study. Its purpose is to determine the exact scope for a *vfm* study and the likely findings. At this stage the auditor liaises with the auditee and identifies what evidence can be collected, examines the activities, identifies the key players and reviews all this material in the light of *vfm* risks. Assuming that the investigation is to proceed, the preliminary study sets the detailed terms of reference and methodology, including confirming timing with the auditee. The preliminary study has to be approved by the C&AG before the next stage begins.

A full investigation, the fourth stage, normally takes up to five months to complete, though there are many variations to this time period. The

---

[77] On access to information, see Ch. 5.   [78] *Supra*, n. 72.

[79] For example, the Limehouse Link study moved from Step 1 (study selection) directly to Step 4 (full investigation), see *London Docklands Development Corporation: The Limehouse Link*, HC 468, 1994–95; while the County Hall study started at Stage 4, see *Sale of County Hall*, HC 314, 1994–95.

audit team typically comprises one director, one audit manager and one or two principal or senior auditors. The team may be supplemented by external experts. For example, in the study of the Metropolitan Police responding to calls, a police officer worked with the audit team.[80] Consultants can be used following a competitive tendering process as, for example, in the study on the Bridge Programme, where engineers acted as consultants.[81] The auditee will usually be consulted in selecting the shortlist for the tendering process, but the ultimate choice rests with the NAO. Potential consultants must declare any conflicts of interest as part of the tendering process.

At the fifth stage, a draft report is drawn up by the audit team. The auditee is provided with the draft report and is given about four weeks to respond. The draft then goes to the C&AG, who may comment on the report. Then, the C&AG formally sends the draft report to the accounting officer of the auditee. This process of sending the draft report to the auditee is known as clearance. Audit institutions world-wide have some form of clearance.[82] It is seen as invaluable as it ensures that when the report goes to the PAC there is agreement between the NAO and the auditee as to the facts, at least.

Where a common ground does not exist, both views can be reflected in the report.[83] Where there is more than one auditee, as with multi-departmental studies,[84] or with a study involving an agency and its sponsoring department, clearance can be more protracted. Interested parties, for instance consultants, might also be consulted and allowed to comment but this is more consultation than clearance.

When it comes to stage six, publication of the *vfm* report, the C&AG has the final say. Generally, a study would be unlikely to get this far and not be published. NAO reports will generally include recommendations to the auditee. While the NAO follows numerous presentational and style rules, there is great variety in form. The aim is to complete *vfm* reports in 12 months, although some reports may be finished in a shorter time. The danger with reports which take a long time is with ensuring that the evidence is up to date and loss of topicality. The C&AG's reporting function to the PAC is discussed further in Chapter 6.

---

[80] NAO, *Metropolitan Police Service: Responding to Calls from the Public*, HC 753, 1994–95. In *Looking after the Financial Affairs of People with Mental Incapacity*, HC 258, 1993–94, a psychiatrist was engaged to assist the audit team.

[81] NAO, *Highways Agency: The Bridge Programme*, HC 282, 1995–96.

[82] Cf. the ECA's contradictory procedure: see, further, Ch. 8.

[83] See, for example, NAO, *Protecting and Managing Sites of Special Scientific Interest in England*, HC 379, 1994–95.

[84] In the 1980s there were some cross-unit studies e.g. personnel, however, because of difficulties with accountability before the PAC and clearance of reports, such central studies are unusual today.

Contracting-out the Audit

Because of the differences between public and private sector audit,[85] it could be argued that private sector auditors are not properly equipped to conduct audits in the public sector.[86] Words such as 'regularity, propriety and probity', and 'value for money' are not within the day-to-day vocabulary of a private sector auditor. In the private sector, the auditor is more concerned with the accuracy of the accounts than with the probity of the transactions which underlie them. However, a certain expertise has built up within the private sector for this type of work, especially within the areas of local government and the NHS,[87] such that today, many of the large accounting firms in the United Kingdom have some form of public service audit division.

It is estimated that 16 per cent, by value, of all NAO financial audit work is contracted out.[88] Where *vfm* work is contracted-out it usually represents only part of a particular *vfm* study; for example, expert engineering advice might be needed, or a consultant might be brought in as part of the audit team. There is evidence that one complete study has been contracted-out but this appears to be the exception rather than the rule. In 1996–97, 13 per cent of the resources used on *vfm* studies were for external consultants.[89] The rationale for contracting-out audit work, as explained by the NAO, is that it allows the NAO to benchmark their costs and methodologies against the private sector, as well as providing the necessary expertise for *vfm* studies.

A New Role?

The NAO describes its constitutional role as twofold.[90] First, and primarily, it 'serves' Parliament by providing independent information, assurance and advice to Parliament on the way departments and other public bodies account for and use public money. Secondly, the NAO 'helps their clients' by developing constructive working relations with departments and other bodies and providing advice on financial management. Traditionally, this latter role has been fulfilled through the use of management letters which follow individual audits and inspections.[91] Furthermore, the

---

[85] See, generally, Ch. 2.

[86] It is interesting to note that whereas previously, the NAO relied on the CIPFA (Chartered Institute of Public Finance and Accounting) qualification for its trainees, for the last five years or so, there has been a shift to the Institute of Chartered Accountants qualification, that is, the more common private sector qualification.

[87] See Ch. 7.

[88] At present, that constitutes 33 accounts: see the PAC, Minutes of Evidence, *NAO Estimates*, HC 383-I, 1997–98. See further NAO, *Annual Report 1997*.

[89] NAO, *Annual Report 1997*.   [90] See, for example, NAO, *Annual Report 1997*.

[91] See, further, Ch. 6.

NAO has previously developed more general advice following individual audits, as was the case following the privatization studies in the 1980s.[92] More recently, examples of a wider 'service to clients' role, suggest that the NAO may be developing a new role as an independent expert consultant to government in general, and more particularly to the executive.

Examples of this new consultative role can be found in relation to the Private Finance Initiative (PFI).[93] When, in 1997, the Labour Government commissioned an external review of the PFI, the NAO gave evidence and made specific recommendations regarding the process to the review though not in the usual form of a *vfm* report. These recommendations were accepted in full by the Government.[94] Further, to address the concerns of public servants seeking to use the PFI, rather than the traditional approach to project procurement, the NAO has taken, in its own words, 'the unusual step' of publishing its approach to the audit of PFI projects. Accordingly, the NAO: supports the concept, because in appropriate cases it offers the prospect of improved *vfm*; recognizes that the PFI requires innovation and risk-taking by public servants; supports well-thought-through risk-taking and innovation. To date, the NAO has produced four *vfm* reports in this area.[95] Two of the above three activities (giving evidence and making recommendations to the external review of the PFI and publishing of the NAO approach to the PFI) clearly go beyond the C&AG's basic statutory audit remit, while the latter represents a sort of *ex ante* stamp of approval from the NAO for the principles and policies of the PFI. Another example of the NAO acting 'beyond the strict call of duty' concerns its advisory role to individual departments on the implementation of resource accounting.[96] In this regard, the NAO is represented on the Financial Reporting Advisory Board of the

---

[92] See NAO, 'The Selection and Use of Management Consultants', (1989); NAO 'Audit of Management Buyouts in the Public Sector', (1991); see, further, McEldowney, J., 'The National Audit Office and privatisation', 54 (1991) *Modern Law Review* 933.

[93] Announced in 1992, the PFI aims to marry private capital with the provision of public services, in a new form of public/private partnership.

[94] See NAO, *Annual Report 1997*, p. 35.

[95] *The Scottish Office: The Skye Bridge*, HC 5, 1997–98; *Contributions Agency: The Contract to Develop and Operate the Replacement National Insurance Recording System*, HC 12, 1997–98; *HM Prison Service: The PFI Contracts for Bridgend and Fazakerley Prisons*, HC 253, 1997–98; and *The Private Finance Initiative: The First Four Design, Build, Finance and Operate Roads Contracts*, HC 476, 1997–98.

[96] This type of activity would appear to be in compliance with INTOSAI *Auditing Standards* (June 1989) where it is stated at para. 57 that: 'A degree of co-operation between the SAI [Supreme Audit Institution] and the executive is desirable in some areas. The SAI should be ready to advise the executive in such matters as accounting standards and policies and the form of financial statements.' A word of warning is included though: 'The SAI must ensure that in giving such advice it avoids any explicit or implicit commitment that would impair the independent exercise of its audit mandate'.

Treasury, which is responsible for drafting and keeping under review the Manual on Resource Accounting.

A more striking example of the NAO's new role was evidenced when it reported, at the request of the executive, on the Assumptions for the July 1997 Budget Projections. In fact, the report was not published by the NAO but as a White Paper by the Government.[97] The purpose of the NAO's work was 'to assist the Government in preparing its forecasts of the public finances by reviewing the assumptions adopted for economic growth, unemployment and interest rates and the conventions used for projecting proceeds from privatisations and from "Spend to Save" expenditure measures'. The C&AG's conclusion, that while the assumptions are not the only ones which could be reconciled with the evidence, they had been arrived at systematically on the basis of the available data and by methods which interpret it in a reasonable way, enabled the adoption of the assumptions by the Executive. This audit was not a one-off. In November 1997, the C&AG, no longer shy of this new role, published *Audit of Assumptions for the Pre-Budget Report*,[98] a report which offered an 'independent opinion' of four further assumptions. The intention is that the NAO will continue to perform this role in the budgetary process.[99] Although the 1997 Report was stated to have been prepared under section 6 (the section on *vfm* studies—see, further, below), and published under section 9, of the 1983 Act, it appears that the 1983 Act may be insufficient authority for this type of work in the future. In its place, the Finance Act 1998 places a duty on the C&AG to report to the House of Commons on such conventions and assumptions underlying the preparation, by the Treasury, of the annual budget documentation.[100] The C&AG's role in the budgetary process clearly goes beyond his traditional audit work and there is evidence to suggest that this wider role could be developed further.[101]

In favour of this new role is the fact that the NAO is well placed to give independent, expert advice to government and the executive. Failure to do so, it could be argued, would mean that full use is not being made of the resource which is the NAO. The publication of the NAO's approach to the PFI, has the effect of altering the NAO's traditional *ex*

[97] *Audit of Assumptions for the July 1997 Budget Projections*, Cm. 3693 (1997).

[98] HC 361, 1997–98.

[99] See *Audit Assumptions for March 1998 Budget*, HC 616, 1997–8. In the Memorandum submitted by the C&AG to the PAC on the NAO Estimate for 1998–99, it is stated that the NAO plans, for 1998–99 to 2002–03, includes a continuing role, as set out in the Government's Financial Statement and Budget Report, for the C&AG in auditing the process of forecasting the prospects for public finances: see Minutes of Evidence before the PAC, *NAO Estimate*, HC 383, 1997–98; see further the Government's Code for Fiscal Stability (1998).

[100] Section 156.

[101] For example, it has been reported that the C&AG has expressed an interest in assessing the criteria for Britain to join a single currency, for example: see *The Times*, 13 February 1998.

post audit, to a type of *ex ante* review. The auditee equipped with this information can then use it in a sort of self-regulatory manner. This, in turn, could facilitate future NAO's audits. Against this has to be balanced the risk to the NAO of losing its independence. For instance, with regard to resource accounting, the NAO may find itself auditing matters which it has previously advised upon. This is already a danger with management letters, though a more private risk because such letters are private between the NAO and the auditee, whereas the C&AG's opinion and report on financial statements is presented to Parliament. A shift from a predominately *ex post* audit (which is not without its critics because of a feeling that the door is being shut after the horse has bolted)[102] to a type of *ex ante* review would represent a significant change in the constitutional role of the NAO and this should not occur without a proper consideration of the above issues. Also, its *extra curricular* activities in the areas of the PFI and the budget assumptions have the potential to draw the NAO into the political process and down from its independent status. The issue of the NAO's independence is discussed further in the next chapter.

THE INSTITUTIONAL AUDIT JURISDICTION OF THE C&AG

A large part of the C&AG's institutional audit jurisdiction is determined by statute: the 1866 and 1921 Acts for financial audit purposes; and the 1983 Act for the purpose of *vfm* audit. In these circumstances, the C&AG must, and it would appear does, operate *intra vires*, that is, within his statutory remit.[103] The extent of this statutory jurisdiction is set out below. The remainder of the C&AG's institutional audit jurisdiction is based on his rights of inspection.[104] The C&AG will generally exercise rights of inspection where the body in question receives public funds but where another body acts as the statutory auditor for the purposes of companies, or other, legislation. This area of the C&AG's institutional audit jurisdiction is unsatisfactory for a number of reasons. Rights of access for inspection purposes are not all statutory; some are granted voluntarily by the auditee, and hence can be withheld. Where rights of access are not statutory, the process of 'negotiating' access is itself inefficient. Also, access can be limited for financial audit, or for *vfm* purposes, only. Accordingly, there is

---

[102] See, for example, Graham, C., and Prosser, T., *Privatizing Public Enterprise*, (Oxford: Clarendon Press, 1991) pp. 59–64.

[103] The authors know of no reported judicial review proceedings against the C&AG and/or the NAO for acting *ultra vires*.

[104] Increasingly, the C&AG conducts other audit work outside his statutory remit, for which he can charge fees. In 1996–97, the NAO audited 53 accounts of major international clients, including UN and Commonwealth bodies. This aspect of the NAO's work indicates its standing in the international field.

little consistency between the various inspection rights granted and the levels of accountability vary on an ad hoc basis. In certain circumstances, there is no access for inspection purposes. Furthermore, the ability of the NAO to follow public monies into private contractors' hands is unsatisfactory, further limiting the effectiveness of the audit. These issues will be addressed below.

Bodies Subject To Financial Audit

The C&AG's core financial audit work is directed at three main groups of accounts:

(1) central government departmental appropriation accounts and/or resource accounts audited under the terms of the 1866 Act;
(2) agency resource accounts audited under the 1921 Act or the Government Trading Funds Act 1973; and
(3) the accounts of other bodies audited under the terms of a specific statute or by agreement.

In 1996–97, the C&AG audited 520 accounts.[105] This process is repeated each year, the only changes occurring where a body subject to the C&AG's audit jurisdiction is newly established, and where a body previously subject to the C&AG's jurisdiction is discontinued. One of the main areas of concern regarding the C&AG's institutional audit jurisdiction for financial audit purposes relates to the introduction of resource accounting (RA) and the question as to what bodies are to be included within the departmental boundary for financial audit purposes.

The Green Paper on RAB proposed 'ownership' as the guiding principle for the boundary of the resource account.[106] Included with the core department were associated executive agencies and trading funds (corresponding to the responsibilities of the departmental principle accounting officer). Excluded were 'constitutionally independent bodies' such as non-departmental public bodies (NDPBs), nationalized industries and local authorities, even though they may have been financially and operationally linked to the department. Following consultation, the Treasury amended its views substantially. The guiding principle in the White Paper was 'control',[107] mirroring practice in the private sector. The 'control' boundary includes executive agencies (which will, however, also continue to publish separate accounts)[108] but not trading funds since these

---

[105] See NAO, *Annual Report 1997*.   [106] *Supra*, n. 60.   [107] *Supra*, n. 61.
[108] Note the C&AG wants core department activities distinguished in the consolidated account, otherwise a lower standard of reporting would apply to core departments (who only report in the consolidated departmental resource account) than to agencies who will continue to report separately and in the consolidated departmental resource account.

are supposed to have an arm's-length relationship with the department. Local authorities, public corporations and nationalized industries are outside the boundary, as are NHS 'providers' (that is, NHS trusts). The purchasers of health care (i.e., health authorities) are within the boundary as are many smaller NDPBs. Executive NDPBs will normally be excluded, unless there are good control reasons to the contrary. Furthermore, wherever the final boundary is drawn, the resource account will show the financial flow between the department and the bodies outside. These latter bodies will continue to produce their own accounts, increasingly on an accruals basis.

It seems right that the criterion for consolidation should be control rather than the formality, and often historical accident, of ownership. This will go some way towards discouraging departments from artificially locating activities outside the boundary. However, if the boundary is not to be arbitrary, clear criteria need to be developed for analysing the relationship between departments and NDPBs, and between NDPBs and the quasi-private sector bodies which undertake certain service delivery. A plethora of 'quangos' exists under a myriad of statutes and regulations. The process of developing criteria for the boundary could itself help to clarify the nature of relationships and result in improved lines of accountability.

The Financial Reporting Advisory Board (FRAB),[109] established to assist the Treasury with the introduction of resource accounting in central government, in reporting on the Resource Accounting Manual, commented on the parameters of the departmental boundary. In effect, FRAB was of the view that the boundary adopted was too narrowly drawn and hence not in close accordance with GAAP.[110] Under GAAP all entities over which bodies exercise a dominant influence would be treated as subsidiaries and would be fully consolidated into a set of group accounts. The reality is that departments exercise a significant influence over trading funds and executive NDPBs due to the manner of funds, among other things. However, in the interests of the prompt introduction of resource accounting, FRAB have accepted the narrower boundary on the condition that the Board would like to return to this issue in due course. This

[109] See, generally, Ch. 2.

[110] See Financial Reporting Advisory Board to the Treasury, *Report on the Resource Accounting Manual*, (1997) para. 2.2. It has been suggested elsewhere that more consideration be given to private sector experience of consolidating organizations to ensure financial reporting is focused upon relevant economic entities: see Heald, D., and Georgiou, G., 'Resource Accounting: Consolidation and Accounting Regulation', 73 (1995) *Public Administration* 571. In the private sector, consolidation brings in the financial position of virtually all subsidiaries: FRS 2 (ASB 1992). A subsidiary is defined in the UK as any company which is controlled, directly or indirectly, by the parent or one over which the parent can exercise dominant influence, meaning that the parent can dominate the subsidiaries operating and financial decisions.

seems a reasonable course of action though all the above evidence points to a widening of the boundary in time.

Bodies Subject To *VFM* Audit

The 1983 Act details the bodies subject to *vfm* audit by the C&AG. Section 6(3) provides that the C&AG has *vfm* jurisdiction over:

(a) any department required to prepare an appropriation account under the 1866 Act;

(b) any body required to keep accounts under s. 98 of the National Health Service Act 1977;[111]

(c) any authority or body whose accounts are required to be examined and certified, or are open to the inspection of the C&AG by virtue of any enactment, including an enactment passed after this Act; and

(d) any authority or body whose accounts are required to be examined and certified, or are open to the inspection of the C&AG by virtue of any agreement made, whether before or after the passing of this Act, between that authority or body and a Minister of the Crown.

Further, section 7 provides that if the C&AG has reasonable cause to believe that any authority or body has in any of its financial years received more than half its income from public funds he may carry out an examination into the economy, efficiency and effectiveness with which it has in that year used its resources in discharging its functions. In effect, bodies can come within the C&AG's jurisdiction one year and escape it the next depending on how it is financed.

Inspection Rights

It is constitutionally important that a public sector external auditor, such as the NAO, can follow and check all public expenditure. Where the C&AG is not the appointed auditor, but the body in question is funded by Parliament, the C&AG has a duty to satisfy himself that the grants made by Parliament are used for the proper purpose. In order to facilitate this, the C&AG has rights of inspection over about 4,000 bodies which receive public money to provide public services.[112] For example, the C&AG has inspection rights over big spenders such as universities, colleges of higher education and grant-maintained schools (GMS). At the same time, a lot of the bodies over which the C&AG has inspection rights are relatively small, for instance the British Chess Federation, and would not be at the forefront of the C&AG's mind in terms of financial regularity, propriety and *vfm*.

---

[111] For the audit arrangements of the NHS, see Ch. 7.
[112] NAO, *Annual Report 1997*.

Inspection rights are different from audit rights though. A private sector auditor will usually perform the statutory audit function at the same time as the C&AG exercises his inspection rights. In terms of outputs following inspection, the C&AG generally reports to the management of the body. In 1996–97, the NAO carried out some 290 examinations, producing the same number of management reports. Where serious problems arise, the NAO may also report to Parliament.

Inspection rights are generally not exercised annually but periodically. They can be for financial audit only or be '*vfm* specific'. In the former case, the focus is not on checking every pound but on particular issues of governance, what was described as 'higher level financial control concerns'. Access for the purpose of inspection can be needed in two different circumstances:

(1) for a *vfm* study of the body in question;[113] or
(2) to complete a financial or *vfm* study of a parent body, access to a subsidiary body may be needed.

Inspection rights are granted either by the statute which established the body or, by agreement. The NAO may find itself seeking access by agreement in two main circumstances: first, where a new body has been established and statutory rights of access are not provided for; or secondly, where the functions and services are provided under contract by a private sector organization. In return for allowing the NAO access to their books of account, the body can benefit from the feedback following the C&AG's inspection. Inspection also allows the body to demonstrate its accountability publicly. It must be remembered that access cannot be forced on a body where it is not provided for by statute. Access must be voluntarily given and hence it can be refused. For instance, access might be refused where a body does not want to subject itself to any more scrutiny than is strictly required by company law. If access is refused, the NAO can enlist the help of the Treasury or the relevant department. The NAO can also seek the assistance of the PAC and the Public Accounts Commission, or it could publish a report itself highlighting the deficiency. In some cases, the lack of access means that the C&AG might have to qualify the audit certificate of the parent body. Ultimately however, access is at the discretion of the body concerned. An example of the difficulties in this area was illustrated when Camelot, the lottery operator, refused the C&AG access to its records in 1997. This lack of access was raised in an NAO report where a 'scope limitation', a form of qualification,

---

[113] Where the C&AG has jurisdiction under any enactment or agreement, to examine and certify a body's accounts, or to inspect those accounts, section 6 of the National Audit Act 1983 gives the C&AG *vfm* jurisdiction over the particular body also: see above. See the following *vfm* reports for example, *Remploy Limited*, HC 267 1996–97; and *The Achievements of the Second and Third Generation Urban Development Corporations*, HC 898, 1992–93.

was put on the C&AG's certificate on the National Lottery Distribution Fund (1995–96) certified in May 1997.[114] The C&AG's report was supported by the PAC in their subsequent report,[115] statutory access is now provided for in section 5 of the National Lottery Act 1998.

The adequacy of the framework of inspection rights will be examined in relation to three categories of bodies in receipt of public funds: executive NDPBs, local spending bodies and private contractors. For the record, the C&AG has no rights of access to Railtrack and the train operating companies, who appoint their own private auditors, as do the other utility companies. The C&AG does have access rights over the regulators though. The former nationalized industries remain outside the C&AG's institutional remit. Publicly owned companies also appoint their own auditors and the C&AG must negotiate access case by case. The current Chair of the PAC, Mr David Davis, has stated that the C&AG should undertake the audit of all publicly owned companies—that is, companies owned by public bodies or the state, in large part or in total. This is currently precluded by companies legislation.

Executive NDPBs[116]

In 1996–97, the C&AG audited the accounts of 154 out of 309 executive NDPBs, such as the higher education funding councils.[117] This audit jurisdiction can be either statutory or based on agreement. All executive NDPBs created since May 1997, have had the C&AG appointed as their statutory auditor. Previous to this, where an executive NDPB was newly established and the C&AG was not the appointed auditor under the relevant legislation, this was a matter largely within the remit of the parent department. In these circumstances, the issue of audit is usually addressed in the particular financial memorandum and management statement. These documents set out, among other things, the terms and conditions which a sponsor department attaches to the funding of a NDPB.[118] Effectively, any grants can be made conditional on the NDPB submitting to audit by the NAO. Where the C&AG is not the auditor, by statute or agreement, the remaining executive NDPBs are audited by private firms, some appointed by the minister, others are self-appointed.[119]

---

[114] C&AG's Report, HC 678, 1995–96. Interestingly, the same problem existed the previous year, the first year of the account, but the account was not qualified then.

[115] PAC Twentieth Report of 1996–97; see also PAC, Forty-First Report of 1995–96.

[116] Other NDPBs, such as advisory NDPBs and tribunals are usually funded as part of the departmental vote, and are not required to produce separate accounts.

[117] See NAO, *Annual Report 1997*.

[118] See Cabinet Office and HM Treasury, *NDPB's: A Guide for Government Departments*, (1992) 5.14; see further *Government Accounting, supra*, n. 3, Annex to Chapter 13.

[119] For example, the Lord Chancellor appoints the auditor to The Legal Aid Board, one of the 'big spenders' often quoted by the NAO where access for inspection is voluntary.

In principle, the C&AG now has access for inspection purposes to all executive NDPBs. In the Green Paper, *Spending Public Money: Governance and Audit*,[120] it was noted that in 1992, the Government agreed that where the C&AG did not audit or had no inspection rights, departments would use their best endeavours to secure such rights. At that time, there were 20 such bodies to which the C&AG had no audit or inspection rights. In the Green Paper, and again in the White Paper, *Governance of Public Bodies: a progress report*,[121] the Government stated that it would ensure that the C&AG had inspection rights over all executive NDPBs which he did not audit, and over companies which are wholly or mainly owned by the NDPB. As a result, at the time of writing, the C&AG had inspection rights to all but 3 of the 270 executive NDPBs in Great Britain.[122] This process of extending the C&AG's jurisdiction continues and although the current position represents an improvement on the position in 1992, for example, it is less than ideal.

The White Paper notes that the C&AG would prefer a statutory right to audit (not just to inspect) all executive NDPBs. This is also the view of the current Chair of the PAC, Mr David Davis.[123] This would mean that the C&AG would formally become the external auditor for all executive NDPBs, though of course he could contract-out some of the work to private auditors. The Conservative Government (1992–97) rejected this more uniform approach because of the large number of legislative changes which would be needed. The Labour Government's decision to appoint the C&AG as statutory auditor from May 1997 of all new NDPBs goes some way to meet the C&AG's needs but a large minority of NDPBs are still audited by private firms appointed by the minister or by the NDPB itself.

Local Public Spending Bodies

This phrase, coined by the Nolan Committee, comprises: grant-maintained schools (GMS) and institutions of further and higher education (including universities); training and enterprise councils in England and Wales (TECs; LECs in Scotland); and registered social landlords in England and Wales (formerly registered housing associations; and registered housing associations in Scotland). These bodies are 'not for profit' bodies staffed mainly by volunteers—members are rarely elected or appointed by ministers. They provide public services at a local level and are largely, or wholly, publicly funded. Very different arrangements for audit exist for TECs and

---

[120] March 1996.   [121] February 1997.

[122] These remaining three bodies are considered relatively small, and not a priority, by the NAO. It is expected that access will be secured in due course. The three are in the Home Office (the Alcohol Education Research Council; the Horserace Betting Levy Board; and the Horserace Totalisor Board). In addition, there are 39 executive NDPBs in Northern Ireland, four of which come under the jurisdiction of the C&AG with the remainder under the jurisdiction of the Northern Ireland Audit Office: see Cabinet Office, *Public Bodies 1997*.

[123] See *Hansard*, Vol. 301 No. 72, col. 480, 20 November 1997, for the annual PAC debate.

registered social landlords in England and Wales, in contrast with local education bodies.

TECs are private companies operating under contract with government (principally, the Department of Education and Employment) to provide certain services. For the most part, TECs subcontract the provision of training to training providers, including local authorities, voluntary bodies and private companies. TECs appoint their own private auditors under companies legislation. Access for inspection purposes depends on negotiations with the department. In practice, the C&AG's right of access to TECs is included in the annual operating agreement between the department and the Council. Hence, access is contractual. Here, inspection rights are only used for the purpose of auditing the parent body.

In England, social landlords must register with the Housing Corporation (in Wales, with Tai Cymru) in order to receive grants. The legal structure of social landlords is not uniform. Any organization can use the name 'social landlord'. Some such organizations are charitable trusts, or companies or industrial and provident societies. Each appoints their own auditors. The C&AG has no rights of access. Again access is voluntary, based on contract and negotiated on a case-by-case basis. Despite access problems, the NAO has published a number of *vfm* reports on particular housing associations.[124]

The area of education (that is, GMS and institutes of further and higher education) is very different. While again these bodies appoint their own private auditors, complete access for audit purposes of parent body is provided for in the relevant legislation;[125] the bodies themselves are also subject to *vfm* studies.[126] The C&AG is also obliged annually to report on any *vfm* studies regarding GMS.[127] There are no logical reasons why access was granted by statute for education and not for social landlords and TECs. This distinction would appear inexplicable as the same point of principle applies in each case. The Chair of the PAC has called for 'independently guaranteed rights' of access to all local spending bodies which would entail legislation being introduced.[128]

Private Contractors

The NAO would like to be able to follow public money into private hands to ensure full accountability to Parliament. This would be for the purpose

---

[124] See, for instance, Tenant's Choice and the Torbay Tenants Housing Association, HC 170, 1997–98.

[125] See Further and Higher Education Act 1992, s. 53; and Education Act 1993, s. 154.

[126] See for example, the *vfm* reports: University of Portsmouth, HC 4, 1997–98; and Governance and Management of Overseas Courses at the Swansea Institute of Higher Education, HC 222, 1996–97.

[127] Education Act 1993, s. 154.

[128] See *Hansard*, Vol. 301 No. 72, col. 480, 20 November 1997, for the annual PAC debate.

of auditing the parent bodies and not the final recipient private body, to ensure that the parent bodies are using public monies for the proper purposes and getting *vfm*. The Conservative Government's White Paper, *Governance and Audit: a progress report*[129] made a commitment to encourage appropriate access to private contractors' books to examine whether audited bodies have managed their functions provided under contract.

At present, the Treasury's Central Unit on Procurement issue Guidance on Model Form Contracts, including a standard term in the contract providing access for the NAO. The Guidance makes clear that the incorporation of the standard clause on access in the contract is 'at the discretion' of the parent/purchaser ('the Authority'). A parent/purchaser might neglect to include such a clause; or it might think that its inclusion is not needed under the terms of the Treasury Guidance;[130] or it might want to avoid having the NAO checking how it is spending public money and intentionally fail to include the clause. Rather than relying on contractual access, the C&AG would prefer a statutory right of access to contractors' books for the purpose of auditing the parent body.

A neat solution to the inconsistencies in this area would be to introduce amending legislation to widen the C&AG's statutory institutional jurisdiction. Under the terms of this proposed legislation, the C&AG could be appointed the statutory auditor for all executive NDPBs, and all publicly owned companies. This would reduce the regulatory burden on the bodies concerned because instead of having both an auditor appointed further to companies, or other, legislation, and the NAO reviewing their financial records, there would only be one auditor, the C&AG. Further, the C&AG could be given guaranteed rights of access to the records of all local spending bodies and private contractors providing public services and functions. Until such legislation is forthcoming, the C&AG will remain the poor relative of other public sector auditors, such as the Audit Commission and the European Court of Auditors, both of which can follow public monies into private hands, with regard to its institutional audit jurisdiction.

---

[129] February 1997.
[130] The Guidance gives examples of when the clause should be included, for example: when contractors process or handle records relating to the operational activities of the Authority; or where contractors' activities include the management of publicly owned assets.

5

Independence

The independence of an external auditor is vital to enable the auditor to perform his functions properly. In the private sector, the auditor's basic role is to certify annually, in a report to members, whether or not the accounts of an organization give a 'true and fair' view of the state of that organization and whether the accounts comply with UK GAAP—Generally Accepted Accounting Practice.[1] If the accounts are to be relied upon, it is essential that they should be true and fair and this is more likely to be the case if someone independent of the organization has vetted and certified them. The importance of the auditors' role, in the private sector, has been emphasized by developments over the last 150 years designed to ensure their professional competence and independence. In 1844, when for a brief time auditors were first made compulsory for registered companies, it was common practice for the auditor to be a shareholder in the company.[2] In 1900, when auditors were again made obligatory for registered companies, it was provided, in an attempt to ensure the auditor's independence from management, that the auditor should not be an officer of the company.[3] It was not until 1948 that a legislative requirement that auditors possess professional qualifications was introduced. The current law, supplemented by ethical rules of practice, seeks to ensure that company auditors are both competent and independent.[4] For instance, in order to be eligible for appointment as a company auditor, persons must be members of a recognized supervisory body and be eligible under its rules to be appointed.[5] These rules require independence from the company concerned and appropriate qualifications.[6] Further, certain relationships with the company

---

[1] See Ch. 2.

[2] Hadden, T., *Company Law and Capitalism*, (London: Weidenfeld and Nicolson, 2nd edn., 1977), p. 137.

[3] Companies Act 1900, s. 21(3).

[4] Companies Act 1985, Parts VII and XI, Chapter V; and as amended by the 1989 Companies Act, implementing the Eighth Company Law Directive on the qualification of company auditors. The main purpose of these sections is to ensure '. . . that audits by persons so appointed are carried out properly and with integrity and with the proper degree of independence', 1989 Act, s. 24(1).

[5] Companies Act 1989, s. 25(1)(b).   [6] Ibid., s. 27, Sch. 11, paras. 4 and 5.

concerned which are fundamentally incompatible with independence are prohibited outright.[7]

Equally, the independence of a public sector external auditor is essential to his ability to perform his role in the accountability process. For the findings of public sector audit, whether financial or *vfm*, to be meaningful, and to be considered meaningful, it is clearly desirable that the auditor is free from the direction or influence of any interested party. The main value of a public sector auditor's findings is that they represent an independent assessment of the government's account and performance. As an independent actor he can present impartial findings. Such objective information is a more powerful tool for those calling government to account and is also more likely to lead to the government remedying shortcomings.[8] It also makes the government's rendering of account more credible. So, whether in the private or public sector, the independence of the auditor is well established as both a legal and professional requirement.

INTOSAI, the International Organization of Supreme Audit Institutions, of which the NAO is a member, states in its *Auditing Standards* that:

The auditor and the SAI [Supreme Audit Institution][9] must be independent.[10]

The Standards further state that an adequate degree of independence from the legislature and the executive branch of government is essential to the conduct of audit and to the credibility of its result. It is interesting to note the use of the word *adequate* regarding the degree of independence of the SAI relative to the legislature and the executive. The Standards do not require an *absolute* degree of independence. This would be unrealistic. Instead, the Standards explore in more detail the relationship between the SAI and these other branches of government advising, for example, that: 'While the SAI must observe the laws enacted by the legislature, adequate independence requires that it not otherwise be subject to direction by the legislature . . .'; and that, 'It is necessary that the legislature provide the SAI with sufficient resources . . .'; and that, 'The executive branch of government and the SAI may have some common interests in the promotion of public accountability. But the essential relationship with the executive is that of external auditor'.

A further dimension to the independence of auditors is highlighted when the distinction between internal and external audit is explored.[11] Auditors themselves conventionally distinguish *internal* from *external* audit. Professional auditors define the mission of internal audit in terms

---

[7] Ibid., s. 27(1).   [8] Note the two meanings of 'government' in Ch. 1.
[9] Supreme Audit Institution is defined in the INTOSAI *Auditing Standards*, as 'The public body of a State which, however designated, constituted or organised, exercise by virtue of law, the highest public auditing function of that State'.
[10] INTOSAI, *Auditing Standards*, (June 1989), Chapter 2, para. 47; see, further, paras. 48–71.
[11] See, generally, Ch. 2.

of improving value for money, avoiding and detecting fraud and checking and improving financial systems. There is clearly some degree of overlap between the work of internal and external auditors. A widely accepted definition is that external audit means the examination of accounts and other activities, conducted from outside an organization by an independent person or body for the purpose of holding managers to account. In contrast, internal audit occurs from within an organization for the review of accounting, and other operations as a basis for service to management.[12] The profession regards the essential difference between the two as the fact that internal auditors are appointed by and report to the management of an organization. Although external auditors may also provide information to management, they are appointed by and report primarily to an external body that holds the organization's management to account. The internal auditor or audit unit is independent in the sense that he or it is professionally independent and separate from those responsible for the activities under review within the organization. However, the internal auditor's independence normally stops there. It can be limited by a number of factors. First, the internal auditor is employed by, and thus, for the duration of the audit at least, is part of the organization which is subject to the audit. Often the internal auditor does not enjoy any physical independence being located 'in-house'—within the relevant organization. Further problems can arise, for instance, as to the scope of the audit, which can be prescribed by the management rather than being determined independently by the auditor. An important feature of an external auditor is the ability to decide the subject matter of the audit and the manner of conducting the audit. Where the auditor can be directed in these matters, as is the usual case with internal auditors, the auditor can easily be diverted from the true financial state of the organization's accounts and performance. The audit exercise can be mere cosmetics in these circumstances. Additionally, the internal auditor can be viewed as a labour resource on which the management can draw during busy periods further diminishing any independence he might seek to preserve for professional purposes.

Nevertheless, from a professional perspective, both internal and external audit must be 'operationally independent'. However, independence cannot be reduced to a matter of professional ethics. External audit in the public sector is, in part at least, a mechanism for calling government to account on behalf of citizens. The independence of the external auditor from government therefore has a constitutional significance and must be embedded in an appropriate institutional framework established through public law. This view concerning the importance of independence

---

[12] Institute of Internal Auditors, *Statement of Responsibilities of the Internal Auditor*, (New York, 1947), cited in Sherer, M., and Kent, D., *Auditing and Accountability* (London: Chapman Publishing, 1983), p. 100.

for public sector external auditors is widely accepted.[13] In Britain, it was partly a recognition of this 'importance of being independent' which led to the introduction of the 1983 National Audit Act (hereinafter the 1983 Act). The 1983 Act reinforced the independence of the C&AG and his staff from the executive. In brief, NAO staff are not civil servants and there are special arrangements for determining the NAO's own budget. The latter go a considerable way towards insulating the NAO from budgetary pressures that might compromise its independence. The Act also defined the method of appointment and status of the C&AG in ways designed to promote his independence from government. These and other matters will be considered in more detail below.

THE MEANING OF INDEPENDENCE

Independence is a complex notion. It is both a political ideal, and a constitutional requirement for various public officials and bodies. At its simplest, it is a status whereby a state, a public body or an official can exist and function free from the direction or control of others. From a more practical perspective, it may not be reasonable to speak of total independence in the sense of being totally free from outside direction or control. A fundamental aspect of the Rule of Law is that no one, including public officials or bodies, is above the law.[14] Hence, public officials and bodies in performing their public functions must be mindful of the law and operate within its parameters. Being independent does not, of course, mean that an official or a body can be arbitrary in the exercise of his or its public functions. The official or body must operate within a legal framework of rules. Where the official or body is given discretion, that discretion should be exercised in a consistent and proportionate manner.[15]

Also, public officials or bodies do not exist in isolation, but as part of a greater whole that is government—government in this sense includes not just ministers, but the whole range of public bodies, such as departments, agencies and non-departmental public bodies, along with the civil servants and other officials who staff them.[16] In certain circumstances

---

[13] For instance, the members of the European Court of Auditors' independence 'must be beyond doubt' (Article 188b, EC Treaty; to be renumbered as Article 247, following the ratification of the Amsterdam Treaty); in Germany the members of the *Bundesrechnungshof* are given a constitutional position similar to judges.

[14] Dicey, A. V., *Introduction to the Study of the Law of the Constitution*, (London: Macmillan, 10th edn., 1959), Ch. X.

[15] On the exercise of discretion see further: Davis, K. C., *Discretionary Justice: a preliminary inquiry*, (Urbana: University of Chicago Press, 1971).

[16] See Ch. 1.

officials or bodies can find themselves on opposing sides;[17] in other circumstances, officials or bodies share a commonality of interests with other officials or bodies. An example of the latter is the long established relationship which exists between the C&AG (and since 1983, the NAO), the PAC and the Treasury. The recognition of this commonality of interest does not necessarily take from the NAO's independence. A closer examination of the respective constitutional roles of these bodies needs to be undertaken to assess the independence, or more precisely the institutional independence of the NAO.

An assessment of the institutional independence of any public body is multidimensional, comprising at least three dimensions. First, is the 'organizational independence' of the body—as an institution of government how is the NAO organized, how is it financed and how does it relate to other institutions of government. A second dimension is the 'personal independence' of the body—here the concern is the extent to which the individuals who staff the office or body are protected from any external influence, in particular from the 'clients' of the institution. And finally, there is the 'operational independence' of the body—how does the body operate or perform its functions on a day-to-day basis, can the body perform its functions without being dependent on any interested party (for example, without having to check its actions in order to maintain the goodwill of an interested party).

THE INSTITUTIONAL INDEPENDENCE OF THE NAO

The constitutional framework of the NAO is intended to provide the degree of independence necessary to allow public sector audit to effectively contribute to the accountability of government. The statutory independence of the C&AG and the NAO is exceptional in the context of the British Constitution.[18] However, the nature of that independence has remained

---

[17] For example, during the PES, each individual department seeks to maximize its spending powers. Once total expenditure is set, this is of course at the expense of other competing departments. At the same time, the Treasury's concern is to minimize costs. See, further, McEldowney, J., 'The Control of Public Expenditure', in Jowell, J., and Oliver, D., eds., *The Changing Constitution*, (Oxford: Clarendon Press, 3rd edn., 1994); and Thain, C., and Wright, M., *The Treasury and Whitehall: The Planning and Control of Public Expenditure, 1976–1993*, (Oxford: Oxford University Press, 1995).

[18] For instance, the Parliamentary Commissioner (the Ombudsman) is appointed by the Government (officially by the Crown: s. 1, Parliamentary Commissioner Act 1967), and now in practice, following consultation with the Chair of the Parliamentary Commissioner Select Committee of the House of Commons. He holds office during good behaviour, to the retiring age of sixty-five years. Unlike the C&AG, he is not an officer of the House of Commons though. And unlike, the NAO, the Commissioner's budget is controlled by the Treasury, and his staff are a mixture of civil servants and some non-civil servants appointed with the approval of the Treasury (s. 3, 1967).

largely unexplored in the constitutional literature. In practice, the C&AG's activities are governed by constitutional conventions and traditions, revealing that the concept of independence is not a simple one.

It is important to note at the outset that the independent legal status of the NAO is statutory only.[19] Unlike other jurisdictions,[20] the principle of independent external audit in the United Kingdom is not enshrined in a constitutional document but it is the subject of long standing legislation and convention.[21] Nevertheless, having a statutory base gives the NAO, as an institution, a degree of protection from a government unhappy with its findings, since it could not be abolished or its duties and powers altered without legislation being passed.

Organizational Independence

Single Head or Collegiate?

In terms of an audit institution's internal organization, a distinction can be drawn between a single head structure and a collegiate structure. Most audit institutions fall into one or other of these categories. The NAO is headed by a single person, the C&AG.[22] The C&AG is, by statute, an officer of the House of Commons and he reports to the House.[23] Schedule 2 of the 1983 Act further specifies that the person for the time being holding the office of C&AG shall by that name be a corporation sole, that is, an artificial legal entity separate from the person holding office from time to time. As corporation sole, the C&AG personifies the office and is responsible in law for its actions—and its omissions—although most of these actions are taken by the staff of the office. The C&AG can sue, and be sued. In theory, the C&AG could, for example, take judicial review proceedings to enforce his legal right of access to documents and information set out under section 8 of the 1983 Act. There is no record of the C&AG being a party to any legal proceedings however. The creation of a corporation sole also ensures the continuity of title and negatives the need to transfer rights and obligations to a successor.

Responsibility for the C&AG's statutory functions vests directly in the C&AG. For instance, in examining and certifying the financial accounts of departments and other bodies, although the actual audit work is done by staff appointed by the C&AG under the 1983 Act, it is the C&AG, or his delegate, who 'signs-off' the accounts. This is the case even where

---

[19] See the National Audit Act 1983.

[20] See, for example, Article 33 of Bunreacht na hEireann (the Irish Constitution); Chapter 12, Article 7 of the Swedish Instrument of Government (which forms part of the Swedish Constitution).

[21] See Ch. 3.   [22] 1983 Act, s. 3(1)(a).   [23] 1983 Act, s. 1(2).

the audit work has been contracted out to a private sector firm. Further, the 1983 Act provides that, subject to any duties imposed on him by statute, the C&AG has 'complete discretion' in the performance of his functions.[24]

In contrast, the European Court of Auditors and the German *Bundesrechnungshof* (Federal Court of Audit), for example, are collegiate bodies where decision-making is a collective process. Further, the independence of the European Court of Auditors and the *Bundesrechnungshof* is judicial in nature.[25]

Established in 1949, the status and functions of the Bundesrechnungshof are outlined in the Basic Law. In 1969, reform of the Budget Law widened the Bundesrechnungshof's remit and extended its role to that of adviser to the *Bundestag* (the directly elected lower house of the legislature), the *Bundesrat* (the upper house of the legislature appointed by the Governments of the *Länder*) and the Federal Government.[26] This reform reinforced its role as the independent audit and advisory body at federal government level. This position is enumerated further in the 1985 Federal Court of Audit Act, which states that the Bundesrechnungshof is the supreme federal authority and an independent institution of financial control subject only to the law.[27] The Bundesrechnungshof's independence is thus constitutionally guaranteed and is thought of in judicial terms. Reference to the Bundesrechnungshof as a 'court' also reflects its collegiate structure. The Bundesrechnungshof has 66 members comprising the President, Vice President, 9 Directors of Audit and 55 Audit Managers.[28] Each member enjoys judicial independence and a constitutional status similar to a judge.

There is no centrally determined and uniform audit approach although the final result from the individual audits is moderated by the collegiate decision-making process. Individual audit decisions are made by colleges (committees) within the Bundesrechnungshof comprising a Director of Audit and an Audit Manager. These two members may be joined by the President and Vice President. Where a college cannot agree on a particular matter, the opposing view is referred upwards to either the Divisional Senate or the Large Senate for decision. The Divisional Senate comprises the relevant divisional Director, all the division's Audit Managers and an Audit Manager from another division. Either the President or the Vice President may attend any Divisional Senate and vote

---

[24] 1983 Act, s. 1(3): see, further, below.

[25] On the European Court of Auditors: see Ch. 8.

[26] See Article 114 of the Basic Law; s. 42 of the Law on Budgetary Principles 1969; and Part V of the Federal Budget Code 1969, in particular s. 88.

[27] Article 1.

[28] The members of the Bundesrechnungshof are supported by over 400 auditors, usually recruited from government.

in any decision. The Large Senate normally comprises 16 members: The President, the Vice President, the Directors of Audit, three Audit Managers and two rapporteurs. As well as this conciliation role, the Large Senate decides the content of the annual report.

It can be seen from the above that in a collegiate structure, the role of any one member, including the President or Vice President, is arguably less significant in maintaining the independence of the institution, than with a single-headed structure. In contrast, the single head structure of the NAO places a greater emphasis on the office of the C&AG and the mechanisms in place to protect his independence. The issue of the C&AG's personal independence will be considered below.

The Budget

The activities of any audit institution will inevitably depend, in part, on the resources available to it. Therefore, control over its budget is an important aspect of its independence. There are obvious reasons why the budget of a public sector audit institution should not be controlled exclusively by the executive. This would allow the executive control over the extent of audit activities, the number and skills of staff which could be employed by the institution and the investments it could make on improving training or technology. The importance of an independent budget-setting process is recognized in Germany, for example. The Bundesrechnungshof's budget is determined by Parliament on an annual basis. The Bundesrechnungshof prepares a draft budget which is discussed with the Ministry of Finance before being presented to Parliament. Where the Ministry recommends a change to the budget, the President of the Bundesrechnungshof has the right to submit comments on the proposed amendments to Parliament through the Ministry of Finance. This gives the President of the Bundesrechnungshof a public right to reply and defend his claim to the resources sought.

The current arrangements, established under the 1983 Act, for the budget of the NAO seem to go further than the German arrangements to minimize the role of the Treasury, and are exceptional within the British Constitution.[29] Prior to the 1983 Act, the budget for the Exchequer and Audit Department, like any other department, was effectively controlled by the Treasury. When proposals to change the funding of central

---

[29] The funding arrangement for the House of Commons is similar to that of the NAO. Under the House of Commons (Administration) Act 1978, the estimate is prepared and laid before Parliament by the House of Commons Commission and hence outside the formal control of the Treasury. See further, Griffith, J., and Ryle, M., *Parliament, Functions, Practice and Procedures,* (London: Sweet & Maxwell, 1989), Ch. 5. Proposals, similar to the budgetary arrangements of the National Audit Office and the House of Commons administration, were made regarding the budget of the Parliamentary Commissioner (the Ombudsman) in 1993–94, but were never acted upon by the Government: see HC 33, 1993–94, para. 32.

government audit were made, the Treasury was wary, not least because of the precedent it set.

The legislation provides that the NAO is funded by an annual Parliamentary vote.[30] The Estimate for the NAO is prepared by the C&AG but it is then taken into the charge of the Public Accounts Commission, a body specifically established under the 1983 Act to protect the NAO's budget from executive control.[31] The Commission consists of the Chair of the PAC, the Leader of the House of Commons and seven other MPs, usually experienced members of the House. Its statutory role includes examining the Estimate for the NAO, making any amendments to it which it thinks fit and laying it before the House. The Commission meets twice a year: once in July to consider the NAO's corporate plan (see, further, below) and once in October to consider the Estimate. The legislation requires the Commission to consult the PAC and the Treasury on the Estimate but it is the Commission which in practice 'controls' the Estimate. In November each year the PAC considers the Estimate (and the corporate plan) in the form of a PAC hearing with the C&AG as a witness. The PAC then reports its findings.[32]

The Treasury

The Treasury's role in the expenditure process is described in previous chapters. Basically, the Treasury's role to date has been to exercise supervision over a decentralized system of financial control. More recent developments, such as the simplification of the estimates from 1996–97 onwards,[33] and the introduction of RAB, indicate an even more strategic role for the Treasury.[34] However, the impact of the Treasury's power to direct the form of the accounts, under section 23 of the Exchequer and Audit Departments Act 1866, should not be underestimated. This affects not only the accounting stage of the expenditure process itself but also affects what happens at the previous stage. The way in which departments, agencies and other bodies actually spend money is profoundly affected by how they must subsequently account for it. This is particularly true with the move from appropriation accounts to resource accounts. But the Treasury's dominance in this area is tempered by the constitutional convention which requires Parliamentary approval for any changes to the

[30] 1983 Act, s. 4. For example, the NAO Estimate for 1998–99 was £40.9 million: HC 383, 1997–98.
[31] See, generally, the 1983 Act, ss. 2, 4 and the First and Third Schedules.
[32] See for example, the Thirty-Ninth Report of the PAC, *National Audit Office Estimate*, HC 176, 1996–97; and HC 282, 1997–98.
[33] See Ch. 3.
[34] See the 1994 Fundamental Expenditure Review of the Treasury: see further Parry, R., Hood, C., and James, O., 'Reinventing the Treasury: economic rationalism or an econocrat's fallacy of control', 75 (1997) *Public Administration* 395.

form of the accounts. This in turn brings the influence of the Financial Reporting Advisory Board into play.[35]

There is an obvious overlap in the interests of the NAO and specific parts of the Treasury. Principles such as propriety, regularity, *vfm* and accountability are at the forefront of the minds of accounting officers, the Treasury Officer of Accounts, as well as the NAO and the PAC. In particular, a concern for *vfm* has driven a number of Treasury initiatives including the *Financial Management Initiative* (1982); the *Next Steps* programme (1988); contracting out and market testing in the *Citizen's Charter* (1991) and *Competing for Quality* (1992); and the drive for delegation in *The Civil Service: Continuity and Change*.[36] It would appear therefore that a natural alliance exists between the NAO and the Treasury. There is no question of one organization seeking to dominate the other. The possibility of Treasury dominance is excluded by the fact that the C&AG has complete discretion in the performance of his statutory duties and the Treasury no longer has any powers of direction over the NAO. The Treasury's powers, under the Exchequer and Audit Departments Act 1921, to direct the C&AG to examine accounts were removed by the 1983 Act.[37] Even where the NAO's budget is concerned, the Treasury's influence is practically of little consequence. This type of natural alliance would therefore appear not to impinge on the independence of the NAO. Indeed, it reinforces the work of the NAO and promotes further the above principles.

The PAC

The relationship between the C&AG and the NAO, and the PAC, is more formalized than that with the Treasury. As an officer of the House of Commons, it is the responsibility of the C&AG to serve the House as a whole. By convention and tradition, he has served the House primarily through the PAC.[38] The expression that the NAO 'serves' the PAC, implies a degree of subservience, but this does not truly reflect the relationship between the two. It might better be described as a 'working partnership', to which each institution brings its own expertise. Describing the relationship as a partnership also implies a common aim or aims.

The 1983 Act contains specific functions for the PAC and its Chair regarding the appointment of the C&AG and the work of the NAO. In effect, section 1(1) of the 1983 Act gives the Chair of the PAC the power to veto the appointment of a new C&AG (see below). Further, section 1(3) of the 1983 Act requires that the C&AG shall consult the PAC on his planned

---

[35] See Ch. 2.   [36] Cmnd. 2627 (July 1994).   [37] 1983 Act, ss. 11, 12 and 14.
[38] 1983 Act, s. 1(2). See also, HC 19, 1989–90, pp. 240–1: 'The control of the issue of moneys is on behalf of the House, certification audit is on behalf of the House and the reports which I make are to the House as a whole.' —Sir John Bourn, C&AG. See, further, Ch. 6 on the use of NAO reports by departmental select committees.

programme of *vfm* studies.[39] The PAC can make requests throughout the year for particular examinations and it has a further opportunity to do so each year when it considers the NAO's two year forward work programme. On the other hand, the 1983 Act underlines the C&AG's independence by providing that ultimately it is at the discretion of the C&AG whether a *vfm* study should be conducted or not.[40] The C&AG is also given statutory powers to report to the House of Commons on any *vfm* investigation.[41] Previous to the 1983 Act, the C&AG communicated to the House mainly through reports on financial accounts and through memoranda to the PAC, which were sometimes published as appendages to PAC reports.[42]

It is apparent from the above that there is a well established and close relationship between the NAO and the PAC. The NAO provides the PAC with the expert information and advice necessary to hold departments and other public bodies to account. The PAC's status adds gravitas to the process. In addition, the PAC has an identity of interests with the Treasury in terms of ensuring that *vfm* is attained from public expenditure. Indeed, since 1895, a Treasury Minister has been regularly appointed as a member of the PAC. This makes the composition of the PAC anomalous; select committees are conventionally made up from backbench MPs. As a matter of practice (or convention), the Treasury Minister (now the Financial Secretary to the Treasury) only attends the Committee for a few minutes of the first meeting of Parliament. Membership of the Committee does however mean that the Treasury retains access to the Committee's working papers. The Procedure Committee questioned this arrangement in its report at the time.[43] It found it 'difficult to see the continuing justification for the presence of a Minister of the Crown on a Committee charged with exercising vigilance on behalf of Parliament over the financial and administrative competence of the Executive and its various agencies'. In addition, it noted that the Treasury Minister's membership of the Committee 'is now merely a device for ensuring that the Treasury retains access to certain of the Committee's working papers— which might be considered an objective of dubious constitutional propriety'. The Procedure Committee recommended that the Financial Secretary to the Treasury should cease to be a member of the PAC. This recommendation was rejected by the then Government. The Treasury Minister's

---

[39] 1983 Act, s. 1(3).   [40] 1983 Act, s. 1(3).   [41] 1983 Act, s. 9.

[42] In a Memorandum to the Select Committee on Procedure from the then C&AG, Sir Gilbert Upcott, in 1946, it was stated that in an extreme case of urgency it would be possible for the C&AG to make a special report to the House of Commons: see HC 189, 1945–46. In evidence to the Procedure Committee in 1946, the C&AG stated his opinion that such a power had never been exercised. The authors know of no example of this power being used since.

[43] HC 19, 1989–90, pp. lxvii–lxviii.

membership of the PAC reflects the close relationship between the Treasury, the PAC and the NAO and any proposals for a change to this arrangement would need to take this into account.

Personal Independence

In analysing the personal independence of the NAO, we first consider the position of the C&AG. While the C&AG is statutorily responsible for the functions of the Office, the actual work is done by teams of auditors. This brings us to the second dimension of the NAO's personal independence: the independence of the individual auditors and their relationship with the C&AG.

The Comptroller and Auditor General

As noted above, the 1983 Act defined the status and method of appointment of the C&AG in ways designed to promote his independence from government. The C&AG is appointed by the monarch, by convention, on the advice of the Prime Minister. When making the recommendation for appointment of the C&AG, the Prime Minister must act with the agreement of the Chair of the PAC of the House of Commons, who by constitutional convention is an Opposition MP.[44] This joint approach to the appointment of the C&AG ensures that the government of the day cannot control the appointment. A candidate agreeable to the government and the opposition must be found. The practice has also arisen of consulting the Chair of the Public Accounts Commission. To date, candidates have been drawn from within government, and, in particular the Treasury. The appointment has no fixed term and so the C&AG need not be concerned about the politics of reappointment. There is no statutory retirement age, though there is a 'gentleman's agreement' that a C&AG should retire between 60–65 years of age, and serve between five to seven years.[45] The 1866 Act describes the C&AG as holding office during good behaviour subject to removal by the monarch on a resolution by both Houses of Parliament.[46] To enhance the C&AG's independent position further, his salary is charged directly to the Consolidated Fund and is not voted upon annually by Parliament.[47]

In a collegiate structure, the independence of the individual members of the court is also important.[48] For example, in Germany, relatively

[44] Exchequer and Audit Departments Act 1866, s. 6 and the 1983 Act, s. 1(1).

[45] There have been seven C&AGs since 1946, with the average tenure being 7.3 years.

[46] Exchequer and Audit Departments Act 1866, s. 3.

[47] Exchequer and Audit Departments Act 1957, s. 1, as amended by s. 6 of the Parliamentary and other Pensions Act 1976. The Speaker of the House is another officer whose independent status is protected by charging his salary directly to the Consolidated Fund.

[48] See Ch. 8 on the European Court of Auditors.

recent measures have been introduced to enhance the personal independence of the individual members of the Bundesrechnungshof. Since 1985 the appointment of the President and Vice President of the German Bundesrechnungshof has been by joint action of the government, the Bundesrat and the Bundestag. Basically, the candidates are proposed by the government and elected by the legislature. An absolute majority is required. Appointments are for 12 years or until the statutory age of retirement of 65 whichever is the earlier. By convention the political allegiances of the President and Vice President tend to reflect the principal parties of the government and the opposition. The remaining members of the Bundesrechnungshof are appointed by the President of the Federal Republic upon proposals made by the President of the Bundesrechnungshof. There is a legal requirement that either the President or the Vice President and one-third of the members should be trained lawyers.

The Auditor

The independence of the individual auditor is multidimensional. The key question when examining the auditor's independence is to ask: independent from whom? Clearly, the auditor must be independent from the auditee. The auditee, that is government, includes government in the broad sense of the civil servants and other officials in the department or body under review in any particular audit; and government in the narrow sense of the executive comprising ministers, or, more narrowly again, the Cabinet. These dimensions of independence are protected by rules of professional ethics and legal rules dealing with the status of NAO staff in the 1983 Act.

We have already noted, from a professional ethical perspective, that external auditors, whether in the private or public sector, must exercise their statutory functions in an impartial and independent manner. A common mechanism, in the private sector, to guard against partiality is the process of rotation. The basic idea is that the regular rotation of an auditor lessens the likelihood of a 'cosy relationship', that might threaten the auditor's independent judgment, developing between the auditor and the auditee. Professional standards, but not the law, require that the partner in charge of an audit must rotate every seven years.

Within the NAO, there is no set maximum for the number of years which a person can audit the same body, but we have been told that it would be unusual for a director (the equivalent to a partner in the private sector) to supervise the same account for more than five years. The Nolan Committee recommended that, in the public sector, the period of rotation should be reduced to at least five years.[49] It is unclear from the Report

---

[49] Nolan Committee First Report, *Standards in Public Life*, Cm. 2850 (May 1995), para. 108.

whether this recommendation applies to the NAO and, if it does, whether it is aimed at directors of audit or at lower levels of auditors: managers or principal auditors, for instance. If it was intended to apply to directors only, the effect of this recommendation, if accepted, would be to formalize what is currently a practice into either a constitutional convention or a legal requirement. A constitutional convention may be said to exist where there is an obligation on the relevant actors to behave in a certain way. A constitutional practice, on the other hand, merely describes how the actors customarily behave.[50] Its effect would be to further distance the auditor from the auditee, that is, government, in the broad sense described above. If this recommendation is accepted it would be important that it would apply equally to a private sector firm contracted to do public sector audit work.

The 1983 Act sought to insulate further the auditors from any influence which would undermine their professional independence. This was achieved by distancing the auditor from the auditee, in the narrow sense of the executive. Staff employed in the NAO's predecessor, the Exchequer and Audit Department, were civil servants. The C&AG was required by the 1983 Act to offer employment, as a member of staff of the NAO, to each person employed in the civil service in the Exchequer and Audit Department immediately before the coming into force of the 1983 Act. As a result the civil servants in the Exchequer and Audit Department were transformed into NAO staff, with one major difference. NAO staff are not civil servants.[51] The C&AG is authorized to appoint such staff for the NAO as he considers necessary for assisting him in the discharge of his functions,[52] and the staff are appointed at such remuneration and on such terms as the C&AG may determine.[53] The statute does specify that in setting remuneration the C&AG have regard to the desirability of keeping the terms of employment of the NAO staff broadly in line with civil servants generally.[54]

The 1983 Act took central government public sector auditors from a central government department under the control of the executive, and more particularly the Treasury. In their place now is the C&AG. This can be viewed from two very different perspectives. As employees of the C&AG, arguably the auditors' independent status is enhanced by the independence of the C&AG. Alternatively, the C&AG's position as employer, with complete discretion in the performance of his duties, effectively means that he can control the audit process. Unlike the legislation governing local government audit,[55] the 1983 Act does not include any explicit powers

---

[50] Brazier, R., 'The Non-Legal Constitution: Thoughts on Convention, Practice and Principle', 43 (1992) *Northern Ireland Legal Quarterly*, 262.

[51] 1983 Act, s. 3(5).   [52] 1983 Act, s. 3(2).   [53] 1983 Act, s. 3(3).

[54] 1983 Act, s. 3(4).   [55] See, further, Ch. 7.

of direction for the C&AG to the auditors, however it is clear that, for example, the C&AG can direct that a *vfm* study be discontinued, or that a particular line of inquiry be dropped. There may be good reasons for such decision: the auditors may be coming close to breaching the prohibition on questioning the merits of policy objectives, for instance. But whatever the explanation, the ability of the C&AG to direct NAO staff brings clearly into question the accountability of the C&AG and his Office. The C&AG and the NAO are agents of accountability but they are also public actors whose own accountabilities need to be considered. 'Independence' therefore has something of a paradoxical character. On the one hand, it is essential for the C&AG and the NAO as an agent of accountability. On the other hand, it risks bringing into question the legitimacy of the C&AG's and the NAO's role. The issue of the NAO's accountability will be considered at the end of this chapter.

Operational Independence

In assessing the day-to-day operational independence of the NAO three areas are considered below: the different jurisdictions of the C&AG; access to information; and reporting powers.

Jurisdiction

As was noted in Chapter 4, the C&AG has two basic roles: Comptroller General and Auditor General. Audit is essentially an *ex post* activity:[56] for instance, in the area of financial audit, money is first spent, next accounts are drawn up and then the accounts are audited. The same is true of *vfm* audit. However, this is not to say that audit only has an effect on what is past; clearly it also has a preventative effect. The mere fact that government decisions and activities may be examined in detail by an auditor acts as a disincentive to financial impropriety in the future and as an incentive to achieve *vfm*. As a result, an auditor's *ex post* examinations can be seen to have an *ex ante* effect.

Furthermore, some public sector auditors have the role of authorizing expenditure in the first place (for example, until recently, the Italian *Corte dei conti*). Generally this involves a check that expenditure is consistent with the purposes approved by the legislature. A small minority of public sector auditors are involved in *ex ante* examinations of the *vfm* being obtained by expenditure. At first sight, this may seem a more effective way of controlling expenditure, by making sure that mistakes do not happen in the first place. But it can have considerable drawbacks in that it involves the auditor in the decision-making process. As a result, some of

---

[56] See Chs. 1 and 2.

the responsibility for the decision can be shifted onto the auditor. This can impact in two ways: first, it may compromise the independence of the auditor in conducting future audit examinations and secondly, it may, to an extent, relieve government of some of the responsibility for the decision to spend in the first place.

As seen in Chapter 4, however, the C&AG's *Comptroller* function could not be described properly as a type of '*ex ante* audit'. Rather, it is a type of 'check' based on the figures and the minimal statutory authority. The propriety, regularity, probity or *vfm* of the requests for credit is not considered by the Exchequer Section. This is left to auditors elsewhere within the NAO. When viewed in this light, it is clear that the C&AG's *Comptroller* function does not undermine the independence of the C&AG and the NAO in the manner described above.

Focusing on the C&AG's audit jurisdiction, this was categorized into two groups in Chapter 4: material audit jurisdiction (that is, the types of audit, such as financial or *vfm*) and institutional audit jurisdiction (that is, the bodies subject to audit or inspection). As was noted, the C&AG's institutional jurisdiction is partly set out in statute and partly determined by agreement. Where the C&AG has statutory institutional jurisdiction to conduct an audit or inspection, the body in question cannot prevent the audit or inspection occurring. However, where the C&AG's jurisdiction is not statutory but based on agreement, access for audit or inspection purposes is 'negotiable'. Having to negotiate access has the potential to undermine the formal independence of the NAO. In such circumstances, the NAO is not 'independent of', but 'dependent on' the audited body for access. This is not to suggest that once access is agreed the auditors conduct their audit in a less than independent fashion. Nevertheless, the position of having to negotiate access is unsatisfactory. This threat to the independence of the Office is further support, if it is needed, in favour of placing all of the C&AG's institutional jurisdiction on a statutory basis.

The other main type of work which the C&AG undertakes and which raises questions about independence is *vfm* audit. Most public sector auditors now do some form of *vfm* audit, examining the economy, efficiency and effectiveness of government activities. Auditors' mandates for examining these issues vary considerably and there is no definitive model for *vfm* audit. VFM audits are more complex than financial audits; the establishment of norms is more difficult and they need to be adapted to a wide range of activities. Many public sector auditors have been involved in debates about exactly what *vfm* audit should be examining, and even whether they should examine *vfm* at all.

In the case of *vfm* work, it is not possible, or desirable, for an auditor to examine the *vfm* obtained from every item of government expenditure.

An audit institution must be selective in such work and it is therefore important that the selection of work undertaken is at the discretion of the audit institution and not the result of direction from the executive. Recommendations may come from the legislature or elsewhere, but it is important that the final decision is made by the audit institution. Otherwise an institution's finite resources could be tied up with studies that avoid real areas of weakness. As already noted, the C&AG, in determining to carry out a *vfm* study, must take into account any proposals made by the PAC. Proposals may also come from other sources including MPs or a particular department or body itself. However, the final decision rests with the C&AG because he is given complete discretion in performance of his duties under the 1983 Act and in particular in determining whether to conduct a *vfm* study.

The issue of audit and policy highlights another area of uncertainty in the C&AG's material audit jurisdiction. There are two approaches to this. Some public sector auditors, including the NAO, operate under an express prohibition not to question the merits of policy objectives. While for others, including Israel's Comptroller and the General Accounting Office in the United States, there is no such prohibition and in practice they do review policy.[57] The basic argument against examining policy is that it brings the audit institution into the political arena and hence compromises its independence. This appears to be the experience in Israel, for example.[58] But even where there is an express prohibition on entering the policy arena, as under the 1983 Act, the matter is not clear-cut. The burning issues then become 'what amounts to policy?' and 'who decides?'. The legislation does little to resolve these questions.

Section 6(1) of 1983 Act empowers the C&AG to carry out examinations into the economy, efficiency and effectiveness with which any department, authority or other body to which the legislation applies has used its resources in discharging its functions. Subsection (2) provides that the C&AG is not entitled to question the merits of the policy objectives of any department, authority or other body in respect of which an examination is carried out. No further explanation of subsection (2) is offered in the legislation. For a better understanding we must look to the NAO's working interpretation of this provision.

While accepting the restriction on questioning the merits of any policy objectives directly, the NAO has carved a jurisdiction for itself around

---

[57] Israel's State Comptroller has offered critiques of policy issues in the sensitive areas of economic regulation, military research and development and the distribution of resources between Jewish and Arab communities: see Sharkansky, I., 'Israel's Auditor as Policy-Maker', 66 (1988) *Public Administration* 77; see also the National Academy of Public Administration Report, 'The Roles, Mission and Operations of the US General Accounting Office: report prepared for the Committee on Governmental Affairs', United States Senate, 1994.

[58] Ibid.

such decisions. This involves a degree of intellectual acrobatics which can bring the NAO close to breaching the statutory prohibition and hence, in theory, threatening its independence. For instance, the NAO considers that it has the authority to examine the accuracy and completeness of the information supplied by departments to ministers before a policy decision is taken.[59] This is not a direct review of whether the right decision was made or not, but rather a review of whether the decision-maker, whatever his decision, was fully and properly informed. Criticizing the quality of this information whilst avoiding questioning the merits of the objectives of the policy finally chosen, can be a potential minefield.

Also within the NAO's self-defined jurisdiction is the manner in which policy is implemented. Here the question is, given the policy adopted, has it been implemented in an economic, efficient and effective manner? But any such assessment requires clarification of policy objectives so that success in achieving them can be judged. Difficulties in ascertaining the objectives of policy may itself lead to implicit criticism of the policy. This formula leaves open the extent to which audit may involve criticism of policy *decisions* on the grounds that they fail to achieve *objectives*. Indeed the distinction between decisions and objectives (like the related distinction between 'policy' and 'implementation') is dependent on specific contexts and purposes.

Discussions surrounding 'policy' during a Procedure Committee's investigation in 1989–90 illustrates how the definition of policy can differ. Robert Sheldon, the then Chairman of the PAC, stated that the PAC:

. . . do not talk about policy, we do not say: Should you have this missile or should you have that? Should you have a nuclear weapon, or not have a nuclear weapon? . . . That is not for us. We say, 'Given that you have decided that you want this missile, are you getting it for the best price in the most efficient and effective way?'.[60]

However, Michael Mates, the then Chairman of the Defence Committee, took a different view:

It is certainly a decision of 'policy' as to whether the United Kingdom has strategic nuclear weapons . . . However, once the basic policy decision has been taken, almost every consequent question is one of *vfm*, and falls squarely within the definitions of economy, efficiency and effectiveness. . . .[61]

His view was that decisions as to the type of nuclear weapons deployed would constitute *vfm* questions within the jurisdiction of the NAO and the PAC. The evidence given by the C&AG, Sir John Bourn, shows that his interpretation of what constitutes policy was in line with that of Robert Sheldon. Indeed, he cites such a careful avoidance of policy as an

---

[59] See NAO, *A framework for value for money audits*, (undated) 8.
[60] HC 19, 1989–90, p. 60.   [61] Ibid., p. 101.

'exact coincidence between my own concerns and the work of the Public Accounts Committee.'[62]

The difficulty in distinguishing the implementation of policy from the merits of the policy objectives was touched on in the debate surrounding the 1983 Act but, as noted above, no definition was offered in the Act itself.[63] This is not surprising. As is shown by the different approaches of Robert Sheldon and Michael Mates quoted above, a clear distinction between the objectives of policy and the policy itself exists only at a high level of abstraction. Its application to concrete circumstances is a matter of judgment on which reasonable opinions may differ.

Furthermore, the answer to the question of whether or not something is 'policy' depends in part on the purpose with which the question is asked and who is asking the question. In the courts, for example, government decisions may be described as 'policy' where the court thinks it inappropriate to subject the decision in question to judicial review.[64] For civil servants, the working definition of policy seems to be 'anything to do with ministers'. In practice therefore, the C&AG must develop his own definition of what constitutes policy for the purposes of external public sector audit. This however is not, and in practice cannot be, a solitary exercise on the part of the C&AG.

The ultimate decision about whether a matter constitutes policy, or not, and hence whether it is within the jurisdiction of the C&AG or not is made by the C&AG under section 1(3) of the 1983 Act which specifies that the C&AG has complete discretion in the discharge of his functions. However, in practice the C&AG and the government together build their own working agreements as to what constitutes policy.[65] This agreement often starts with a dialogue between the NAO and the department concerned during the planning stage of the *vfm* study and so it is dealt with on a case-by-case basis. Some NAO reports push the boundaries further than others[66] but it is unlikely that they would be pushed so far as to provoke serious confrontation.

---

[62] Ibid., p. 243.

[63] See Garrett, J., 'Developing State Audit in Britain', 64 (1986) *Public Administration* 421.

[64] See, e.g., *Bushell* v. *Secretary of State*, [1980] 2 All ER 608, especially the speech of Lord Diplock at p. 615.

[65] HC 19, 1989–90, pp. 243, 247; see also *Government Accounting: a guide on accounting and financial procedures for the use of government departments*, (2 vols., loose leaf) (London: HMSO, 1989 and seven amendments 1989–97) 7.1.29–30. The Chairman of the Procedure Committee queried whether a document setting out the NAO's guidelines as to what constitutes policy existed. The C&AG's deflection of the question suggests that if such a document were in existence, it would not be readily available: HC 19 Session 1989–90, p. 243.

[66] See, for example, NAO, *The elderly: information requirements for supporting the elderly and implications of personal pensions for the National Insurance Fund*, HC 55, 1990–91; or more recently, NAO, *The Work of the Directors General of Telecommunications, Gas Supply, Water Services and Electricity Supply*, HC 645, 1995–96.

It is important that the decision as to what constitutes policy is a co-operative exercise between the NAO and government because, in reality, much of the NAO's work benefits from the existence of a co-operative relationship—not least the issue of access to information, explored further below. In addition, if departments feel that policy itself is being challenged it is unlikely that recommended changes would be implemented. An antagonistic relationship would not serve the NAO's long-term aims and arguably, there are enough non-controversial areas where the NAO could be well employed.

A final aspect of the C&AG's material jurisdiction, which is germane to the independence of the NAO, is his potential new role as a sort of management consultant, highlighted in Chapter 4. Increasingly, public sector auditors are being used in a consultancy capacity in efforts to improve efficiency and effectiveness. Auditors have an important role in developing and improving systems of internal control and financial management and have expertise in the area. By establishing adequate systems and procedures they go some way in ensuring that sound financial management is a matter of course. They do not have the resources to audit all government activities every year and so part of their responsibility should be to ensure mechanisms of self-regulation are working well. The consultancy role does however raise the issue of conflict of interests. Auditors may find themselves auditing systems which they have advised in setting up. Arguably, objectivity can be maintained by setting up 'Chinese walls' within an audit institution, but it is not clear that this removes entirely a conflict of interest. Parallel practices in the private sector are attracting increasing criticism and it is an issue public sector auditors need to address.

There is no separate division, within the NAO, with responsibility for this type of work. Much of what can be termed management consultancy work takes place as part of the audit process. Management letters, for instance, are in effect a report to management on the financial control and mechanism for achieving *vfm*. Because these are not published, this side of the NAO's work remains private. Arguably, there are more overt examples of this type of work. For instance, the NAO has advised departments on the move to resource accounting and it has published its approach to the Private Finance Initiative.

The British position contrasts sharply with the position in Sweden where the combination of management consultancy and audit roles in their SAI, the *Riksrevisionsverket*, has led to questions about the propriety of these two functions being located in the one audit organization. The Riksrevisionsverket is an agency which operates within the Swedish Ministry of Finance. It is divided into departments including the Financial Audit Department, the Performance Audit Department and the Financial Management and Accounting Department. It is this last department which is of interest to us here.

In Sweden, the public administration is very decentralized. Ministries, where policy is formulated, are small with many employing only a few hundred staff. Agencies, employing around 320,000 staff, execute this policy. Although agencies exist within departments they are given a wide degree of independence in how they implement policy. There is little direct control by ministers, rather control is exercised through a system of management by results. The basis for this system has operated in Sweden for over 200 years. Prior to 1961 the financial management division was a separate agency under the Ministry of Finance. In that year it was transferred to the Riksrevisionsverket. The rationale for this coupling is to allow problems of financial management and audit to be resolved within the one institution. If the functions are separated into two agencies, any problems which might arise during an audit would have to be resolved, at a higher level of operation, in the Ministry of Finance. Such a marriage is far less problematic where the SAI is already formally part of the Ministry of Finance. Development of such a separate role for the NAO however, should not occur without considering fully the implications it might have for the independence of the C&AG and the Office.

Access to Information

Sufficient rights of access to information are essential to the effectiveness of public sector audit. If public sector auditors cannot get access to all the information relevant to their investigations, then their findings lose value as a contribution to accountability. A 'right of access', however, is far from being a simple concept. Operationally, auditors have to rely, to a varying extent, on the voluntary co-operation of the bodies they are auditing; even those with the strongest powers of access cannot investigate activities or examine papers that they do not know exist. Most audit institutions seek to build constructive relationships with the bodies they audit, both to allow the work to progress smoothly and to make the body's acceptance of the auditor's findings more likely. In addition, as noted above, there are restrictions on the extent to which most auditors can consider the merits of policy objectives—and, the line between policy and the implementation of policy is not a clear one. As a result, the papers or information to which an auditor can legitimately claim rights of access may not always be clear. Arguably, an auditor should have access to all papers, and restrict himself to examining matters of policy implementation, but this is a sensitive area and governments are generally reluctant to give an auditor more access than is necessary.

Rights of access to information necessary for an audit institution's work are usually included in the institution's statutory framework. But generally, the way these rights are interpreted, in practice, is more important than what is actually stated in the legislation. It is difficult to separate, with any precision, the information that an auditor can legitimately seek to obtain, from the information that a government can legitimately keep to itself. As a result, if a government refuses access, an auditor may find it difficult to compel it to change its decision.

The problem with defining exactly what 'rights of access' should entail also makes it difficult to pursue access through the courts. The main weapon for some audit institutions where access is being denied, is external pressure through the legislature. The relationship between the audit institution and the legislature is therefore important: if there is a strong working relationship, the legislature is more likely to get involved in putting pressure on the government and to act as an informed defender of the audit institution's powers. In most cases, however, it is in the interests of both the audit institution and the government to resolve such disagreements between themselves. For the government, such disputes are unwelcome publicity. For the auditor, they may damage their working relationship with government and, in the longer term, reduce the effectiveness of the audit.

In recent years, the Canadian Auditor General (AG) has experienced some difficulties in exercising his statutory rights of access, although it should be noted that the AG identifies such instances as exceptional. The most prominent case concerned Petro-Canada's (a state-owned oil company) acquisition of Petrofina Canada Inc. The AG reported in 1982 and 1983 on the lack of evidence that due regard for economy had been exercised in the purchase. Discussions were held with Petro-Canada, the Department of Energy, Mines and Resources, the Department of Finance and the external auditors of Petro-Canada to obtain information about the purchase. Access to such information was repeatedly refused and, in 1984, the AG decided to invoke the access to information provisions in the Auditor General Act 1976–77.

For the purposes of carrying out his examinations, section 13 provides the AG, *inter alia*, with the powers to require such information, reports and explanations from the public service of Canada as he deems necessary for the fulfilment of his responsibilities. Section 14(1) permits the AG to rely on the report of the duly appointed auditor of a Crown corporation 'in order to fulfil his responsibilities as the auditor of the accounts of Canada'; while section 14(2) permits him to obtain information from the corporation's offices and directors. If the information in insufficient, he can, under section 14(3), ask the Governor in Council to direct disclosure.

The AG made a request under section 14 but Petro-Canada and the Governor in Council both refused. Following further requests to government ministers, the AG wrote to the Prime Minister, who replied that the information requested constituted confidences of the Queen's Privy Council for Canada and that the AG was not entitled to access to such confidences. The AG then commenced an action in the Federal Court of

Canada seeking access.[67] The Federal Court found that the AG was entitled to access to information, including Cabinet documents, that he considered necessary to fulfil his responsibilities under the Auditor General Act. This decision was overturned by the Federal Court of Appeal,[68] a ruling which was then appealed by the AG to the Supreme Court.[69] The Supreme Court held that the AG has no recourse to the courts in the event of the refusal by ministers and the Governor in Council to make documentation available. This ruling was made on the basis that there is a linkage between the AG's asserted right of access and the AG's duty to report to the House of Commons whether he receives all the information and explanations required to fulfil his duties. The Supreme Court concluded that this linkage and 'the extent to which the reporting remedy is part of a comprehensive remedial code, indicate that the remedy was meant to be exclusive'. This means that the AG's final remedy is to report to the House of Commons any difficulties in obtaining information.

One result of this case was that, in 1985, the Government directed that the AG be given access to a wide range of Cabinet documents. This has enabled what the AG describes as 'a constructive relationship' between the government and the AG in the following years. However, the AG has experienced further difficulties relating to access and it is by no means clear that the exclusive remedy of reporting to Parliament is at all adequate. In 1989–90, the AG experienced difficulty gaining access to information on ministers' expenses. In accordance with the Supreme Court ruling, this denial of access was reported to the House of Commons. The Standing Committee on Public Accounts subsequently recommended that access should be given to the necessary information but, in March 1991, the Government stated that it was unable to accept this recommendation. This was despite considerable pressure from Parliament. This incident illustrates how, if a government is willing to pay the political price, access can be effectively denied.

Under the 1866 and 1921 Acts, the C&AG has free access, at all convenient times, to the books of account and other documents relating to the accounts of departments and other bodies.[70] The 1983 Act provides that the C&AG has statutory rights of access, at all reasonable times, to all such documents in the custody or under the control of the department, authority or body, as he may reasonably require for his *vfm* work.[71] In theory, the NAO cannot be obstructed in such work; in practice, its

[67] *Auditor General* v. *Minister of Energy Mines & Resources*, 23 DLR (4th) 210.
[68] 35 DLR (4th) 693.   [69] 61 DLR (4th) 604.
[70] Exchequer and Audit Departments Act 1866, s. 28; and the Exchequer and Audit Departments Act 1921, s. 9(2). The issue of access to private contractors' accounts is dealt with in Ch. 4.
[71] 1983 Act, s. 8: for the meaning of reasonable see *Associated Provincial Picture Houses Ltd.* v. *Wednesbury Corporation* [1948] 1 KB 223.

access is determined by government co-operation. Different opinions on what constitutes policy may cause the government to refuse access to documents and flexibility is needed on both sides. The NAO accepts that there are some documents that it cannot see. For instance, until 1997, the marking 'Not for NAO eyes' was used by departments in accordance with an agreement between the Treasury and the NAO, under which current documents relating to the handling of relations between departments, the NAO and the PAC were not automatically available to the NAO.[72] In July 1997, the Labour Government, as part of its commitment to 'open government', announced that the use of this designation would be dropped with retrospective effect.[73]

In 1994, an amendment to the *Accounting Officer Memorandum*, following the NAO and PAC reports on the Pergau Dam, extended further the range of information which must be made available to the C&AG.[74] Accordingly, further to the accounting officer's general duty to advise the minister on all matters of financial propriety and regularity and more broadly regarding economy, efficiency and effectiveness, the accounting officer is now required to communicate to the C&AG (and the Treasury), without undue delay, the papers relating to all cases where ministers issue instructions, against the advice of the accounting officer, on matters involving economy, efficiency and effectiveness. Previous to this amendment, it was only where a minister planned a course of action which the accounting officer considered would infringe the requirements of propriety or regularity, that the accounting officer had a duty to send the papers to the C&AG (and the Treasury). In practice, about two or three examples of this occur each year. So, while the volume of information made available to the C&AG has not significantly increased by this amendment, it has had the effect of equating financial matters with those of *vfm*.

Reporting Powers

One of the main functions of public sector audit is to provide a source of expert information about government accounts and activities which can be used by others to hold government to account. The provisions governing an audit institution's freedom to report its findings therefore impact on how effective audit is as a means of delivering accountability. With financial audit, the C&AG is usually required by statute to report

---

[72] See *Hansard*, 3.12.93, Written Answers, c.746, 747, 753, 756, 763, 766, 785, 793, 798–9, 809, 819, 854; and 27.1.94, Written Answers, c.361.
[73] See Treasury Minute, Cm. 3714, following the PAC's Twenty-Second Report, 1996–97.
[74] See Appendix 1, NAO: *Pergau Hydro-Electric Project*, HC 908, 1993–94, (relevant extract); and *Government Accounting*, *supra*, n. 65, 6.1.5, and see paras. 13–15 of the *Memorandum* reproduced following 6.1.

annually to Parliament. With *vfm* audit, he has a discretion. In this section, we concentrate on the drafting of *vfm* reports and the timing of their publication. The issue of the audience(s) for audit reports is considered in the next chapter.

An important consideration in reporting is the likely reaction of the body being audited. If the body being audited does not feel that it has been fairly represented in the report, the audit findings may prompt a discussion about their validity and the methods by which they were reached, rather than about how the body's shortcomings could be remedied. In an attempt to avoid these problems, it is common practice for audit institutions to 'clear the facts' of their *vfm* reports with the auditee, in advance of publication. Where this process involves a 'negotiation' of the facts, it could be argued that the independence of the audit institution is undermined. The NAO's clearance procedure was described in Chapter 4. In practice, this is not a negotiating process. Where there is no 'meeting of the minds' on a particular point, both views are reflected in the report.

The question of when reports are issued may be a sensitive one if the findings are politically damaging. This may place an audit institution in a difficult position. If an audit institution were to publish a critical report, at a politically sensitive time, it might be accused of political involvement. On the other hand, it would clearly be an infringement of an institution's independence if the government could dictate when, or indeed, if, the report was to be published. To avoid the accusation of political interference, some audit institutions are restricted to reporting at a fixed date each year. The disadvantage of this approach is that audit findings may be so dated that they have lost their relevance. This was part of the problem which led to reform of the reporting arrangements in Canada.

Until recently, the Canadian Auditor General (AG) was restricted to making one annual report. Additionally, the AG could, under section 8(1) of the Auditor General Act 1976–77 submit special reports to the House of Commons on any matter of pressing importance or urgency. However, this appears to have been interpreted as a provision which should be used only in extreme situations. The fact that a report might be more timely, and hence more effective, was not regarded as meeting the criteria. Over the intervening years, various proposals were made to change the reporting arrangement and to allow the AG to report more frequently. Although supported by chairpersons of the Canadian Public Accounts Committee and recommended by other committees, from both the Canadian House of Commons and the Senate, the proposals were blocked by successive governments. As recently as 1990, the government refused to introduce legislation allowing the AG to report at any time. The arguments against such a change included that control over the timing of the reports could bring the Office of AG too close to the political process; that it could lead to a loss of focus; and that it would be out of step with the annual expenditure cycle.

These arguments did not hold sway however, and, in June 1994, the reporting arrangements were finally changed, when a Private Member's Bill amending the Auditor General Act received Royal Assent.[75] The Bill was introduced by a former chair of the Public Accounts Committee and as a result the AG is able to report more regularly. The AG continues to publish an annual report, but is able to publish up to three additional reports. The AG envisages replacing the previous annual report, of approximately 30 chapters and 600 pages, with three or four reports of approximately eight chapters each. This change should allow Parliament, and in particular the Public Accounts Committee, to make greater use of the AG's findings. In the past, the Committee examined only three to four of the 20–30 subjects in the annual report. Smaller, more regular reports will spread the Committee's workload more evenly throughout the year and ensure that the findings are not out of date. It is hoped that this will produce a more sustained and detailed scrutiny of public expenditure rather than the once a year spotlight and overload of information which happened previously.

The legislation in Britain goes one step further. The decision to publish, and when to publish, *vfm* reports is at the C&AG's 'complete discretion'.[76] Rather than reporting once a year, or four times a year (as in Canada), there is no limit on the number of times that the C&AG can report. The C&AG actually publishes about 50 separate *vfm* reports annually. This figure does not take into account the C&AG's reports on accounts. As well as being a more effective system of reporting to the PAC, the C&AG's 'complete discretion' in this area is seen as an important aspect of his independence.

INDEPENDENT, YET ACCOUNTABLE?

While the C&AG and NAO are commonly perceived as agents of accountability, that is, they are part of the process of holding government to account, on behalf of the electorate, there is also the issue of how they are made accountable: who audits the auditors? Many audit institutions have some sort of supervisory body, normally part of the legislature, overseeing their activities. Typically, such a body would examine

[75] Section 7(1) of the Auditor General Act now allows the Auditor General to report annually and in addition to any special report under ss. 8(4) or 19(2) . . . , not more than three additional reports in any one year to the House of Commons.

[76] 1983 Act, ss. 1(3) and 9.

the institution's budget, past performance and future plans of work. Also, private auditors are often used to audit the institution's accounts and performance. It is important that these relationships are concerned with the accountability of the institution and not with exercising control over its activities. In addition to external scrutiny, most audit institutions have an internally driven desire to be seen to be accountable and accordingly they publish annual reports and other information about their performance.[77]

The Public Accounts Commission, established under the 1983 Act, exercises such a supervisory role in relation to the NAO. As mentioned above, it effectively controls the NAO's budget. It also reviews the NAO's corporate plan, covering the next five years, every July, for the following year commencing in April. The NAO's annual accounts and the auditor's report thereon are also available at this time. The Commission can use this budgetary process and financial information as a mechanism of accountability. In order to receive future funding the NAO must be able to account for past expenditure, with an emphasis on outputs as well as an eye on future medium-term plans. The Commission currently reports once every two years to the House of Commons on its functions.

The Commission appoints the accounting officer for the NAO—the C&AG.[78] The accounting officer is responsible for preparing the annual accounts of the Office, which are audited by persons appointed by the Commission.[79] The Commission has adopted a policy of rotating auditors for these purposes. Originally, auditors were appointed for a term of six years. More recently, from the start of the financial year 1996–97, auditors have been appointed for a three-year period, renewable for two years, following a competitive process.[80] These auditors conduct financial audit of the accounts, and *vfm* studies (usually one per year), of the NAO.[81] Following these audits, the auditors report to the Commission.[82] While the NAO accounts and the report thereon are published, any *vfm* studies are not published, though some have been referred to in the Commission's own reports to the House of Commons.[83] For example, in their Eighth Report in 1996, the Commission commented briefly on a study in

---

[77] Some audit institutions are better than others at this: see Pollitt, C., and Summa, H., 'Reflexive Watchdogs: How Supreme Audit Institutions account for themselves', 75 (1997) *Public Administration* 313.

[78] 1983 Act, s. 4(4).   [79] 1983 Act, s. 4(5).

[80] Interestingly, this ties in with the recommendation in the Nolan Committee's First Report that the rotation period should be reduced to at least five years: *supra*, n. 49.

[81] 1983 Act, Schedule 3, s. 2.   [82] 1983 Act, Schedule 3, s. 4(2).

[83] The NAO has also in the past commissioned internal management reports in an attempt to improve the workings of the organization. For example, the Cubbon Report (April 1992), examined the impact of the NAO and PAC process on value for money in government departments. This report is not publicly available and so cannot be used as a mechanism of accountability.

1994 on NAO Accommodation Services; on another study on the provision of professional training at the NAO; and on a third study on the areas selected by the NAO for *vfm* audit. The fact that *vfm* reports on the NAO are not published makes the reports appear more like internal management reports rather than a mechanism for holding the NAO accountable. This may also make the NAO appear less accountable than those other public bodies, subject to the jurisdiction of the C&AG, whose *vfm* reports are published. *VFM* reports on the NAO should be fully published and not just referred to in public. Their publication represents no threat to the independence of the institution and would add to its accountability. As an agent of accountability, the NAO should be, and appear to be, totally accountable for every penny of public money spent, both in terms of regularity and propriety, and *vfm*.

Another potential mechanism for holding the NAO to account is the annual PAC debate. In this debate, the Chair of the PAC reports to the House on the working of the NAO, indirectly. All PAC reports to which the Government has responded through a Treasury Minute, since the previous PAC debate, can be considered in this debate, but the Chair usually restricts himself to using about six PAC reports, as examples. This debate happens around October/November each year.[84] Because of the setting for this debate the emphasis can be on the 'scandals' that have come to light during the year. The more important points, from an audit perspective, are often ignored. This is not always the case though. During the 1997 PAC debate, the new Chair of the PAC raised the issue of access to the records, of certain executive non-departmental public bodies, local spending bodies and private contractors, for the purpose of inspection.[85] However, the focus of this debate is mostly on the auditee and not the auditor. Accordingly, the PAC debate has not been used to hold the NAO accountable in any real sense.

Parliamentary Questions can be asked of the NAO. These questions are not addressed to the C&AG—the C&AG never appears before the whole House—nor to the Chair of the PAC. By convention, it is the Chair of the Public Accounts Commission who answers these questions, following a briefing from the NAO.[86] This appears to be a result of mere practice; there is no legal requirement as such.[87] In this regard, the Chair of the Commission acts as a buffer between the House and the NAO, protecting the independence of the C&AG and the NAO. Because the Commission's remit covers NAO resources, Parliamentary Questions to the Chair

    [84] See, for example, *Hansard*, Vol. 301 No. 72, col. 480, 20 November 1997.
    [85] See, generally, Ch. 4.
    [86] Question time is shared with the Church Commissioners.
    [87] *Erskine May's Treatise on the Law, Privileges, Proceedings and Usages of Parliament*, Limon, D. W., and McKay, W. R., eds., (London: Butterworths, 22nd edn., 1997), p. 296.

should also be limited in this respect. This limitation is not always strictly observed. In the Commission's Eighth Report, covering a two-year period, 1994–96, it was noted that 24 questions were tabled, 17 of which were answered orally. The average is 2 to 4 questions per month. Viewed over a period of time, the questions can be repetitious and range from 'How many economists are employed by the NAO?' to queries concerning more interesting areas such as the jurisdiction of the C&AG to follow money into private hands and the modernization of audit of government.

A final avenue of accountability is the NAO annual report. This is a 'stand alone document', in the sense that the report is not made to any-one in particular, such as a committee of the House of Commons. Rather, it is a general report to Parliament and the public. Indeed, the NAO is not obliged to publish such a report. However, it is seen by the NAO as an account of their work. In 1996–97, for instance, it is reported that the financial audit work of the NAO generated savings of £13 million. In the three years to 1997, the *vfm* work led to savings of £858 million. The 1997 Annual Report notes that the total savings over the previous three years has amounted to £7 saved for every £1 spent on running the Office. As a mechanism for holding the NAO accountable, this type of reporting is of limited value. A more effective alternative would involve the NAO's annual report being considered by one of the Committees of the House. The PAC might seem an obvious candidate at first sight but there are strong reasons why the PAC should not perform this function. First, the PAC cannot appoint any specialist advisers. The NAO is the PAC's specialist adviser. To enable the PAC to comment on the work of the NAO it would have to be able to appoint specialist assistance. Further, the introduction of another such specialist or specialists could upset the close relationship and the institutional balance which exists between the NAO and the PAC. Reporting to the Treasury Committee, for example, would avoid these difficulties.

6

The Audience(s) for Audit

THE NEED FOR AN AUDIENCE

Auditors report and make recommendations. Also, some auditors may have executive or quasi-judicial functions as, for example, in the case of local government where the legislation provides for a power to surcharge a person, or to issue a prohibition order to prevent unlawful spending.[1] However, such powers are not inherent in the audit function but are additional to it. Usually, for the work of an auditor to have any real impact there must be an audience. The primary function of the audience is to use the audit information to hold the auditee to account. In addition, having an identifiable audience enables the auditor to tailor his findings to the needs of that body.

Who the audience is, and the exact nature of their role, can vary tremendously. In the public sector, there are two distinct roles which an audience can seek to fulfil. First, an audience can help to secure democratic accountability, whereby, on behalf of the electorate, it uses the audit information to hold government to account for its spending. Secondly, an audience may act as an instrument of managerial accountability, enabling government to use the information to police internal financial control mechanisms and to enhance value for money.[2] These two roles are not necessarily mutually exclusive—some audit arrangements are such that the audience performs both a democratic accountability *and* a managerial accountability function.

The remainder of this chapter focuses on the question of what audiences exist for the findings of central government audit. Our main concern will be the relationship between the NAO and its principal audience, the PAC, and how the combination of these two institutions delivers accountability to the public for its spending, *and* enables central government to police itself. In addition, other audiences, such as the

---

[1] In relation to surcharge see ss. 17 and 18 of the Audit Commission Act 1998, and for prohibition orders see s. 20 of the Audit Commission Act 1998. The Government is currently reviewing these functions: see the Department of the Environment, Transport and the Region's Consultation Paper, *Modernising Local Government. A New Ethical Framework*, (1998); see, generally, Ch. 7.

[2] For a definition and understanding of both democratic accountability and managerial accountability, see Ch. 1.

public as citizens, government itself, and departmentally related select committees will be considered. In the following chapters, similar issues surrounding the identification of an audience and the role of the audience will be addressed in relation to local government in England and Wales (Chapter 7), and the European Union (Chapter 8).

THE PAC AS AUDIENCE

The National Audit Act 1983 states that the C&AG is an officer of the House of Commons and it is his responsibility to serve the House as a whole.[3] As described in previous chapters, by convention and tradition, he has served the House primarily through the PAC. Accordingly, at present, both types of NAO reports, financial and *vfm*, are directed towards the needs of the PAC. Other than providing a specific focus for NAO reports, the PAC has a very real role to play in achieving both democratic accountability and managerial accountability. The main mechanism used to do this is a public hearing, whereby officials from the department, agency or other public body in question, are brought to answer before the PAC. The detail of the hearing process will be dealt with below before going on to consider how the PAC contributes to the accountability of government.

The Work of the PAC

The PAC is assisted in its work by a small staff, including a committee clerk, who, in general, provide procedural and administrative support to the Committee. The majority of the PAC's work is taken up by hearings based on NAO financial and *vfm* reports.[4] The PAC also publishes reports in its own right, usually following a hearing based on an NAO report. As well as holding hearings and publishing reports, the PAC annual debate is an important feature of the PAC's constitutional role. The different aspects of the PAC's work are set out below.

Planning the Hearings

The PAC plan their programme of hearings, for two months at a time, in consultation with the NAO. This programme may be reviewed a number of times each year to enable NAO reports and PAC hearings to remain synchronized. Adherence to the annual programme is usual. However, on occasion—when, for example, the NAO report in question is not

---

[3] National Audit Act 1983, s. 1(2).
[4] For the detail on these reports, see, generally, Ch. 4.

completed in time to allow the accounting officer(s) to prepare for the hearing, or where the subject matter of the audit is considered politically sensitive at that time—deviations from the annual programme may occur. In such circumstances, reserves (that is, replacement reports) are brought in.

Preparing for a Hearing

PAC hearings usually require a considerable amount of preparation, both by the members of the Committee and by those who are called as witnesses. The PAC's preparation is based on a briefing by the NAO, and any independent research that a particular member may undertake. The members are not assigned any specific portfolios according to their particular interest or expertise. Instead, they are each responsible for every NAO report. Typically, one week before the hearing the NAO will provide a Chairman's brief (which may be circulated to all members) and a member's brief. In these briefs, the NAO may suggest areas for questioning and, on the whole, these areas are generally covered by the PAC during the course of the hearing. In addition, some members may pursue a different line of questioning based on any independent research that they have conducted.

The main witness at the hearing is the relevant accounting officer. If an agency is the subject of the NAO report, the chief executive, as accounting officer, will attend. The accounting officer of the relevant department may also attend. The PAC is not limited to calling the accounting officer as a witness but can call anyone else to appear before it. However, the PAC does not call ministers to give evidence. In terms of preparation, the accounting officer is usually briefed by the Treasury Officer of Accounts[5] in addition to the preparation conducted by the department, agency or other public body. This preparation can include a 'PAC damage limitation' exercise, whereby the accounting officer 'rehearses' the hearing in advance. In addition to the accounting officer, as the main witness, the C&AG and Treasury Officer of Accounts, or their deputies, attend every hearing as witnesses.

The Hearing

The PAC holds approximately two hearings a week when Parliament is in session, each hearing lasting about two to three hours. The Committee cannot sit when Parliament is in recess. The annual number of reports varies, but the PAC produces about 35–40 per annum. In terms of timing, the PAC will usually aim to hold a hearing about four weeks after the NAO report is published.

---

[5] See, generally, Ch. 3.

Normally, the Chairman of the PAC starts the proceedings at the hearing by questioning the relevant witnesses, mainly the accounting officer, for about 30 minutes. The Chairman's questions are followed by those of the most senior member of the party in Government. Members other than the Chairman are generally limited to 15 minutes in which to ask questions. This differs from other select committees and quite clearly this time restriction has its shortcomings. It provides the witness being questioned with the opportunity to exhaust the member's allocated time by talking at length on a particular issue, and preventing that particular member from asking further, perhaps more probing, questions. However, the time limit does ensure that hearings can be completed in an afternoon and hence maximizes the overall output of the PAC. Many of the questions asked by the PAC appear to be largely concerned with whether the public expenditure was regular and proper, and thus it has gained the reputation of being a 'rule enforcer'.

The PAC Report

The minutes of evidence of the hearing are published a number of weeks after the hearing, once they have been checked for accuracy by the witnesses. The draft report then follows. The Chairman is responsible for drafting the report although, in practice, he is assisted by the NAO. The clerk of the PAC may also assist with the drafting. When the draft is prepared the PAC have a deliberative hearing,[6] where any amendments can be made and, if there is unanimity, the report can be adopted and published. Unanimity is seen as very important, as a unanimous report adds strength to the Committee's influence. In the past, some reports have been held back until unanimity was obtained. This means that the timing of the publication of the final report after the hearing can vary.[7] The PAC report will encompass the recommendations of the Committee, based on the hearing. Many of the recommendations will have already been dealt with by the department, agency or other body before the report is published, indeed often before the hearing is held. Dealing with particular issues raised in the NAO report before the hearing, enables the accounting officer to deflect some of the PAC's criticism.

A major limitation on the scope of PAC reports is that the PAC operates a practice (or convention) that it does not consider the merits of policy objectives. This is unlike departmentally-related select committees, which can examine expenditure, administration and policy. The inability of the

---

[6] As well as being used to finalize reports based on PAC hearings, deliberative hearings may also be held to discuss matters of procedure.

[7] For example, there was a hearing on the Royal Palaces in 1995 but the report was not published until 1998. See PAC's Eleventh Report, *Responsibilities for Occupied Royal Palaces*, HC 406, 1997–98.

PAC to examine policy objectives is in line with the same restriction placed on the NAO by the legislation. Although at first sight this may appear to limit the capacity of the PAC to hold government to account, it does in fact enable the PAC to operate more effectively, because it reduces the likelihood of disagreement between members.

The Government's Response

The government's official response to the PAC report comes in the form of a Treasury Minute. This is published usually 2–3 months after the PAC report and it outlines which of the PAC's recommendations the government accepts and will act on, and those which it simply notes (that is, which will not be acted on). If the department or body in question does not accept any PAC recommendations, the Committee can return to the issue at a future date. The Treasury Officer of Accounts supervises the production of the Minute but the main responsibility for the drafting of the Minute lies with the department or body under examination, not the Treasury.

The PAC Annual Debate

As well as reporting on their hearings, the PAC also reports annually to Parliament. This takes the form of a debate, in full session, which normally focuses on a selection of PAC reports, and the government's responses thereto. The debate is concluded by a 'take-note' motion. Although such debates are not usually well attended, an annual debate of this sort—a privilege not granted to other select committees—is a reflection of the importance which is accorded to the work of the PAC.[8]

Delivering Democratic *and* Managerial Accountability

The model of democratic accountability outlined in Chapter 1, is similar to the agency theory model in the private sector.[9] When this model is applied to central government, the public, who entrust their money to the government (as agent) to spend, are represented by Parliament. An independent auditor (the NAO) examines the accounts and performance of the government and reports to the public, through their representatives, in this case the PAC of the House of Commons. The PAC is then responsible for calling government to account, thus completing the circle of accountability.

The PAC hearing, the subsequent reports, and the annual debate are all part of the process of holding, and being seen to be holding,

---

[8] See Flegman, V., 'The Public Accounts Committee: A Successful Select Committee?', (1980) *Parliamentary Affairs* 166.

[9] See Dunn, J., *Auditing—Theory and Practice*, (London: Prentice Hall, 1996), Ch. 1.

government to account. This is the public or democratic face of account-ability. The hearings are normally in public and some hearings and reports receive much media attention. The PAC works on behalf of Parliament to ensure that any irregular or improper spending, or lack of value for money resulting from spending decisions, is publicly addressed so as to ensure that the taxpayer's money is correctly used in the future. However, the managerial accountability aspect of the PAC's work is as important, if not more so, in actually improving financial management and control in government.

A key element in the continued dominance of the PAC as the audience for NAO reports is that it provides not only democratic accountability but also helps to secure managerial accountability. The combination of these roles within the PAC reflects the mutual aims sought by Parliament (democratic accountability) and the Treasury (managerial accountability). As set out above, the PAC's role as audience comes into play largely in the form of a public hearing. It is this public display of accountability which provides democratic accountability. However, there are also a number of aspects of the hearing process which serve to enhance managerial accountability.

For instance, unlike other select committees, and as noted above, it is not the relevant minister but the relevant accounting officer, who appears as the witness before the PAC. If democratic accountability was the sole aim of the process then the minister would attend and answer questions, in keeping with the principles of ministerial responsibility.[10] However, it is the accounting officer who is responsible for the finances of the department. The accounting officer is accountable to his minister but not to anyone else, democratically or otherwise. Hence, the presence of the accounting officer as the main witness before the PAC demonstrates the importance of managerial accountability in the whole process. Removing the minister from the arena also contributes to the PAC's largely non-partisan nature. Moreover, the fact that the PAC acts in a non-partisan way is itself representative of the PAC's awareness of its function not only to secure democratic but also managerial accountability.

The Treasury has an integral part to play in the whole process. The Treasury, as outlined in Chapter 3, has general responsibility for the internal financial control of other government departments. Its position in the external audit process is a continuance of this role and ensures that managerial control is achieved through the audit arrangements. A number of officials from the Treasury are intrinsically linked to the PAC, and sit on both sides of the fence, so to speak. For example, as noted in Chapter 5, the Financial Secretary of the Treasury is a member of the PAC in an

---

[10] See Ch. 1.

ex officio capacity. Although, in practice, the Financial Secretary only attends the first meeting of the newly formed Committee each session, for the first few minutes, this automatic membership is a reflection of the close relationship between, and shared aims of, the PAC and the Treasury. In addition, the Treasury Officer of Accounts, whose role it is to promote a high standard of propriety, regularity and effective accountability,[11] attends every PAC hearing. The Treasury Officer of Accounts is also involved in briefing the accounting officer before the PAC hearing. Finally, once the PAC have reported, it is the Treasury which formally responds by way of a Treasury Minute. The response does not come in the name of the particular department or body. Although in practice it is the department or body which drafts the response, it is again indicative of the Treasury's intrinsic involvement in the process, and reflects the emphasis placed on managerial control.

The PAC's role is therefore notable in that it seeks to fulfil both a democratic and a managerial accountability role. But, although the PAC is the primary audience for NAO reports, it is not the sole audience. Two other audiences can be identified, and in distinguishing them we are able to see more distinctly the split between democratic accountability and managerial accountability. These audiences are the citizen (adding to democratic accountability) and government itself (adding to managerial accountability).

OTHER AUDIENCES

Reporting to the Citizen

Both NAO and PAC reports are published and available to the wider public. In more recent years, it seems that, at least on behalf of the NAO, there has been a move towards selecting more consumer orientated topics, for example, hospital catering,[12] and towards making the reports more reader-friendly, colourful and pictorial. This development appears to be linked to 'open government',[13] and the development of the *Citizen's Charter* (1991), with the emphasis on being a consumer as well as a citizen. The Audit Commission takes a similar approach—it does not have a specific audience comparable to the PAC, but instead directs its reports towards the public.[14] Reporting directly to those to whom government is

---

[11] See Ch. 3.

[12] *National Health Service: Hospital Catering in England*, HC 329, 1993–94.

[13] See more recently the White Paper, *Your Right to Know: The Government's Proposals for a Freedom of Information Act*, Cm. 3818 (1997).

[14] See, generally, Ch. 7.

accountable, rather than to their democratic representatives, cuts out the intermediary. Democratic accountability thus appears to be served.

In local government, this system appears to work because, despite the lack of a dedicated audience for the auditor's reports, the reports carry the threat, not often used, of a reduction in funding from central government if the reports are not adhered to.[15] However, this is not the case for central government departments and it is submitted that this consumer-based approach alone could never be an effective alternative to the current system whereby the PAC acts as an surrogate for the public interest. Any mechanism of reporting directly to the public should be seen as supplementary to the role of the PAC. In any event, it can be argued that a consumer approach in itself is inadequate because public objectives must be rationalized and may not conform to the wishes of individual members of the public.

Government Policing Itself—Management Letters

Managerial accountability is usually accomplished when the auditor reports directly to the auditee. In these circumstances, the auditee is the audience. This is the practice with the C&AG's reports in New Zealand, and with the reports of the *Riksrevisionsverket* in Sweden.[16] In the United Kingdom, as well as managerial accountability playing a vital part in the traditional accountability model involving the PAC, it is also sought in a more explicit way by the NAO. To this end, in addition to reporting to the PAC, the NAO reports its findings to the auditee, commonly in the form of a management letter.

A management letter follows every financial audit and can feature in *vfm* work, though this not as common. In effect, the *vfm* report is itself a form of management letter. The management letter is a formal document. When it follows a financial audit it contains a summary of the results of the audit, highlights the areas of risk and includes recommendations which the NAO believe should be implemented following the audit. The management letter is accompanied by a covering letter from the audit manager which highlights the important issues which have arisen from the audit. It is common for the management letter to contain three main aspects—the weaknesses or risks, the relevant recommendations and the response from the audited body. This third aspect is usually dealt with informally at a meeting of the audit team and the auditee and is then returned to the NAO. It will set out whether the department or body accepts the NAO's recommendations or not. If a recommendation is not accepted the NAO can either choose to acknowledge the fact, if, for example, it is

---

[15] See, further, Ch. 7.   [16] See, further, below.

minor, or, if it concerns a more important issue it can pursue the matter with the auditee. A final option open to the NAO, if a department or body refuses to accept the recommendation, is to qualify the account.

Given the importance of management letters and the effect they can have on central government, arguably they should be published.[17] Knowing the auditee's reaction to NAO recommendations in advance could also aid the PAC in its role when holding departments to account during a hearing. However, this does not require publication of the management letter. The NAO already has the ability to communicate this information to the members of the PAC in its pre-hearing briefing. Publication of management letters might also cause problems for the relationship between agencies and their sponsoring departments. When an agency is the subject of the NAO report, whether the management letter is copied to the department or not is at the agency's discretion.[18] The automatic publication of management letters would take control in this regard from the agency.

By reporting its findings to the auditee, the NAO's role is perhaps closer here to that of an internal auditor or private management consultant, than an independent external auditor.[19] This point should not be overstated, though. There is more to the distinction between external and internal audit than the audience for audit reports. Other significant differences relate to the independence of the auditor and whether the auditor is subject to the direction of another.[20] External auditors usually have the power to select the subject matter of the audit, whereas internal auditors, and the like, are normally employed and directed in their work by the auditee.

In seeking to attain better managerial accountability, a primary consideration is whether this dual role of external auditor *and* management consultant leads to conflict for the NAO. It has been suggested, for example, that not all NAO *vfm* reports should go to the PAC, the implication being that a PAC hearing is not always productive in achieving better managerial accountability.[21] At present, not all NAO *vfm* reports result in a PAC hearing but this is a result of the limitations of the PAC's annual timetable.[22] If more reports went directly to the auditee, any pressure on the PAC's time would be eased but democratic accountability would not

---

[17] For a discussion of the use of management letters in local government see Bowerman, M., Gray, I., and Reedman, M., *Audit Management Letters in Local Government. Aspects of Accountability*, Research Papers in Accounting No. 2, (Sheffield: Sheffield Hallam University, 1996); see, further, Ch. 7.

[18] *Government Accounting: a guide on accounting and financial procedures for the use of government departments*, (2 vols., loose leaf) (London: HMSO, 1989 and seven amendments 1989–97), 7.1.21.

[19] It should be noted that reporting to the auditee is an Auditing Practices Board requirement for all external auditors, private or public: see SAS 610.

[20] See, further, Ch. 5.   [21] See the Cubbon Report, (unpublished, 1992).

[22] See, further, below.

be served. As seen from above, reporting to the PAC serves both demo-cratic and managerial accountability. Reporting to the auditee serves man-agerial accountability alone. Any change in the NAO practice of reporting would need to take this fundamental difference into account.

AN EVALUATION

Evaluating the audience for audit, in particular the PAC, is a multifaceted task. First, it is necessary to review the actual mechanics of the PAC hear-ing process, and to consider what alterations, if any, can be made to improve the current system. However, this cannot be done in isolation. Account must also be taken of the effects which the introduction of Resource Accounting and Budgeting (RAB) will have on the ability of the PAC to hold government to account. Finally, alternatives to the current system will also be considered.

The Current System

The close and effective working relationship between the NAO and the PAC often produces powerful criticism. The non-partisan, all-party nature of the PAC ensures that, at least in the first instance, it is not used for party political point scoring. This means that the relationship between the PAC and government whilst not cosy, is constructive. One of the perceived strengths of the PAC is the fear which witnesses supposedly feel when having to appear at a hearing. Many commentators cite the threat of having to answer questions before the PAC as an incentive for account-ing officers and others to act with probity and seek to achieve *vfm*.[23] However, within the system, some believe that this is a 'myth of account-ability', and that, in reality, the PAC does not command as much respect as is commonly stated.

Nonetheless, the PAC is made up of backbenchers who have wide experience which, together with the technical know-how of the NAO, creates an expert body able to scrutinize those responsible for spending public money.[24] This is particularly effective for issues of probity. Unlike other select committees, the PAC rarely divides on party political lines. This, along with its access to documents, and its ability to call anyone as a witness adds to the effectiveness of the system. The PAC and its hear-ings provide the public face of accountability, and the political clout needed to make the NAO's report effective.

[23] See Robinson, A., 'The Financial Work of Select Committees', Ch. 17 in Drewry, G., *The New Select Committees*, (Oxford: Clarendon Press, 1985).

[24] It is interesting to note that seven of the current Committee members were new MPs at the 1997 Election.

There are, however, some shortcomings to the current system which may limit the PAC's impact. One major criticism is the *ex post facto* nature of the PAC hearing and report—the PAC examines expenditure once it has already been spent, and can do nothing to recover wrongly spent money. It was assumed until relatively recently, that accounting officers could be held personally liable for expenditure not properly charged to a Vote. In practice, this rarely happened,[25] but it is a mistake to judge the importance of a sanction by how often it is used. However, in 1980, with the agreement of the PAC, the reference to the personal liability of accounting officers was dropped from the *Accounting Officer Memorandum.*[26]

With or without the power to surcharge accounting officers to recover misspent money, the criticism of the *ex post facto* nature of the PAC's powers remains. However, this criticism is one made of the system as a whole and cannot be aimed only at the PAC. But there are other limitations which are specific to the PAC. First, it appears to be widely recognized that the PAC represents a 'bottleneck' in the system of central government audit. On the current schedule of two hearings per week, when Parliament is in session, the PAC is severely limited in the number of hearings it can have and reports it can publish. The NAO already produces more reports than the PAC can examine. The PAC could deal with more NAO reports and reduce the bottleneck if it were prepared to alter the way in which it operates. It could, for instance, divide into subcommittees, giving each subcommittee the responsibility for considering different reports based on division according to subject matter.[27] However, this might be unpopular with the members of the PAC, in that a hierarchy could develop, with one subcommittee being considered more prestigious than the other. An alternative would be for the PAC to be able to sit when Parliament is in recess. Or, more radically, the PAC could examine written evidence, and avoid having an oral hearing altogether. On a similar note the PAC could require departments and other bodies to respond to NAO reports within a given time, for example six months, again without a hearing taking place. These two alternatives could, however, reduce the esteem with which the PAC is held and mitigate one of its strengths—the fear it apparently causes in those who have to appear before it. There might also be less media attention given to the PAC, and hence the PAC's public image would diminish. Nevertheless, it would seem to make sense to have some sort of hierarchy of NAO reports. Those which

[25] The last recorded instance appears to have been in 1920, when an accounting officer repaid £101 6s 3d that the PAC had considered to be not properly chargeable to a Vote. See PAC, Third Report 1921, para. 14 (Epitome I, p. 624).

[26] See PAC, First Special Report, 1980–81.

[27] The current Standing Order prevents the PAC from forming subcommittees: see S.O. 148.

deal with more serious financial control issues, and give most cause for concern, could be subject to a full-blown hearing. Those reports which throw up less serious problems could be subject to a report based on written evidence, or simply contain a requirement that the department concerned has to respond to the NAO report. A further alternative which would, it is argued, make better use of the NAO whilst easing pressure on the PAC's time, would be for departmentally related select committees to examine NAO reports.[28]

The second shortcoming of the current system is related to the first— that is the problem with delay. Often PAC reports are published so long after the event in question that those responsible are no longer in the department and cannot be held to account, or brought to answer for their actions. The person who is actually brought before the PAC can represent the department and answer for the department but personally can be absolved from responsibility. If a hierarchy of NAO reports as outlined above were to be introduced this would also address the problem of delay.

Other than the above problems, a potential difficulty for the PAC arises in relation to the introduction of RAB in British central government. Here the continued effectiveness of the relationship between the NAO and the PAC is more immediately at risk. The NAO and the members of the PAC will have to adapt to a new method of accounting and, as a result, a new language of accountability.

Resource Accounting and Budgeting

In terms of ensuring public accountability for the spending of public money, Parliament must have the information it needs to influence decisions and to give its 'informed consent' to the voting of funds. Also, it must have the knowledge to hold government to account, particularly after the spending has taken place. Fundamental to both these functions is the provision of the right information or, rather, the best information. The question is, does Parliament get the information it needs? As noted above, in terms of the *ex post* control of expenditure, NAO reports provide the information on which accountability of government by Parliament is based. NAO *vfm* reports are aimed at the PAC, and consequently, given that the membership of the PAC is made up of parliamentary backbenchers, who, although they may have an interest in financial matters, are not accountants, the NAO reports are relatively short and contain conclusions which are designed to be developed into recommendations by the PAC. The Conservative Government's proposals on RAB aimed to provide Parliament, and the relevant managers, with *better* financial

---

[28] See, further, below.

information.[29] However, there are a number of points which need to be considered further on this issue.

A New Language

One of the aims of the NAO in preparing its reports is to act as an 'interpreter' for the PAC. It takes often complex accounting information and produces it in the report in a way which can be easily understood by the members of the PAC. The NAO is the accounting expert, and members of the PAC are not expected to be qualified accountants. Nevertheless, members of the PAC must have a basic understanding of the accounting system to make proper use of the information provided, particularly when it comes to being able to effectively question witnesses who appear at the hearing. Changes to the methods and language of public sector accounting, which will result from the introduction of RAB, could undermine the above long-standing and constructive working relationship between the NAO and the PAC. Such changes are an inevitable feature of RAB: accounts will no longer simply follow the flows of cash (a concept most of us can appreciate); the accounts will concern the use of resources (not just the use made of public funds) and they will involve more judgment. Hence it may be more difficult to interpret this information in a meaningful and user-friendly way.

Potential Conflict

One area of uncertainty is whether government and Parliament can get, or indeed want, the same things from RAB. For government, RAB is about a better way to manage—an internal function. In contrast, Parliament's primary concern is ensuring accountability—an external checking function. Although, as outlined above, the PAC helps to ensure both types of accountability, RAB raises the possibility that the increased emphasis placed on managerial accountability may have the effect of diminishing democratic accountability.

The potential for conflict between these two concerns is evident in the PAC's Ninth Report of 1996–97, *Resource Accounting and Proposals for a Resource-Based System of Supply*. In that report the PAC laid stress on the external dimension when it set out the two objectives of financial reporting, as follows:

(1) to demonstrate to Parliament that public monies have been used for the purposes intended by Parliament; and
(2) to provide Parliament with reliable information with which to consider the levels of finance voted for services and to examine how policies, functions and the programmes have been carried out.

[29] See, generally, Ch. 2.

The PAC further noted the Government's additional financial reporting objective to '... help Government in the planning, monitoring and management of public expenditure ...'. The Report then stated that the Government's additional objective should be entirely consistent with the other objectives of financial reporting to Parliament, but should there be any conflict between objectives, those designed to provide Parliament with information would need to take precedence. However, despite this reference to the primacy of Parliamentary accountability, it is quite clear that the driving force behind the adoption of RAB is internal. In the White Paper, the Treasury emphasized that RAB would improve departmental management and value for money. RAB is the natural next step in the succession of initiatives which have focused on management in UK central government: the *Financial Management Initiative* (1982); the *Next Steps* programme (1988); contracting out and market testing in the *Citizen's Charter* (1991) and *Competing for Quality* (1992). Given that the PAC's primary concern appears to be issues of probity the potential for conflict is very apparent. One of the central questions which needs to be asked about RAB is whether it will promote, or at any rate preserve, the distinctive features of accounting and audit in the public sector, in order to meet the requirements of accountability to Parliament. In other words, can the PAC continue to deliver democratic accountability when the accounting procedures themselves are being altered in a way which so obviously serves the needs of managerial accountability more?

An Alternative Audience: Departmentally-Related Select Committees?

The two main issues highlighted above—the restrictions on the operation of the PAC due to workload and the challenges presented by RAB—might be resolved if the NAO also reported to departmentally related select committees. The United Kingdom is not unique in having a specific body to which the supreme audit institution reports,[30] though not all countries with a Westminster-style government follow the PAC model. In New Zealand, for instance, there is no specific parliamentary committee to which the C&AG reports. Instead, the C&AG can report to any minister of the Crown, and to 'any other person'.[31] However, this means that there is no guar-

---

[30] Canada, for example, has a Public Accounts Committee similar to the one in the United Kingdom.

[31] In New Zealand, the provision for reporting to ministers evolved out of the obligation in the Public Revenues Act 1910 to 'communicate with the Minister [of Finance] upon all matters arising ... relating to the collection, receipt, issue and payment of public moneys', and a right '... in such yearly report or in any special report which [the Controller and Auditor-General] may at any time think fit to make [to] offer any suggestions for the better collection and payment of public moneys and the more effectually and economically auditing

antee that a Parliamentary body, or any other body, will take up the auditor's report.

In the United Kingdom, in contrast, the Parliamentary scrutiny of government expenditure has traditionally been the preserve of the PAC. The introduction of departmentally-related select committees ('departmental committees') in 1979, with a remit to examine 'expenditure, administration and policy',[32] prompted the proposal that the NAO should serve these committees as well as the PAC. This issue was discussed in a 1990 Procedure Committee Report on the select committees.[33] The Report recognized the importance of the traditional ties between the NAO and the PAC, but recommended that improved use could be made of the NAO's resources if they were occasionally made available to departmental committees. In some cases this would mean that an NAO report would be taken up by a departmental committee instead of the PAC. It was also recommended that co-operation between the PAC and the departmental committees be improved and that this should extend to the PAC allowing departmental committees access to unpublished memoranda from the C&AG. The then Government agreed to the main substance of these proposals.

These proposals underline the extent of the C&AG's statutory independence, which in terms of the British Constitution is exceptional. The main statutory restrictions are that the C&AG shall not 'question the merits of policy objectives' in conducting *vfm* examinations,[34] and that access to documents and information for *vfm* purposes is subject to a test of reasonableness.[35] Both these terms are open to interpretation and, in practice, are defined in a process of constant negotiation between the NAO and government.[36] The constitutional conventions which form the context for this process are not rules which could, in principle, be written down. Rather they are expectations that behaviour will be governed by a traditional understanding of the roles of ministers, civil servants, and Parliament.

The objections to the proposal that the NAO should serve departmental committees illustrate the point. It was argued that NAO reports would provide the basis for a more searching examination of policy by the committees (who are not restricted as the NAO and PAC are from questioning the merits of policy objectives) and that this would alter the context within which negotiations over access took place. As a result the

and examining the public accounts and stores, and any improvement in the mode of keeping such account, and generally [to] report upon all matters relating to the Public Accounts, public moneys and stores.'

[32] S.O. 152(1) (since 1997, previously S.O. 130).
[33] Select Committee on Procedure, *The Working of the Select Committee System*, HC 19, 1989–90.
[34] 1983 Act, s. 6(2).   [35] 1983 Act, s. 8.   [36] See, generally, Ch. 5.

NAO might find its access reduced. Even though it remained within its statutory remit it would be perceived to have overstepped traditional constitutional understandings. Further, the NAO could be seen as being drawn into this policy debate which in turn could impinge on its independent constitutional status.

Others have argued that NAO reports are a rich source of expert information which is being under-utilized in holding government to account and that the NAO could serve departmental committees without causing problems of this kind. The key point of difference is a matter of constitutional interpretation. Those in favour of the NAO serving departmental committees attach importance to the fact that, in carrying out his functions, the C&AG is independent not only of government, but also of Parliament itself. The PAC (perhaps not unnaturally) attaches greater importance to its own role in the delicate web of convention and negotiation.

The current position is that the vast majority of NAO reports are taken up by the PAC with other select committees making some use of the NAO, either using an NAO report but not exclusively, or seeking advice from the NAO on a particular point. While other committees are making more use of the NAO, the principal user by far remains the PAC. An alternative way of tackling the specific needs of the departmental committees would be to create one or more additional sources of independent audit-type information. The proposal that the NAO should serve other select committees is a recognition of the contribution independent and authoritative reports can make to the scrutiny of government. By making it possible to work from an accepted foundation of independent findings, rather than political claims, such a development might offer further encouragement to departmental committees to act in a non-partisan way.

There is no question that, if departmental committees were to take on the role of primary audience for those reports falling within their area of expertise, more NAO reports could undergo detailed Parliamentary scrutiny, increasing the potential for democratic accountability. However, there are two reasons why departmental committees should *not* replace the PAC and become the primary audience for NAO reports. First, the NAO would probably not be able to 'educate' its new audience in the same way that it has educated the PAC. There would simply not be the resources to spend the time briefing all the departmental committees to ensure that they would be sufficiently familiar with the relevant accounting and audit principles and other financial issues. Nor would it be possible for the NAO to nurture an effective close working relationship with so many committees. Equally, the members of the departmental committees would not be able to be 'educated' in such a specialized way, given the diversity of their work, and their need to deal with issues other than finance.

Secondly, and more importantly, if departmentally-related select committees were to be the main audience for NAO reports, given the political framework within which they operate, there is the very real danger that NAO reports would be used as political ammunition. As a result, the NAO would inevitably be forced to make political judgments in its reports, with the increased risk that governmental pressure could be placed on the NAO not to include certain information which could be used against it. So, rather than departmental select committees becoming less political because they are provided with independent information, the more likely outcome is that NAO reports would have to be adapted to avoid being used as political ammunition. This could, in turn, undermine the link between democratic and managerial accountability because reports might be less worthwhile in a managerial sense.

An Alternative Model—the Swedish Example

Rather than exploring the different audiences for NAO reports, a more far-reaching alternative would be to reconsider the basic PAC model whereby the Committee combines the functions of providing democratic *and* managerial accountability. A useful alternative model can be found in Sweden where these two functions are separated and performed by two separate audit institutions: the *Riksrevisionsverket (RRV)*, the national audit institution which serves government, and the *Riksdagens Revisorer*, the Parliamentary auditors who serve Parliament.[37] The existence of these two separate audit institutions appears less to do with any fundamental incompatibility in coupling the above roles, and more to do with the development of the particular system of government in Sweden.

Most of the work of government in Sweden is carried out by agencies or companies. The actual central ministries themselves are relatively small.[38] For over 200 years, agencies have been a feature of Swedish government. In this time, the trend has been to decentralize the public service in Sweden from ministry to agency; and from the centre to local levels.[39] There is no 'framework document' as such, between a ministry and an agency. The relationship is regulated by government ordinances. Also, as part of the agency's annual budget, performance targets are attached.

---

[37] Similarly, in Finland, two sets of auditors exist: one to serve the government and a second dedicated to Parliament.

[38] There are about 320,000 staff in the agencies and companies compared to only 2,500 staff in the 13 central ministries.

[39] Other audit institutions exist at lower levels: at the lowest level of governance there are locally elected parliamentary auditors for the municipal councils; and at a regional level—the *Landsting*—a similar system operates. Where central government agencies have local and regional offices, the RRV has jurisdiction.

Agencies are free to work within the framework of the ordinances and have considerable freedom of operation from the ministries including the freedom to use the resources at their discretion. However, they must report on their spending and the achievement of the targets set. Audit and the RRV is one means by which the ministries can control the agencies.

The RRV is itself one of the agencies under the Ministry of Finance.[40] While the Ministry has some control over the RRV's budget,[41] it does not direct the RRV in its audit work. But, the Ministry does specify that *all* agencies must be audited annually and the audit must be conducted in accordance with certain standards. The RRV performs an annual audit (financial audit and, since 1988, this includes an audit of performance measures) for each agency; and, in accordance with another Ministry target, produces about 15–20 performance (*vfm* type) reports annually.[42] Excluded from the RRV's jurisdiction are the ministries themselves; legislation; and 'administrative practice'.[43] Significantly, the RRV does not report to a body independent of government, there is no independent audience. Instead, its reports are addressed to the agency itself, and the relevant ministry.

The other Swedish audit body, the Riksdagens Revisorer or Parliamentary Auditors (PA), comprises 12 parliamentarians, 12 professional auditors and about 25 other staff. The Parliamentarians are selected at the same time as membership of standing committees with each new government, every four years.[44] The Office is a parliamentary *agency*, along with the central bank and the ombudsman. It is one of three institutions established under the Constitution dealing with 'Parliamentary Control'.[45] The PA audit the central ministries and the civil service on behalf of Parliament. Financial audit represents about 5 per cent of their work and the PA usually contract-out this type of work to a private firm. Their main interest is performance audits—in promoting the most economic use of government funding and ensuring that assets are used on a rational basis.

[40] The RRV's legal status is weak because there is no founding legislation governing the RRV. But, by convention, its budget cannot be reduced without consulting Parliament; and no decision to appoint a new Auditor General or remove a current Auditor General can be taken without consulting Parliament. At the time of writing, the legal position of the RRV was under review and legislation may be forthcoming.

[41] The Ministry provides the RRV with 50% of its funding, which is approved by Parliament. Any agency which is '50% plus' financed by fees must pay the RRV for their audit.

[42] See further Swedish National Audit Bureau, *Performance Auditing at the Swedish National Audit Bureau*, (Stockholm: 1993).

[43] This last element belongs within the remit of the Standing Committee on the Constitution: see further Chs. 8 and 12 of the Instrument of Government 1974.

[44] Article 7, Ch. 12 of the Instrument of Government 1974. See also Article 11 of the Riksdag Act.

[45] See Instrument of Government 1974—Ch. 12. The other two are the Parliamentary Ombudsman and the Standing Committee on the Constitution. All three institutions date from 1809.

The PA produce about 12–14 performance reports per year, following an relatively open investigation and drafting process. These reports are sent to Parliament but there is no specific committee dedicated to dealing with all PA reports. Instead the reports go to the relevant standing committee. The committee may hold a hearing with the minister, and other experts are called as witnesses. The committee then makes a series of recommendations which can be adopted by the Parliament, in plenary session. The standing committees are responsible for following-up their recommendations. At the same time, the PA follow-up earlier reports and can report on any matter in their annual report.

In terms of providing democratic accountability for public sector expenditure, the responsibility rests with the PA. Arguably, the PA have a number of advantages over the RRV. First, their position is constitutionally secured.[46] Secondly, and unlike the RRV, which is limited to the ministry/agency relationship, the PA can follow public money from Parliament, to the ministry, to the agency, to local levels. And thirdly, the PA report directly to Parliament. But, in Sweden, the real business of government is carried out in the agencies and this is where the RRV dominates. The RRV is recognized by INTOSAI as the Swedish Supreme Audit Institution. Also, the RRV operates on a totally different scale to the PA, with over 500 staff as compared to about 50 in the PA's Office. In terms of language familiar to constitutional lawyers, the Parliamentary auditors' work can be described as a 'dignified' aspect of the Swedish constitution, compared to the RRV's more 'efficient' role.[47]

Arguably, having two separate bodies responsible for audit would help avoid any potential conflicts between providing democratic and managerial accountability. However, it must be recognized that this split would probably result in a disparity between the two bodies as is the case in Sweden. The lion's share of the resources would be allocated to the body responsible for managerial accountability, while the body providing democratic accountability would have a role only insofar as it fitted into the dignified aspect of the constitution. Accordingly, the importance currently attached to the role the PAC plays in providing democratic accountability is largely derived from the fact that the same process also serves the needs of those ensuring managerial accountability. Any split designed to separate the processes for achieving democratic accountability and managerial accountability could result in a diminution of the PAC's role, since it would only retain responsibility for attaining democratic

---

[46] At the time of writing, the constitutional role of the PA was under review, one issue being whether the PA should be more independent from Parliament: see the Final Report from the Audit Committee to the Speaker's Conference (1998).

[47] Bagehot, W., *The English Constitution*, with an introduction by Crossman, R. H. S., (London: Fontana, Collins, 1963).

accountability. Democratic accountability would also suffer as a result. In order to avoid this and to maintain the position of the PAC in the United Kingdom constitution, there should be no such division in the accountability process. Therefore, although there are some faults in the current system, at present no viable, better alternative exists.

7

The Audit Commission

INTRODUCTION

The focus of the book so far has been on the role which the C&AG, the NAO and the PAC play in holding central government to account for its spending. The following two chapters will widen this focus by examining, in turn, the constitutional role of public sector audit at a sub-national, or local, level and, at a supra-national, that is European Community, level.

At a local level, some form of checking of money spent has existed since the seventeenth century. In 1846, the District Audit Service was established to audit the accounts of money spent under the Poor Law.[1] The District Audit Service continued to be responsible for local government audit until 1982 when the Audit Commission was established. This chapter will look at the Audit Commission, or to give it its full legal title, the Audit Commission for Local Authorities and the National Health Service in England and Wales.[2] We will consider how the Audit Commission holds local government and national health service bodies to account, drawing on some of the themes raised in relation to audit at central government level—namely, jurisdiction, independence and audience.[3] The origins of the Commission will be outlined first. Secondly, various relationships will be analysed to evaluate the independence of external audit in the areas for which the Commission is responsible. This involves looking both at the Commission and at the auditors that it appoints. Next, the audit process and its role in delivering accountability will be examined. A key issue here is the audience for audit work; that is, the person or persons to whom the auditors' reports are addressed. In contrast to the NAO, the Audit Commission has no direct relationship with Parliament and there is no equivalent of the PAC to receive audit reports about local government and NHS bodies. Finally, the significance of this difference for the

---

[1] See Couchman, V., 'The Audit Commission', in Sherer, M., and Turley, S., *Current Issues in Auditing*, (London: Chapman, 1997), Ch. 17; and Jones, R., *Local Government Audit Law*, (London: HMSO, 1985).

[2] There is a separate body for Scotland: the Accounts Commission. In Northern Ireland, the Audit Office assumed responsibility for local government and NHS audits from 1 April 1997.

[3] See Chs. 4, 5 and 6 respectively.

effectiveness of the Commission as an independent agent of accountability will be addressed.

THE ORIGINS OF THE AUDIT COMMISSION

The Audit Commission was established by the Local Government Finance Act 1982 to undertake a range of functions in relation to the external audit of local government. In particular, it appoints auditors and itself conducts national *vfm* studies. In 1990, the National Health Service and Community Care Act extended the Audit Commission's remit to include national health service bodies.[4] The relevant legislation has been consolidated in the Audit Commission Act 1998, which received the Royal Assent on 11 June 1998, and, in accordance with section 55, came into effect at the end of the period of three months beginning with the day on which it was passed (hereinafter the 1998 Act—references shall be made to the provisions of the 1998 Act *and* to the now repealed provision of the 1982 and 1990 Acts).[5]

When it began work in 1983, the Commission took over responsibility for the local government District Audit Service from the Secretary of State for the Environment. District auditors had exclusive responsibility for the audit of local government for approximately 130 years, until the Local Government Act 1972.[6] The 1972 Act gave local authorities the choice of whether to have their accounts audited by a district auditor or by a private firm of auditors. In 1976, however, the Layfield Committee concluded that it was wrong for any public body to be able to choose its own auditors.[7] It recommended that auditors should be completely independent of both central and local government and proposed the creation of a new body to which auditors should report. These proposals were rejected by the Government of the day. The PAC and the Expenditure Committee of the House of Commons subsequently suggested that the District Audit Service should become the responsibility of the C&AG.[8] This idea was also rejected and the arrangements for local government audit remained unchanged until the Audit Commission was established.

---

[4] The Commission now covers some 480 principal local government bodies, 11,000 minor bodies (such as parish councils), 600 health service bodies and 4,400 GP fundholders: see Audit Commission, *Annual Report*, 1997, p. 8.

[5] The 1998 Act repeals, *inter alia*, ss. 11–36, s. 38(5) and (6), Sch. 3, 5, and Part IV in Sch. 6, of the 1982 Act; and ss. 20(1) and (3)–(8), and Sch. 4, of the 1990 Act.

[6] See, generally, Jones, R., *supra*, n. 1.

[7] Layfield Committee, *Local Government Finance. Report of the Committee of Inquiry*, Cm. 6453 (1976).

[8] First Special Report of the Committee of Public Accounts, HC 115, 1980–81; and the Eleventh Report of the Expenditure Committee, HC 535, 1976–77. See, generally, Ch. 3.

The Commission was created at a time when conflict between local and central government was particularly acute. It was widely seen as part of the first Thatcher Government's package of measures to curb local powers and was regarded with suspicion and hostility by many people in local government. Over the past decade, however, the Commission has increasingly come to be seen as an independent body.

INDEPENDENCE AND THE AUDIT COMMISSION

The independence of an external audit body is integral to its role in the accountability process.[9] The main value of a public sector auditor's findings is that they represent an objective assessment of the government's accounts and performance. We saw in Chapter 5 how the independence of the NAO is secured. However, we cannot simply transfer the model applied to the NAO on to the Commission in order to assess its independence. In terms of its structure and functions, the Commission is a very different creature from the NAO. The Commission is responsible for the appointment and regulation of auditors but, unlike the NAO, the Commission does not itself audit any accounts. Instead, it appoints either a district auditor or a private firm of auditors to do the work. This means that questions about the 'independence' of the audit are multidimensional. Any examination of the independence of the audit involves distinguishing the Commission from the individual auditor, and looking first at the constitutional status of the Commission, and in particular its relationship with ministers; and secondly at the status of the individual auditor. The latter must in turn be viewed from two perspectives: the individual auditor's relationship with the Commission; *and* the individual auditor's relationship with the audited body.

The Constitutional Position of the Audit Commission

The Commission is a statutory corporation, listed in *Public Bodies* as an executive non-departmental public body, and sponsored by the Department of the Environment, Transport and the Regions,[10] the Department of Health and the Welsh Office.[11] Having a statutory base gives

---

[9] See, further, Ch. 5.   [10] Formerly the Department of the Environment.

[11] There is no provision in the Government of Wales Act 1998 concerning the role of the Audit Commission though, the relationship between audit and Welsh devolution will probably be considered as part of the Financial Management and Policy Review of the Commission currently being conducted by the Department of the Environment, Transport and the Regions.

the Commission, as an institution, a degree of protection from a minister unhappy with its findings, since it could not be abolished or its duties and powers altered without legislation being passed. The Commission's own accounts are audited by the NAO.[12] At the other end of the expenditure process, the Commission is self-financing in the sense that its revenue comes from audit fees and not from its sponsoring department.[13] Fee levels are prescribed by the Commission itself, but the Secretary of State has statutory authority to replace the scale of fees: this reserve power has never been exercised.[14] Since ministers have no direct control over its budget, the Commission is less vulnerable than most quangos to financial pressure from their department. However, other means of controlling or directing the Commission are available to ministers, including the power of appointment of members of the Commission, and a series of ministerial powers provided for in the 1998 Act.

Appointment

The Commission consists of between 15 and 20 members, including a chairman and deputy chairman.[15] At present, there are 16 members, drawn from (though not representing) local government, the health service, the accountancy profession, industry, and trade unions.[16] The members of the Commission make up a number of standing panels which include: District Audit Supervisory; Purchasing and Quality Control; Citizen's Charter; and Audit. They are appointed by the Secretaries of State for the three sponsoring departments, following a statutory consultation process.[17] The legal duty to consult merely requires the Secretaries of State to consider the views expressed, so the final power of appointment rests with government ministers. Since the composition of the Commission is controlled by government ministers, in theory at least, a compliant Commission could be engineered. In sharp contrast, the Prime Minister's recommendation to the Crown for appointment of the C&AG must be agreed with the Chair of the PAC, who by constitutional convention is an Opposition MP. This means that a consensus has to be reached

---

[12] The 1998 Act, Sch. 1, para. 11 (see previously the 1982 Act, Sch. 3, para. 12). The Accounting Officer for the Commission is the Controller of Audit.

[13] The 1998 Act, s. 7 (see previously the 1982 Act, s. 21): the Commission charges the auditee and then reimburses the auditor for his work, keeping a percentage of the amount for itself.

[14] The 1998 Act, ss. 7(8) and 7(9) (see previously the 1982 Act, ss. 21(7), and 35).

[15] The 1982 Act, s. 11 originally provided for between 13 and 17 members of the Commission. This was increased to 15–20 members by the National Health Service and Community Care Act 1990, Sch. 4, para. 1. See now the 1998 Act s. 1(1).

[16] See Audit Commission Home Page: http://www.audit-commission.gov.uk/

[17] The 1998 Act, s. 1(4) (see previously the 1982 Act, s. 11(2)). The bodies consulted include: the local government associations, the CBI, the TUC and the Consultative Committee of Accountancy Bodies.

between the government and the opposition on the appointment of the C&AG.[18]

Once appointed, a member's position is safeguarded to the extent that he can only be removed by the Secretary of State on one of the limited grounds specified in the statute.[19] However, members are appointed for the relatively short period of three years and appointments are renewable; hence a member who wants to continue beyond the initial three-year period has a strong incentive to be responsive to ministerial wishes. Renewal of membership is quite common.[20] Indeed, the previous Chairman, David Cooksey, held office for nine years.

The chief executive officer of the Audit Commission is the Controller of Audit. The Controller is appointed by the members, with the approval of the Secretary of State.[21] Like the members of the Commission, he is, in practice, appointed for a three-year renewable term. He enjoys no special statutory protection against dismissal.

The members' role is non-executive and part-time, meeting on a monthly basis. The members are in a position similar to that of non-executive boards and chairmen of some other public sector quangos. Potentially such boards have a dual role. On the one hand, they can insulate the chief executive from ministerial pressure. On the other hand, they may act to keep the chief executive in line. Often the role is a mixture of both elements. The members of such boards are more likely to exercise independent judgment if they are themselves insulated from direct ministerial pressure.

Other Ministerial Powers

INTOSAI, the International Organization of Supreme Audit Institutions, has developed criteria which can be used for assessing a Supreme Audit

---

[18] See, further, Ch. 5.

[19] The 1998 Act, Sch. 1, para. 4 (see previously the 1982 Act, Sch. 3, para. 4). The grounds are that the member has: become bankrupt or incapacitated; has been absent from meetings for six months without an approved reason; or is, in the opinion of the Secretary of State, otherwise unable or unfit to discharge the functions of a member.

[20] Five members of the Commission whose appointments were due to expire on 30 June 1997, had their appointment extended until 31 October 1997 to enable the new Labour Government to consider the range and balance of appointments to the Commission. The five members were: Clive Thompson (the Deputy Chairman, a member since April 1991, now working for a small management consultancy firm); Iris Tarry CBE (a member since 1 September 1994, currently Chair of Hertfordshire Police Authority); Peter Soulsby (a member since 1 September 1994, currently Labour Leader of Leicester County Council); Jeremy Orme (a member since February 1989, Chartered Accountant and head of Enforcement and Legal Services for the Securities and Investment Board); and Tony Travers (first appointed in February 1992, Greater London Group Research Director at the London School of Economics). Three of these have since been reappointed: Iris Tarry; Peter Soulsby; and Jeremy Orme (as Deputy Chairman).

[21] The 1998 Act, Sch. 1, para. 7 (see previously the 1982 Act, Sch. 3, para. 7).

Institution's (SAI's) independence.[22] The Audit Commission does not belong to INTOSAI: the NAO is the UK member. Nonetheless, the criteria are relevant since many SAIs are responsible for the audit of local, as well as central government. It is therefore instructive to apply the criteria when looking at the Commission's independence from the executive. INTOSAI requires in particular that:

> . . . *it is important for the independence of the SAI that there be no power of direction by the executive in relation to the SAI's performance of its mandate. The SAI should not be obliged to carry out, modify or refrain from carrying out, an audit or suppress or modify audit findings, conclusions or recommendations.*[23]

There are a number of provisions of the 1998 Act that are not compatible with this standard. Specifically, the Secretary of State may: (i) sanction items of account contrary to law and where there has been a failure to bring sums into account;[24] (ii) require the Commission to direct an extraordinary audit;[25] and (iii) give directions to the Commission as to the discharge of its functions, with which it must comply.[26]

The powers to direct an extraordinary audit and to give directions have not been used.[27] However, the impact of provisions of this kind is not limited to their formal use. In other situations, the existence of such powers has been taken as a reason to accept informal and less publicly visible forms of control (as, for example, in the case of the so-called 'lunchtime directives' that ministers used to give to chairmen of the old nationalized industries).[28] The legislation does provide that any direction must be published and this goes some way to protect the independence of the Commission.[29]

In 1994, the Commission and the Departments for the Environment, Health and the Welsh Office produced a 'joint statement of responsibility and accountability'.[30] This document emphasizes the Commission's independence from government. However, it also states that the government has a responsibility to ensure 'that the Commission's management processes are robust and secure'.[31] Sponsoring departments must also satisfy themselves that the Commission has adequate systems of financial control. In

---

[22] INTOSAI, *Auditing Standards*, (June 1989), paras. 47–71.

[23] Ibid., para. 56. Authors' emphasis.

[24] The 1998 Act, ss. 17(1) and 18(1) (see previously the 1982 Act, ss. 19(1), 20(1)).

[25] The 1998 Act, s. 25(2) (see previously the 1982 Act, s. 22(2)).

[26] The 1998 Act, Sch. 1, para. 3 (see previously the 1982 Act, Sch. 3, para. 3).

[27] Department of the Environment, Department of Health, Welsh Office and the Commission, *Accounting for Independent Audit—A Joint Statement of Responsibility and Accountability*, (1994), p. 6.

[28] See Prosser, T., *Nationalized Industries and Public Control*, (Oxford: Blackwell, 1986).

[29] The 1998 Act, Sch. 1, para. 3(5) (see previously the 1982 Act, Sch. 3, para. 3(4)). A similar safeguard operated in *Brind* v. *Home Office* [1991] 1 AC 696.

[30] *Supra*, n. 27.   [31] Ibid., p. 1.

practice, there are twice yearly meetings between the Department of the Environment, Transport and the Regions and the Commission in which the Department comments on the Commission's strategy and corporate plan. According to the joint statement, the Commission is 'ultimately answerable to Parliament'. This proposition could as well be intended to emphasize the ultimate right of ministers to control the Commission as to refer to some supposed limitation of that right. The meaning of the joint statement taken as a whole, however, is clearly that ministers regard the Commission as having a considerable degree of independence. It is less clear just what constitutional significance should be attached to this fact. The independence of the Commission from the government can be analysed in terms of a constitutional practice, but it would be hard to make a case that it is a matter of constitutional convention.[32] Clearly, however, because this practice has been publicly expressed, it would be improper for the government or the Commission to act in ways inconsistent with the joint statement, unless and until the statement itself is expressly withdrawn or revised.

Auditors and the Audit Commission

The Code of Audit Practice specifies that auditors must act independently of the Commission.[33] Yet the relationship between the auditor and the Commission is not simply an arm's length one. The Commission has many duties regarding auditors: it appoints them; it regulates the quality of audit; and it can also direct an extraordinary audit.

Appointment

As already noted, when first established the Commission took over responsibility for the local government District Audit Service. It was similarly required to offer employment to auditors from the Department of Health and the Welsh Office when it received its NHS functions in 1990. Since November 1994, the Commission's audit staff have been managed in an agency known simply as 'District Audit'. The relationship between District Audit (DA) and the Commission is intended to be similar to that between a 'Next Steps' agency and a government department. That is, the agency has managerial independence, within the terms of a Framework Document.[34] As with other agencies, the establishment of DA

---

[32] A constitutional convention may be said to exist where there is an obligation on the relevant actors to behave in a certain way. A constitutional practice, on the other hand, merely describes how the actors customarily behave. See Brazier, R., 'The Non-Legal Constitution: Thoughts on Convention, Practice and Principle', 43 (1992) *Northern Ireland Legal Quarterly*, 262.

[33] See Code of Audit Practice, para. 9.

[34] See District Audit *Framework Document*, (undated).

was not intended to involve any formal legal change of status and the staff of DA remain employees of the Commission. The Commission appoints either DA or an approved private firm of accountants to audit each local authority and health service body.[35] In practice, about 70 per cent of the work is done by DA. The choice between DA and private firms is not made, for the most part, on the basis of price competition.[36]

The independence of the audit is more complicated when the auditor comes from DA because DA is 'owned' by the Commission. The Commission has two roles as regards DA. First, it acts as the purchaser of audit, through its Purchasing and Quality Control Panel, selecting either DA or a firm to conduct the audit and setting the fees. Secondly, it is the 'owner' of DA and it exercises its ownership rights through the District Audit Panel. To maintain a distance between these two roles, there is a convention that the members of the District Audit Panel are never also members of the Purchasing Panel. Two areas are particularly relevant to DA's independence—its financial contribution to the Commission and its management accountability. As the in-house audit service for the Commission, DA pays to the Commission the usual percentage from the audit fees, plus an additional sum 'to reflect a rate of return to the Commission as "owner" of District Audit'.[37] The Commission therefore receives a higher financial benefit when it appoints DA to conduct an audit than it does when it appoints a private firm. Secondly, the District Audit Panel, which consists of the Deputy Chairman and four other members of the Commission, acts as the strategic governing board of DA and agrees DA's budget as prepared by the chief executive. It also sets DA's income and contribution targets based on a forecast number of audit days, as well as setting quality and performance targets.[38] There does appear to be some potential for conflict between these two roles. However, DA is a wholly owned agency of the Commission and, as such, is not intended to be totally independent of the Commission. It is accountable to the Commission in managerial terms. The next steps model seeks to achieve this accountability whilst allowing DA greater freedom to manage itself within an agreed framework. This does not, of course, directly affect the professional independence of individual auditors. All appointed auditors, whether from DA or a firm, are equally professionally independent in conducting their statutory responsibilities.

---

[35] The 1998 Act, s. 3 (see previously the 1982 Act, s. 13). The approved firms, in order of size, are: Coopers & Lybrand; Price Waterhouse; KPMG; Ernst & Young; Deloitte & Touche; Robson Rhodes; Binder Hamlyn; and Kidson Impey.

[36] To date, the Commission has engaged in four 'market testing' exercises for a small proportion of the work available (the Commission gave us the figure of 1–2 % of total audit days) which enables the Commission to check that standards and prices are generally reasonable. Any profit (or loss) from market testing is borne by the Commission and not the audited body.

[37] *Supra*, n. 34, p. 6.   [38] Ibid., p. 4.

Regulation

As a regulator, the Commission is responsible for drawing up and reviewing, at least once every five years, a Code of Audit Practice for auditors supplemented by an annual guidance letter. The Code is subject to Parliamentary approval.[39] The Code and the annual guidance letter are prepared by the Commission's Purchasing and Quality Control Directorate.[40] This Directorate is also responsible for the appointment of auditors and for carrying out quality control reviews, based on a sampling method.[41] The results of the quality control reviews are taken into account in deciding whether or not to reappoint an auditor.[42]

A related issue is the procedure for dealing with complaints. To protect the independence of auditors, the Commission, when dealing with complaints, does not question the merits of an auditor's decision but reviews only the process of the audit. Some complaints, however, may lead to a special quality control investigation, and hence are relevant to decisions about reappointment.[43] The complaints procedure has been codified and centralized in the Purchasing and Quality Control Directorate.

Extraordinary Audit

If it believes that it is desirable to do so, the Commission may instruct the auditor of a local authority or an NHS body to carry out an extraordinary audit.[44] In the case of local authorities, this can be done in response to an application made by a local government elector for the area of that body. The Commission's power has two aspects. First, it may order an extraordinary audit, even if the auditor does not think it necessary. More significantly, the auditor has no power to conduct an extraordinary audit unless instructed to do so. If the auditor does wish to conduct an extraordinary audit, therefore, he must apply to the Commission, which can in effect veto his request. It should be noted that where the Commission directs that an extraordinary audit should be conducted there is no change of auditor, nor does the auditor have any special powers. The Commission defines the scope and content of the extraordinary audit, but it cannot direct how the audit should be carried out. Within the bounds of the audit, the auditor's professional independence remains intact.

[39] The 1998 Act, s. 4(4) (see previously the 1982 Act, s. 14(3)). The first Code appeared in 1983 and was revised in 1988, 1990 and 1995.

[40] There are five directorates in all: Local Government Studies; Health and Personal Social Services Studies; Audit Support; Resources; Purchasing and Quality Control.

[41] See Audit Commission, *Annual Report*, 1997, pp. 10–11. The aims of these reviews are to: check that audits are being carried out in accordance with the Code; examine audit achievement against the targets set by the Commission in its annual guidance letter; assess audit performance with a view to taking remedial action if necessary and; identify and spread best practice.

[42] Code of Audit Practice, p. 4.   [43] Audit Commission, *Annual Report*, 1997, p. 11.

[44] The 1998 Act, s. 25(1) (see previously the 1982 Act, ss. 22(1) and (4A) as inserted by the 1990 Act, Sch. 4).

The Commission has only twice ordered an extraordinary audit. In practice, the extraordinary audit seems to be an anachronism, left over from the days when such a direction was needed to empower current audit work. As auditors are now able to undertake current audit work, its usefulness has greatly reduced. The power remains because elector's rights only apply at a late stage in the audit process. Extraordinary audit brings those rights into play at the stage when such an audit is directed.

The various factors discussed above mean that the Commission has an influence on the auditor and his work. This fact can be looked at in two ways. If the Commission is itself seen as an independent audit body, then the powers which it has over individual auditors are almost certainly less than those which, for example, the C&AG has over his staff. On the other hand, if the Commission is seen as an agent of central government, then its powers may appear as a possible source of interference with the independence of the auditors.

This potential ambiguity in the role of the Commission has, in the past, appeared in relation to the giving of legal advice by the Commission to the auditors of local authorities. Radford gives examples of occasions when the Commission gave legal advice, both to the auditors and to local authorities, which appeared to go beyond the strict legal requirements.[45] It is very difficult for a local authority to ignore the legal advice of an auditor or the Commission, given the impact of the *ultra vires* principle on local government and the possibility of surcharge (see, further, below). The relationship between the Commission and the auditors regarding legal advice has more recently been changed, to promote further the independence of auditors. Previously, if auditors were seeking legal advice on specific cases this could be obtained from the Commission's own solicitor, who would then treat the auditors as private clients. His experience in dealing with individual cases was then used to develop more general advice which the Commission could pass on to other auditors. However, since 1995 the Commission has decided that auditors can no longer receive formal legal advice on specific cases from the Commission's solicitor. Whether these changes will resolve the problems highlighted by Radford remains to be seen, since the Commission will continue to give general guidance to auditors on legal issues.

Auditors and Audited Bodies

The Code of Audit Practice provides that auditors must carry out their duties independently of the body being audited.[46] The 1998 Act gives the

[45] Radford, M., 'Auditing For Change: Local Government and the Audit Commission', 54 (1991) *Modern Law Review* 912.
[46] See Code of Audit Practice, para. 9.

auditor access to all documents that he may require, as well as the power to demand explanations from individuals concerned. Failure to comply with the auditor's requirements is a criminal offence punishable by a fine.[47]

The power of appointment of the auditor rests solely with the Commission. There is a statutory requirement to consult local authorities, but not NHS bodies. In practice, the Commission consults both types of auditee and seeks to accommodate any reasonable objections that may be put forward against a proposed auditor. The Commission awards a particular audit to either DA or to a private firm and informs the auditee accordingly. It is then DA or the firm that selects the particular auditor to carry out the audit. A list of these individual appointments is approved by the Commission annually.

The period of appointment of DA or the private firm is normally five years. This period is cost-effective from the point of view of the Commission, since every new auditor takes time to get to know the auditee's operation.[48] It also allows for continuity. The period of appointment can be extended, to offer further continuity where the auditee is undergoing extensive change (following a merger in the NHS, for example). However, even if the appointment period is extended, the individual auditor and audit manager must change every seven years unless there are exceptional circumstances.[49] This requirement of 'rotation' is considered essential to ensure the independence of the auditor from the auditee. As noted earlier in the book, the Nolan Committee recommended that the period of rotation for auditors in the public sector should be reduced from seven to five years.[50] In 1995, the Commission invited a former senior partner of KPMG to conduct an independent review of its performance and make recommendations for increasing its impact. The resulting Butler Review was published in September 1995.[51] According to the Review, when the time comes to rotate, most audited bodies prefer to keep the same auditor. This is understandable, since a new auditor means uncertainty and costs for the auditee in establishing a new relationship. The Butler Review concluded, nevertheless, that the Commission should attempt to implement the Nolan Committee's recommendation.

---

[47] The 1998 Act, s. 6 (see previously the 1982 Act, s. 16). The maximum fine is £200 plus an additional £20 for each day the offence continues. This is similar to the French administrative law concept of *astreinte*. Astreinte has been defined as a judgment that requires a person to pay a certain sum of money for each day of delay in the fulfilment of an obligation: see Depuis, G., Guedon, M. J., and Chretien, P., *Droit Administratif*, (Paris: Armand Colin, 5th edn., 1994).

[48] Audit Commission, *Who Audits the Auditors*, (London: HMSO, 1994).

[49] In the private sector, professional standards require that the partner rotate every seven years. No reference is made to managers.

[50] Nolan Committee First Report, *Standards in Public Life*, Cm. 2850 (May, 1995), para. 108.

[51] Butler Review of the Audit Commission, February–July 1995.

One of the main contributions of auditors to the accountability process is to provide expert information which can be used to hold government to account. While the Audit Commission and the auditors it appoints produce many reports of various types, their route as vehicles of accountability is less well defined than that of NAO reports. Before describing the various audit outputs in the Commission's field of responsibility, it is first necessary to outline the legal framework within which audit is conducted.

When auditing local government and NHS bodies, individual auditors have a number of specific duties under the 1998 Act, which can broadly be classified into two functions: first, to check the legality and regularity of the expenditure and the accounts (financial audit)[52] and secondly, to examine the arrangements for securing *vfm* of their expenditure.[53] There are however, some features of audit that are specific to local government and others that are peculiar to the NHS.

Auditing Local Government

In order to understand why auditors enjoy certain powers as regards local government audit that they do not possess in relation to NHS bodies, it is necessary to consider the historical development of local government. Two features of the legal position of local authorities and their members are particularly significant: the *ultra vires* principle and the liability of local councillors to surcharge.

Unlike the Crown, local authorities do not enjoy a general legal competence. They only have those powers which are conferred on them by statute or which are reasonably incidental thereto. Actions that do not fall within those powers (that is, which are *ultra vires*) are unlawful. The practical impact of this principle is mitigated by the fact that many statutory powers of local authorities are very widely drawn. As regards budgetary matters, however, there are two factors that give special significance to the *ultra vires* rule. First, the courts have developed the principle that local authorities owe a fiduciary duty to their taxpayers, so that by ignoring 'value for money' considerations, an authority may act *ultra vires*. In *Roberts* v. *Hopwood*,[54] for example, the House of Lords upheld the view of the district auditor that the authority had acted unlawfully in raising the wages

---

[52] The 1998 Act, s. 5(1) (see previously the 1982 Act, s. 15(1)(a) and (b)).

[53] The 1998 Act, s. 5(1) (see previously the 1982 Act, s. 15(1)(c)). The current split between regularity and *vfm* work is about 70/30 in any individual audit.

[54] [1925] AC 578. In *Bromley London Borough Council* v. *Greater London Council* [1983] 1 AC 815, Lord Wilberforce said that *Roberts* v. *Hopwood* 'remained authoritative as to principle'.

of its employees to a level which was above that of comparable employees in the area. The second factor, which reinforces the first, is that the *ultra vires* rule may give rise to financial and other penalties on individuals through the power of surcharge.

Auditors of private sector bodies do not have the power to impose personal liability on someone who is responsible for incurring a loss. Nor is this a power which all public sector audit bodies possess. For example, the C&AG does not have power to surcharge. However, local auditors in the United Kingdom have had the power to surcharge for 150 years. Arguably, it gives them a potent weapon to ensure the legality of local financial management.

Surcharge is governed by sections 17 and 18 of the 1998 Act.[55] Section 17 allows the auditor to apply to the court for a declaration that an item of account is contrary to law, except where it is sanctioned by the Secretary of State. If the court makes the declaration, it may also order the person responsible for incurring the expenditure to pay back, in whole or in part, the amount which was unlawfully spent. However, the court must not make an order for repayment if it is satisfied that the person acted reasonably, or believed the expenditure was authorized by law. Section 18 concerns the recovery of an amount that has not been accounted for by law. If the auditor believes that a person has failed to bring into account any sum which should have been included and the failure has not been sanctioned by the Secretary of State, or that a loss has been incurred or deficiency caused by the wilful misconduct of any person,[56] the auditor must certify that that sum is due from the person responsible and may recover that sum for the benefit of the body who suffered the loss. There is provision for appeal to the court against the auditor's decision.[57] This system of surcharge has been criticized for giving the auditor powers to be investigator, prosecutor and judge. In his third report, Lord Nolan recommended the abolition of surcharge to be replaced by a new statutory offence of misuse of public office.[58] At the time of writing, a consultation process was underway and it was not clear whether Parliament would abolish the surcharge power.[59] Although there may be faults in the current system, these do not necessarily present a strong case for abolition, rather reform. Surcharge provides a powerful incentive for councillors to ensure that they spend public money

[55] See previously the 1982 Act, ss. 19 and 20, respectively.

[56] For example, the refusal of some councils to set rates in the 1980s as a protest against rate capping.

[57] For recent example, see *Porter, and ors* v. *Magill*, (unreported, High Court, 19 December 1997). See, further, *Guardian*, 6 October 1997, p. 10 leave to appeal has been granted.

[58] Nolan Committee Third Report, *Standards in Public Life*, Cm. 3702 (July 1997).

[59] See the Department of the Environment, Transport and the Region's Consultation Paper, *Modernising Local Government. A New Ethical Framework*, (1998), pp. 34–5.

correctly, even if it is not often used. Indeed, it is a power which, we have elsewhere argued, could and should be given back to accounting officers at central government level.[60]

In addition to *ex post* controls, such as the power to surcharge, a local auditor also has power to act *ex ante* to prevent an illegality from occurring. The Local Government Act 1988 gave the local authority auditor the power to issue a prohibition order.[61] This can be done where the auditor believes that a decision has been made, or is about to be made, which would result in illegal expenditure, or if the auditor wants to prevent a loss, deficiency or entry of an item into account which would be unlawful.

The power to issue a prohibition order can only be effective if the auditor becomes aware of potential illegalities in time and has the power to obtain further information. The local authority chief finance officer has a specific duty to report to the auditor any proposal for unlawful expenditure, or for the entry into account of an unlawful item.[62] Furthermore, the auditor has power to carry out examinations throughout the year ('current audit') rather than just at the end of the financial year when the accounts have been prepared.

Another *ex ante* power of the auditor is to bring judicial review proceedings against an audited body.[63] The auditor has *locus standi* to apply for judicial review if it is reasonable to believe that any decision by that body, or any failure of that body to act, would have an effect on the accounts of that body. This power was introduced in response to late rate setting, where a remedy of *mandamus* (rather than a prohibition order) was needed to compel compliance with the statutory duty.

The *ex ante* powers, the *ultra vires* principle and the possibility of surcharge mean that auditors have a significant executive role in the regulation of local government as well as in the provision of information and analysis about its performance. There are two factors that make this a potentially difficult combination of roles. First, the Code of Audit Practice states that auditors may not question lawfully adopted policies, but only the effects of the policies and the arrangements by which policy decisions are reached.[64] In practice, however, the *ultra vires* principle and in particular the fiduciary duty mean that there is sometimes room for uncertainty about whether a policy is 'lawfully adopted'. Secondly, even where the boundaries of legality are clear, they are sometimes created by legislation that is seen, by local government at least, as a weapon used against it by

---

[60] See Harden, I., White, F., and Hollingsworth, K., 'Value for Money and Administrative Law', [1996] *Public Law* 661.

[61] The 1998 Act, s. 20 (see, previously, the 1982 Act, s. 25A).

[62] Local Government Finance Act 1988, s. 114.

[63] The 1998 Act, s. 24 (see, previously, the 1982 Act, s. 25D, inserted by the Local Government Act 1988).

[64] Code of Audit Practice, para. 43.

central government in a political struggle. This can make policing such boundaries an uncomfortable task.

Auditing the NHS

Before the National Health Service and Community Care Act 1990, the audit of NHS bodies was governed by the National Health Service Act 1977. Under section 98 of the 1977 Act, the accounts of NHS bodies were audited by auditors appointed by the Secretaries of State for Health and for Wales. The C&AG had the power to examine all of the accounts and any report of the auditor on them,[65] and under section 98(4) he had to examine and certify the summarized accounts prepared by the Secretary of State. The audit of health service bodies thus appeared to straddle the boundary between internal and external audit.[66] Rather than report directly to an external body which was independent of the auditee, the auditors reported instead to the Secretary of State, who was the minister responsible for the management of the body.

The relevant provisions of the 1990 Act were said to be intended to increase the independence of auditors and to place greater emphasis on *vfm*.[67] The Audit Commission was given responsibility for the audit of NHS bodies, whilst the C&AG retained the power to examine the accounts and the records relating to them and any report of the auditor on them,[68] and the power to examine and certify the summarized accounts. Under the National Audit Act 1983, the C&AG can also look at the economy, efficiency and effectiveness with which health authorities and other NHS bodies have used their resources in discharging their responsibilities.

Since NHS bodies are funded through the Department of Health budget, voted by Parliament, an obvious alternative to appointment of NHS auditors by the Audit Commission would have been for the NAO to carry out all the necessary audits. However, one of the perceived advantages of the Commission was that it already had the necessary facilities available to audit bodies throughout the country. Regional health authorities, audited by the Commission, have now been replaced by NHS regional offices, which are to be audited by the NAO. Other NHS bodies continue to have auditors appointed by the Commission. Both the Commission and the NAO claim that the rather complex division of labour causes little difficulty in practice. But in the area of *vfm*, the dividing line between the Commission and the NAO can be unclear, and issues of overlap and wasted

---

[65] The 1977 Act, s. 98(1).   [66] See Ch. 2.
[67] See remarks by Lord Henley, *Hansard HL*, Vol. 520: col. 265, 12 June 1990.
[68] The 1990 Act, s. 20(2)(a).

resources have arisen in the past.[69] As evidence of their good working relationship, the Commission and NAO issued a joint news release in January 1995, detailing future 'collaboration ventures'.

In relation to health service bodies, the auditor does not have the same powers as are given the local government auditor under sections 17 and 18 of the 1998 Act, and so does not have *locus standi* to apply for judicial review or prohibition orders. However, the auditor does have reporting duties to the Secretary of State, in certain circumstances. Where, for instance, the auditor has reason to believe that the body, or an officer of the body, is either about to make, or has made, a decision which involves or would involve the incurring of expenditure which is unlawful, he must refer the matter to the Secretary of State.[70] And, where the auditor has reason to believe that the body, or an officer of the body, is about to take, or has taken, a course of action which, if pursued to its conclusion, would be unlawful and likely to cause a loss or deficiency, he must refer the matter to the Secretary of State.[71] As a matter of formal agreement rather than statutory requirement, the NAO receives copies of all such reports on NHS bodies automatically, as well as of 'public interest' reports (see, further, below).

The Outputs of Audit

The outputs from financial and *vfm* audit are outlined below, with particular reference to two questions. First, is the information in the public domain? Secondly, to whom is the information addressed? Later in the chapter, we assess the answers to these two questions in examining the relationship between accountability and democracy.

Certificates and Opinions on Financial Accounts

The 1998 Act requires that when an audit is concluded, auditors shall enter on the annual accounts a certificate that the audit has been completed in accordance with the legislation, and an opinion. If the auditor decides that the accounts accurately represent the financial position he will issue an unqualified audit opinion.[72] Auditors should also report to officers, in the

---

[69] See Bowerman, M., 'The National Audit Office and the Audit Commission: co-operation in areas where their value for money responsibilities interface', 10 (1994) *Financial Accountability and Management*, 47.

[70] The 1998 Act, s. 19 (see previously the 1990 Act, s. 20(3)).   [71] Ibid.

[72] As regards local authorities, this states that 'In my/our opinion the statement of Accounts set out on pages——to——*presents fairly* the financial position of the authority at 31 March 19——and its income and expenditure for the year then ended'. The opinion for NHS trusts is a *'true and fair'* opinion. In the financial year 1995–96, the AC audited the accounts of 448 principal local authorities, of which 8 were qualified; and 677 NHS bodies.

form of *memoranda*, on issues arising from financial audit, including recommendations for improvement.

Management Letters

Each year the auditor summarizes the main message of the audit in a so-called 'management letter'.[73] As the name suggests, this letter is primarily addressed to those responsible for the management of the audited body, which, in the case of local authorities includes both officers and elected members. The letter is also sent to the Audit Commission and in the case of NHS bodies, to the NHS executive or the Welsh Office.[74] Management letters concerning an NHS body are sent to board members and formally considered by the body's audit committee. In local authorities, the method of distribution of the management letter to elected members is generally left to officers to organize, but the auditor may personally issue a copy to all members if he considers it necessary to do so.

There is some confusion about whether management letters to local authorities should be publicly available. Section 49 of the 1998 Act (which prohibits the disclosure of information obtained in the course of the audit, barring special circumstances) has been claimed to be a bar to publication;[75] while section 8 can be used to support the argument that the letter, as an auditor's report, is in the public domain as of right.[76] The better view would seem to be that management letters are not public interest reports under section 8 unless the auditor expressly provides so. Hence, the Commission's view is that management letters are restricted under section 49 unless and until published by the authority. In practice, the management letter is not published, but it normally comes into the public domain by being put on the agenda of a council meeting.[77] Further, under section 11 of the 1998 Act,[78] the auditor can insist that certain management letter recommendations—but not the letter itself—are brought

There were no qualified opinions of any trusts, health authorities, or family health services authorities. However, the accounts of the newly established NHS Litigation Authority were qualified due to the inadequacy of underlying records, and at 45 NHS bodies auditors added explanatory paragraphs to their opinions to draw readers' attention to matters of concern: see *Annual Report*, 1997, pp. 13–14.

[73] Now also referred to as an annual report of audit.

[74] See, further, Bowerman, M., Gray, I., and Reedman, M., *Audit Management Letters in Local Government. Aspects of Accountability*, Research Papers in Accounting, No. 2 (Sheffield: Sheffield Hallam University, 1996).

[75] See, previously, s. 30 of the 1982 Act.

[76] See, previously, s. 15(3) of the 1982 Act; and s. 24 which provided a right of inspection to a local government elector to audited accounts, statements and reports.

[77] Agenda items for local authority committees are open to inspection under s. 100B of the Local Government Act 1972 and s. 1(4) of the Public Bodies (Admission to Meetings) Act 1960. They can be removed from the public domain only by resolution or if the letter is classified as material of a 'confidential nature'.

[78] Sec, previously, s. 5 of the Local Government Act 1992.

to the attention of the public.[79] In their 1997 Annual Report, the Commission again stated its belief that authorities should make management letters publicly available, in accordance with the seven principles of public life laid down by the Nolan Committee.[80] It also noted that 79 per cent of public authorities had considered the management letters at an open meeting and 85 per cent said they would make them available to the public on request, even though there was no legal requirement to do so.[81]

Local VFM *Studies*

Local *vfm* studies undertaken by appointed auditors must be distinguished from the national studies which the Audit Commission itself produces and which are discussed below. Section 5(1)(e) of the 1998 Act provides for auditors to examine whether proper arrangements exist for securing the '3Es' of economy, efficiency and effectiveness.[82] However, local *vfm* reports are not automatically published. Instead, the auditor gives either a written or an oral report to the officers, and where appropriate to the members.[83] Increasingly, such reports are debated or reported to members in public session, and so become public documents in this informal and ad hoc manner. The reports may have recommendations and an action plan, and a response by the local authority or NHS body, and they must be referred to in the management letter. They are followed up in future years to see if the action plan is being followed.

Public Interest Reports

After examining the accounts, the local government auditor may issue an immediate report to draw attention to any important matter—good or bad—if they consider it to be in the public interest to do so.[84] The Code of Audit Practice gives examples of when it would be in the public interest to make a report. These include, amongst other things: failure to comply with statutory provisions; misconduct or fraud; delayed preparation of accounts; and absence of, or weaknesses in, arrangements for securing the 3Es in the use of resources.[85] This report is sent by the auditor to the body concerned. The report must accompany the agenda of the meeting at which it is to be discussed and must not be excluded from material required to

[79] In 1996, 10 such recommendations were made: see Audit Commission, *Annual Report*, 1997, p. 13.
[80] Ibid. For the seven principles, see the Nolan Committee First Report, *supra*, n. 50, p. 14.
[81] Ibid.   [82] See, previously, s. 15(1)(c) of the 1982 Act.
[83] See Code of Audit Practice, para. 55(d). When it is 'appropriate' is left to the discretion of the individual auditor.
[84] The 1998 Act, s. 8 (see previously the 1982 Act, s. 15(3)). Ten public interest reports were issued regarding local government accounts for 1995–96: Audit Commission, *Annual Report*, 1997, p. 13.
[85] Code of Audit Practice, para. 74.

be supplied to newspapers. The auditor may supply a copy of the report to persons he sees fit and the Commission may publish information on it. Further, the local authority has to advertise the existence of the report.[86]

Similar requirements exist in the NHS for public interest reports but the reporting lines are very different. The reports are copied to the Secretary of State and the body concerned.[87] Although these reports invariably become public, the Nolan Committee has recommended that the Commission should be authorized to publish such reports on the NHS at its own discretion.[88] The Conservative Government (1992–97) accepted this recommendation but no legislation has been forthcoming to date.[89]

National Studies on VFM

The Commission itself undertakes national *vfm* studies under two statutory powers. Section 33 of the 1998 Act requires the Commission to undertake or promote studies into economy, efficiency, and effectiveness in the provision of services.[90] Studies under section 33 are comparative and make recommendations as to how the auditees could improve their performance. Section 34 requires the Commission to report on the impact of statutes and of ministerial directions and guidance on the 3Es in the provision of services, or on financial management, by local authorities.[91] This provision does not extend to health service bodies. Nonetheless, when carrying out studies of NHS bodies under section 33, the Commission may take into account the implementation by that body of any particular statutory provisions and any directions or guidance given by the Secretary of State.[92] However, this is not to be construed as entitling the Commission to question the merits of the policy objectives of the Secretary of State. There is no equivalent provision concerning questioning the merits of policy objectives for section 34 reports on local government. The Commission must send copies of reports made under section 34 to the C&AG, who can require the Commission to give him the information obtained by it in connection with the preparation of the report, although information concerning the activities of individual authorities must not be given.[93] The C&AG may report to the House of Commons on matters arising out

---

[86] The 1998 Act, s. 13 (see previously the 1982 Act, s. 18A(2), inserted by the Local Government Finance (Publicity for Auditors' Reports) Act 1991).

[87] For 1995–96, there were no public interest reports for the NHS but auditors reported to the Secretary of State on 10 occasions where unlawful expenditure had been or was about to be incurred: Audit Commission, *Annual Report*, 1997, p. 14.

[88] Nolan Committee First Report, *Standards in Public Life*, Cm. 2850 (May 1995), Recommendation 51.

[89] *Spending Public Money: Governance and Audit Issues*, Cm. 3179 (1996), para. 19.

[90] See, previously, the 1982 Act, s. 26.   [91] See, previously, the 1982 Act, s. 27.

[92] The 1998 Act, s. 33(3) (see, previously, the 1982 Act, s. 27(6)—as amended by the 1990 Act, Sch. 4).

[93] The 1998 Act, ss. 34(3) and 34(4) (see, previously, the 1982 Act, s. 27(3)).

of such information.[94] The C&AG also has the right to request the Commission to provide him with all the material relevant to a study of health service bodies carried out under section 33. In practice, the Commission does not issue separate reports under sections 33 and 34. Reports on a particular subject draw on both powers, though they contain separate recommendations to local government and central government.

The national *vfm* studies are comparative management studies. They examine particular areas rather than individual bodies. The national reports can be divided into two main groups: local government (including the police) and the NHS. Each of these areas are the responsibility of the Local Government Studies Directorate and the Health and Personal Social Services Studies Directorate respectively, each of which produces about four to five national studies per year.[95] A core of two people usually work on a study under the supervision of an assistant director and with the assistance of other experts. On average, a national study takes up to two years to complete. The Commission has been criticized in the past for the length of time it takes to complete studies. In a fast changing environment, studies can quickly become outdated. Selection of topics is on a rolling basis, following consultation. Among the selection criteria, the Commission is concerned to cover the different areas under its remit, to achieve a balance of the 3Es and to ensure that the topics should be susceptible to significant improvement and be relevant up to three years after their selection. In the past, these studies have influenced government legislation, for example, on Community Care and Special Educational Needs.[96] The studies also have a more local impact, with bodies taking on board recommendations, often in the knowledge that the audit process will follow up on the national reports.

Performance Indicators

The Local Government Act 1992 gave the Commission additional responsibilities, including a duty to direct local authorities to publish comparative indicators of performance on an annual basis.[97] The Commission does not have the same powers of direction in respect of health service bodies. Under the *Patient's Charter*, however, provider units (such as, NHS

---

[94] The 1998 Act, s. 34(5) (see, previously, the 1982 Act, s. 27(4)).

[95] The Commission also publishes bulletins, which are updates on the national reports, and management papers, which look at the wider issues which span across all service departments (such as personnel issues) and are concerned with highlighting best practice. To date, it has also produced occasional papers, containing quicker reviews of smaller aspects of local authority services and three papers about IT issues.

[96] See Butler Review, *supra*, n. 51, para. 32.

[97] This was as part of the *Citizen's Charter* programme, initiated by Cm. 1599 (1991). The Audit (Miscellaneous Provisions) Act 1996 allowed local authorities to publish their performance indicators in free newspapers. See now the 1998 Act, ss. 44–47.

Trusts and remaining directly managed units, if any) must report their performance against seven key indicators. The results are used to compile published league tables. The responsibility for establishing the indicators and compiling the tables lies with the Department of Health and not with the Commission. However, the Department has asked that the auditors appointed by the Commission should carry out checks on the data collection systems.[98]

ACCOUNTABILITY TO WHOM?

In the years that it has been functioning, the Audit Commission has established itself as a key player, alongside the NAO, in ensuring proper accountability for the use of public money. The combined annual spending of the bodies within its remit is about £90 billion; that is a third of the Control Total for public expenditure, or 15 per cent of Gross Domestic Product. The development of the Commission has been largely a matter of pragmatic adjustments, tempered by the requirements of the accounting profession. In previous parts of this Chapter we have looked at the relationships between the various actors and at the process of audit. Here, we take stock of the current position from a constitutional perspective. The core value of independent audit findings is that they represent a source of expert information that can be used to hold those responsible for spending decisions to account. Accordingly, the key questions addressed in this part of the Chapter are the extent to which audit information should be publicly available and whether a specialist audience should exist to maximize the use made of such information.

For the purposes of analysing these two questions, it is useful to distinguish three dimensions of accountability. These are: the democratic accountability of government to citizens; managerial accountability, in which public officials in government departments, agencies, and local government are held to account by their hierarchical superiors; and legal accountability, consisting of the monitoring and enforcement of rules and principles laid down in advance to guide behaviour.[99] These dimensions of accountability overlap both in theory and in practice. For example, the relationship between DA and the Audit Commission is modelled on that between executive agencies and government departments. This relationship is partly managerial and partly legal, in the sense of being

[98] Audit Commission, *Annual Report*, 1995, p. 31.

[99] See Ch. 1 on types of accountabilities; see, further, White, F., Harden, I., and Donnelly, K., 'Audit and Government Accountability—a Framework for Comparative Analysis', Working Paper No. 2, (University of Sheffield: Political Economy Research Centre and Department of Law, August 1994).

based on rules established in advance (even though the rules have no—or at any rate no clear—public law status).

The process of audit provides information that can be relevant to all three dimensions of accountability. It may also involve a judicial or executive role in relation to legal accountability, as for example, in the case of prohibition orders and surcharge. As regards managerial accountability, there is clearly an overlap between the work of the auditor in evaluating systems for achieving *vfm* and the work of management, which is responsible for delivering *vfm*. This overlap creates a potential confusion; is the role of the auditor to provide information to help management, or information by which others can evaluate the performance of management? The distinction between 'internal' and 'external' audit does not entirely resolve the question since, as has been shown above, even external auditors provide information to management. This leads to a practical problem: does the public have the right to see the information that an external auditor provides to management?

Information in the Public Domain

In relation to local government, there is a strong prima facie case that all audit information that is relevant to democratic accountability should be publicly available on request, even if it is not formally published. Citizens and local taxpayers have a legitimate interest in knowing what the external auditor thinks of the authority's performance. The present position is that the auditor's certificate and opinion on the local authority's accounts and any public interest reports are automatically published. Local *vfm* reports, however, are not published, although inadequate arrangements for *vfm* will normally be the subject of a public interest report. Citizens and taxpayers have as much interest in *vfm* at local as at central government level and the national studies published by the Commission do not contain detailed studies of particular authorities. Even the Commission would not argue that performance indicators are an adequate substitute for local *vfm* reports. Either the *vfm* studies add no significant new information to the indicators—in which case their publication is harmless—or they do add significant new information—in which case local citizens and taxpayers should have a right to see them.

There is no legal requirement to publish management letters though the Commission supports such action.[100] A recent study also recommends

[100] See Audit Commission, *Annual Report*, 1997, p. 13. Note the impact that freedom of information legislation may have in this area. The White Paper on freedom of information extends to local government and private contractors carrying out statutory functions. There are seven specified categories of material which may be exempt and six of those categories are subject to a substantial harm test. It is unlikely that local *vfm* reports and management

publication due to the fact that they both contain rich information and provide an independent view of important matters affecting the authority.[101] The study further suggests that it is unclear whether, at present, management letters are intended as a report to members on the actions of officers; as a reflection on the actions of members; as a mixture of both; or indeed whether they serve as a reflection on the auditor's own work.[102] This apparent confusion over the status and purpose of management letters leads to a fundamental question: who or what is the primary audience for the outputs of audit? This is an issue that affects the Audit Commission as well as the auditors themselves.

The Audience(s) for Audit

At central government level, the contribution made by audit to accountability depends not just on the audit information being in the public domain but also on the existence of a specific audience to whom the auditor's reports are addressed. NAO reports on accounts and its *vfm* studies are addressed to Parliament, through the PAC. As seen in Chapter 6, the role of the PAC as an official audience for the NAO brings together a number of different elements. Because its work is, by convention, bipartisan, the PAC represents Parliament in calling government—in the broad sense—to account.[103] Again, due to its bipartisan nature, the PAC is not a forum for political criticism of ministers. Its objectives—regularity and legality of expenditure, *vfm*—are ones that ministers themselves can hardly refuse to share. Furthermore, the PAC and the NAO are—for much of the time and on many issues—pushing in the same direction as the Treasury, in the latter's role as internal regulator of the public expenditure process. By focusing these different and overlapping elements, the PAC provides a considerable amount of 'political clout' for the audit work of the NAO and a mutually supportive link between managerial and democratic accountability. At the same time, the role of the PAC operates as a discipline on the NAO. Although it is essential for the NAO to be independent, it would be undesirable for it to be able to develop a political agenda of its own. Were it able to do so, questions about its accountability could hardly be avoided. In practice, the characteristics of the PAC as the official audience for NAO reports operate as an institutional constraint on the NAO, preventing such questions arising.

---

letters, even if they fall within one of the specified areas, would meet the substantial harm test: see the White Paper, *Your Right to Know: The Government's Proposals for a Freedom of Information Act*, Cm. 3818 (1997).

[101] *Supra*, n. 74.   [102] Ibid., p. 27.
[103] For the different meaning of the word 'government', see Ch. 1.

Within the area of the Audit Commission's responsibilities, audit find-ings do not have an official guaranteed audience of the kind that the PAC provides for the NAO. The Commission itself reports annually on the discharge of its functions to the Secretary of State for the Environment, Transport and the Regions, who lays the report before Parliament.[104] Neither its own national *vfm* reports, however, nor reports by the appointed auditors of local government and NHS bodies, are presented to Parliament. Nonetheless, audit findings can achieve 'clout' in a num-ber of different ways.

As regards questions of legality, the scope of the *ultra vires* principle and their own regulatory role together provide the auditors of local authorities with quite powerful instruments of enforcement. However, although some *vfm* reports raise issues of legality, this is not always the case and most audit findings cannot be made effective in this way. The Audit Commission itself and the reports of the auditors it appoints get some indirect clout from the constitutionally subordinate position of local government. Lurking in the background is the possibility of legis-lation, or more likely the exercise of existing ministerial powers, to require or induce local authorities to act, or not act, in particular ways. The same is true for the NHS.[105] However, this indirect form of clout is obviously of no relevance when the Commission criticizes the effects of central government policy. Furthermore, the possibility of legislative or ministerial intervention is too remote to give clout to audit findings in the ordinary run of events.

Audit committees exist in NHS bodies, executive non-departmental public bodies, and a few local authorities. Amongst other functions, such committees provide a forum for the discussion of audit reports. A consultation paper issued by the Conservative Government (1992–97) sug-gested extending audit committees to all local authorities.[106] It would be a mistake, however, to think that such committees could easily fulfil a role analogous to that of the PAC at central government level. In the NHS, audit committees are not an instrument of democratic accountability because they do not act on behalf of, or report to, either elected persons or to the public generally. They are primarily an instrument of manage-rial accountability within the structure of the particular NHS body.

In local government, the role of audit committees is less clearly defined. At one level, they are, like NHS audit committees, about man-agerial accountability within the administrative structure. At another

---

[104] The 1998 Act, Sch. 1, para. 14 (see previously the 1982 Act, Sch. 3, para. 15).

[105] Commission reports can lead to legislative changes: see for example reference to legis-lative changes on Community Care and Special Needs Education in the Butler Report, *supra*, n. 51, para. 32.

[106] *Spending Public Money: Governance and Audit Issues*, Cm. 3179 (1996).

level, they appear to be about the accountability of officers to elected members. They are not, however, a mechanism through which the local authority as a whole is democratically accountable to its electorate. Furthermore, there are two major obstacles to the development of such a role. The constitutional obstacle is the absence of any analogy at local level to the concept of the accountability of government to Parliament. The political obstacle is the weakness of the opposition in many local authorities.

At the Parliamentary level, Charter 88 has suggested that the Audit Commission, like the NAO, should report to the PAC.[107] The Labour Party, when in Opposition, also suggested more parliamentary involvement, with the Commission reporting to the Select Committee on the Environment.[108] These proposals need to be evaluated carefully. The triangular relationship between the PAC, Treasury and NAO works as a way of linking democratic and managerial accountability because all the actors involved are basically pushing in the same direction and because party politics is largely excluded. In contrast, central–local relations in Britain are characterized by endemic conflict, not least over finance. It seems unlikely that Audit Commission reports bearing on the relationship between central and local government could be examined by Parliament in a bipartisan way.

INDEPENDENT BUT ACCOUNTABLE?

Over the past decade, the Audit Commission has established itself alongside the NAO as an agent of accountability. Its independence from ministerial control is essential to its ability to fulfil this role. From the analysis above, however, it can be seen that there are a number of aspects of the present position that are less than satisfactory. Most striking are unfettered ministerial patronage in appointments and unconfined ministerial powers of direction under the Audit Commission Act 1998.

As regards the former issue, there are a number of ways to enhance the independence of the Commission. First, there could be a longer term of office for members of the Commission and the Controller of Audit, say five years, without the possibility of renewal. Parliamentary involvement in the appointment process is also desirable. This could take the form of requiring the consent of the chair of the PAC, as with the appointment of the C&AG. A further measure of parliamentary involvement that might be considered is to allow the Public Accounts Commission, which determines the NAO's budget, to comment on a budget proposal from

[107] In a joint report with Democratic Audit and Professor Patrick Dunleavy, *Reinventing Parliament—Making the Commons More Effective*, (1995).
[108] The Labour Party, *Renewing Democracy, Rebuilding Communities*, (London, 1995).

the Audit Commission. This would facilitate useful comparisons and could also remove the need (or at any rate confine and structure the potential use of) the ministerial power to set fee levels.

As regards the powers of direction, the 'joint statement of responsibility and accountability' contains, in effect, a promise by government that the existence of such powers will not be used to compromise the Commission's independence. What purpose, therefore, is served by having such powers? The obvious answer is that, unlike the NAO, the Audit Commission is not subject to the discipline of having the PAC as an official audience. The ministerial power of direction therefore serves to deflect accusations that the Commission is an 'unaccountable quango' by constraining the Commission from developing its own political agenda.

An alternative approach to the Commission's accountability would be to regard its legitimacy as depending not upon ultimate accountability *to someone*, but upon the absence of such accountability: that is, on its independence in carrying out its statutory mandate. The question of accountability would then become one of monitoring and enforcing the Commission's adherence to that mandate. Provided the mandate were adequately defined this could be a matter of legal accountability, enforced through the process of judicial review.[109] Although unusual in the British context, this approach would be preferable to attempting to extend the role of the PAC, which would risk damaging one of the seemingly few successful parts of the British Constitution.

---

[109] In such circumstances the issue of *locus standi* would need careful consideration.

8

The European Court of Auditors

INTRODUCTION

Large sums of money pass through the accounts of the European Communities.[1] Poor control, inadequate accountability, waste and fraud are
favourite themes of those hostile to the European Union. But those who
want further expansion of the Union's powers cannot afford to ignore
such issues. Nor can those who are more agnostic about the extent and
pace of further integration. Enlargement of the Union eastwards and
southwards is being negotiated. This can hardly be a zero-cost exercise,
although the scale of new spending is a matter for future conflict and bar-
gaining. Whether the Community is to spend more, or a lot more, European taxpayers and voters are unlikely to accept its legitimacy without
a strong system of financial control and accountability.

The Treaty on European Union (TEU) addressed the issue of financial
control and accountability by amending the provisions of the EC Treaty
concerning the European Court of Auditors (ECA).[2] In particular, it
raised the Court to the status of a Community 'institution' alongside the
European Parliament, Council, Commission and Court of Justice.[3] The
significance of this change is mainly symbolic.[4] However, a substantive
change was also made to the Court's functions. It must now provide the
European Parliament and the Council with a statement of assurance as

---

[1] The European Union has no budget, though certain expenditures under the common
foreign and security pillar and the justice and home affairs pillar can be charged to the
Community budget (Articles 28 and 41, Treaty on European Union (TEU), previously
Articles J 11(2) and K 8(2)). *All references hereinafter to the TEU shall be the references as amended
by the Amsterdam Treaty. Article 14 of the Amsterdam Treaty states that the Treaty will enter into
force on the first day of the second month following that in which the instrument of ratification is
deposited by the last signatory state. References to the pre-Amsterdam Treaty provisions are also
provided, in parentheses and italicized.*

[2] See, generally: House of Lords, Select Committee on the European Communities, *The
Court of Auditors*, HL 102, 1986–87, and *Financial Control and Fraud in the Community*, HL
75, 1993–94; Kok, C., 'The European Court of Auditors: The other European Court in Luxembourg', 26 (1989) *Common Market Law Review* 345; O'Keeffe, D., 'The Court of Auditors',
in Curtin, D., and Heukels, T., eds., *Institutional Dynamics of European Integration*, (Dordrecht:
M. Nijhoff, 1994).

[3] Article 7 EC (previously Article 4). *All references hereinafter to the EC Treaty are the references as amended by the Amsterdam Treaty. References to the pre-Amsterdam Treaty provisions are
also provided, in parentheses and italicized.*

[4] See also Declaration 21 TEU.

to the reliability of the accounts of the Community and the legality and regularity of the underlying transactions.[5] Amendments concerning the ECA under the Amsterdam Treaty are less significant.[6]

From a British perspective, it seems natural to respond to problems of public sector financial management by strengthening external audit arrangements. However, the ECA is not the NAO transferred to Luxembourg. Even the name can be misleading. In other languages, based on different domestic analogies, the Court is a court of *accounts* (*Corte dei conti, Cour des Comptes*).[7] This is more than a mere nuance of translation. It reflects a different culture of public sector organization, which emphasizes accountability based on formal legal requirements. The legality of expenditure is of fundamental importance in Britain,[8] but financial control and accounting procedures are not prescribed in detail by law, nor are they implemented through judicial processes.[9] The NAO, for example, does not sit in judgment on the legality of the actions of individuals.

It would be wrong, however, to imagine that there is a unified continental model of financial control and accounting to provide a context for understanding the ECA.[10]

Despite the existence of international organizations,[11] there is no 'European audit fraternity' to provide a basis for the work of the ECA comparable to the 'European monetary fraternity'[12] of central bankers which informs the work of the Monetary Committee and the European Monetary Institute. For example, although based on similar concepts, the Italian system is very different from the French and the Corte dei conti has a different role from the Cour des Comptes. Until recently, the Italian

---

[5] Article 248 EC (*Article 188c(1)*).

[6] The ECA is mentioned, along with the other institutions, in Article 5 TEU and Article 230 EC (judicial review); Article 248 on the ECA now provides that the Statement of Assurance shall be published in the Official Journal; express provision is made for the ECA to report on any cases of irregularity; and the ECA's rights of access are spelt out; Article 276 on budgetary discharge to the Commission now requires the Parliament to consider also the Statement of Assurance. See, further, Articles 274 and 280.

[7] We owe this point to Sabino Cassese.	[8] See, in general, Ch. 4.

[9] See Ch. 2 and in particular, *Government Accounting: a guide on accounting and financial procedures for the use of government departments*, (2 vols., loose leaf) (London: HMSO, 1989 and seven amendments 1989–97). This contrasts with, for example, Germany, where financial control and accounting are governed by a comprehensive body of statute law.

[10] See, generally, Keemer, P., 'State Audit in Western Europe: A Comparative Study', M. Phil. thesis, (University of Bath, 1985).

[11] The main bodies are INTOSAI (the International Organization of Supreme Audit Institutions) and EUROSAI (the European Organization of Supreme Audit Institutions). There is also a Contact Committee of Heads of National Audit Bodies in the EU, of which the President of the Court is also a member.

[12] See Kees, A., 'The Monetary Committee as a promoter of European integration', in Bakker, A. F. P., et al., eds., *Monetary Stability through International Co-operation: essays in honour of André Szász*, (Dordrecht: Kluwer, 1994).

Court had responsibility for *ex ante* control over some five million administrative acts each year, as well as conducting an *ex post* audit of accounts. None of its work took into account *vfm* considerations.[13] The work of the French Court, on the other hand, is exclusively *ex post* and includes a concern for the quality of financial management.[14] It is also important to recognize that the ECA does not have the judicial functions that its name suggests and which are often exercised by Courts of Accounts, or by bodies closely associated with them such as the French *Cour de discipline budgétaire et financière*.

We argue in this chapter that the Court's real contribution to the proper use of Community resources is more limited than its status as an 'institution' would suggest. The limitations on its role result from the broader institutional framework of which it is part and from internal weaknesses. It operates in an environment of ill-defined and complex patterns of accountability, in which it is struggling to define clearly the scope and purpose of its own activities and its relationship to other actors in the Community. The Chapter begins with a brief overview of the budgetary and financial control processes of the Community. It then examines the structure, powers and duties of the Court and its relationships with its various audiences.

BUDGETARY AND FINANCIAL PROCEDURES IN THE COMMUNITY

The procedures for establishing and implementing the Community budget and for presenting and auditing accounts are laid down by the EC Treaty,[15] the Financial Regulation (FR);[16] and a Commission Regulation (CR)[17] made under powers delegated by the FR.[18]

DG XIX of the Commission is responsible for preparing the Commission's budget proposal following in bilateral discussions with the

---

[13] See Cassese, S., ed., *I Controlli nella Pubblica Amministrazione*, (Milan: il Mulino, 1993). For the changes to the Court's role made by Law n. 20/1994 (14 January 1994) see Perez, R., 'Il nuovo sistema dei controlli sulla spesa pubblica e il ruolo della Corte dei conti' in Banca d'Italia, *Nuovo sistema di Controlli sulla Spesa Pubblica*, Atti del convegno tenuto a Perugia il 9–10 giugno 1994.

[14] See Raynaud, J., *La Cour des Comptes*, Presses Universitaires de France, 'Que sais-je?', 1980.

[15] Part Five, Title II.

[16] Financial Regulation of 21 December 1977, as amended. A consolidation of the Financial Regulation and amendments was published at OJ C80 1991. For the latest amendment (Regulation 2730/94) see OJ L 293/7 1994.

[17] Commission Regulation 3418/93, OJ L 315 1993.

[18] See, generally, Strasser, D., *The Finances of Europe*, (Luxembourg: Office for Official Publications of the EC, 3rd English edition, 1992); Henderson, R., *European Finance*, (London: McGraw-Hill, 1993); Laffan, B., *Finances of the European Union*, (London: MacMillan, 1997).

spending directorates-general. The Commission's preliminary draft goes to the Council which establishes the draft budget, acting by a qualified majority. The draft budget is placed before Parliament, which can make amendments. It then returns to the Council. Approximately half the budget is spent on 'compulsory expenditure' (mostly agriculture) and in the event of disagreement between the Council and Parliament, the former's view prevails. Parliament has the last word only in respect of 'non-compulsory' expenditure.

A key feature of Community public finance is that, despite the Commission's formal responsibility for implementation of the budget,[19] some 80 per cent of expenditure is actually disbursed by national administrations to its final recipients. Budgetary authority in the Community is shared between the Council and Parliament.[20] The Council and the Parliament examine the reports of the ECA as part of the procedure by which the Parliament gives 'discharge' to the Commission in respect of budget implementation (see below).

The system of financial control established by the FR is based on a separation between *ordonnateur, comptable* and *contrôleur financier*.[21] Each institution has the function of ordonnateur. The ordonnateur's function as regards revenue is to determine the sums due and to issue an order for the amount to be recovered. As regards expenditure, the ordonnateur makes financial commitments and orders payments. The distinction between commitments and payments is of fundamental importance in the Community financial system. In Britain, parliamentary appropriations relate only to payments. The Community budget, however, contains appropriations both for commitments and for the actual payments that eventually result from the commitments.[22] Financial control, accounting and audit procedures relate to both types of appropriation. The comptable recovers revenue that has been checked as being due by the ordonnateur and makes payments which have been properly committed and subsequently authorized by the ordonnateur.

Each recovery of revenue, commitment of expenditure and payment order requires the prior approval (*visa préalable*) of the contrôleur financier. The FR provides that each institution shall appoint a contrôleur

---

[19] Article 274 EC (*Article 205*). Each of the other Community institutions implements its own budget, under powers conferred by the Commission (Article 22(2) FR). The sums involved are relatively small compared to those handled by the Commission itself.

[20] Article 272 EC (*Article 203*). The Community has no power to borrow to finance its current expenditure, so the budget must balance.

[21] The three separate roles were recognized by the TEU: Article 279c EC (*Article 209(c)*). See generally Cogliandro, G., 'La responsabilité des fonctionnaires chargés de la gestion des deniers publics dans l'union européene', in Modeen, T., ed., *La responsabilité des fonctionnaires*, (Brussels: International Institute of Administrative Sciences, 1995).

[22] The German and Italian budget systems are similar.

financier to be responsible for monitoring, the commitment and authorization of expenditure and the establishment and collection of revenue.[23] The contrôleur of an institution is expressly required to be 'completely independent' in carrying out his duties under the FR. [24]

The Commission's contrôleur financier is the director general of DG XX. The FR's requirement of independence puts him in a different position from other directors general. In relation to his functions as contrôleur (as opposed to his administrative role in the Directorate-General) he is subject to instructions neither from the Commissioner for financial control, nor from the Commission as a whole. Furthermore, he has in practice a much higher degree of security of employment than other directors general.[25] The FR allows each institution to appoint one or more assistant contrôleurs.[26] Unlike the European Parliament, the Commission has never appointed such assistants, though it has appointed a deputy contrôleur. The 160 staff of DG XX who deal with the 60,000 or so commitments and 300,000 payment approvals each year act in the name of the director general, although they are referred to informally as 'controllers'.

Where the criteria set out in the FR are not met,[27] the contrôleur has a discretion (not a duty) to withhold the *visa*. If the visa is refused, a written statement of reasons must be given and the institution notified accordingly.[28] Unless the refusal is because appropriations are not available (because the budget line in question has already been exhausted), the institution can overrule the contrôleur.[29] If it does so, reasons must again be given and the Council, Parliament and the ECA must be informed. A basic principle of this *ex ante* control, therefore, is that the institution has the final executive authority over the spending of budgeted amounts. The requirement of prior control is primarily intended to serve an internal management function, enabling the institution as a whole to control the individuals and units within it. It also has an external political function: if the contrôleur refuses a visa, he can only be overruled openly and transparently.

---

[23] Articles 24, 37 and 47 FR; Article 34 CR.   [24] Article 39 CR.

[25] See Article 24 FR, Title V CR. When the ECA appointed their contrôleur financier only for a two-year period there was criticism from the Parliament that this undermined his independence.

[26] Article 24(a) FR and Article 35 CR.

[27] Article 38 FR, for example, deals with commitments and requires the contrôleur to establish that: (a) the expenditure has been charged to the correct item in the budget; (b) the appropriations are available; (c) the expenditure is in order and conforms to the relevant provisions; (d) the principles of sound financial management referred to in Article 2 [*of the FR*] have been applied.

[28] Article 39 FR.

[29] While the ordonnateur's role may be delegated according to the institution's own internal rules of procedure, the decision to overrule the contrôleur financier's refusal of a visa cannot be delegated.

In practice, it is rare for the *visa* to be refused for commitments and almost unknown for payments. There is considerable support in the Commission for the idea of amending the FR so that the contrôleur's role in relation to payments and commitments could be based on *ex post* sampling and an audit of systems. Indeed, since 1996, DG XX has been using *ex ante* sampling techniques in relation to payments.[30] However, many people still regard the prior control of *commitments* as an important safeguard.

In evaluating the prior control of commitments, it would be a mistake to look only at the number of refusals of the visa. More frequent than a formal refusal is that when the contrôleur raises a query the dossier is withdrawn and not subsequently re-presented. Furthermore, the system is not formalistic. If the requirements of the FR are not met by the dossier as presented, the 'controller' will offer positive advice as to what steps are necessary to enable the *visa* to be given. A decision to refuse a *visa* is a major step, with potential political significance. It can only be made personally by the *contrôleur financier* or, in his absence, his deputy.

However, prior control of commitments is focused exclusively on legality and regularity. The system was not designed to promote *vfm* and the ECA has argued that it has the opposite effect, by encouraging an institutional culture in which those who make spending decisions regard the visa of the contrôleur as absolving them from further responsibility. The contrôleur's assessment of whether expenditure is regular and legal is supposed to take into account the 'principles of sound financial management'.[31] Since 1990, these have included 'cost-effectiveness', a concept which is closely related to the idea of *vfm*. It would be unrealistic, however, for the dossier accompanying requests for a *visa* to contain a piece of paper specifically relating to cost-effectiveness. Instead, the requirement for the contrôleur financier to take into account issues of cost-effectiveness is dealt with through internal audit.

Internal Audit

The Court has frequently criticized the absence of an effective internal audit function in the Commission. In response, the Commission has given the task of internal audit to the contrôleur financier.[32] The work is carried out by a specific unit in DG XX, whose annual work programme

---

[30] See Annex 1 of the unpublished Memorandum to the Commission from M. Gradin, in agreement with the President, 6 November 1996 (see, further, below).

[31] *Supra*, n. 27.

[32] The relevant Commission decision, made in 1990, is unpublished.

is approved by the Commission as a whole.[33] The intention is that between four and six Directorates-General will be examined each year. Internal audit reports are issued in the name of the contrôleur,[34] and they can be made available to the Parliament and the ECA, on request.

THE COURT OF AUDITORS

The system of financial control described above is essentially self-contained. Its functioning is in no way dependent on the work of the ECA. In this respect the ECAs' position may be contrasted with that of the NAO in Britain. The NAO and the PAC complement the system of Treasury control over spending departments. Questioning and criticism at PAC hearings, based on NAO reports, is an important aspect of the accountability of the executive to Parliament. But it is not just that. It also provides a kind of informal sanction which supports the system of Treasury control of spending departments. In contrast, the ECA plays no direct role in the enforcement of the obligations of ordonnateurs, comptables and contrôleurs financiers.

The ECA was established in 1977,[35] replacing the Audit Board for which the original Treaty of Rome provided. The role of the Audit Board was recognized to be marginal to the main business of financial control.[36] Its replacement by the ECA was not part of a general reform of the system of financial control. It was a gesture of appeasement to the Parliament, to console it for the limited extension of its budgetary powers in the second budgetary treaty.[37] This meant that the new Court did not have a ready-made role to play in the Community institutional system. Furthermore, it was burdened with a number of competing sets of expectations about its functions, derived from doubtful analogies with different national institutions. In dealing with this unfavourable external environment, the Court has not been helped by its own structure and organization.

[33] The Commission has a further level of internal control in the form of an Inspectorate General of Services whose main function is to examine and evaluate the appropriateness of staffing levels in different parts of the Commission. It also examines the performance of the Commission, covering aspects of economy, efficiency and effectiveness. This includes an evaluation of the impact of Community legislation and the extent to which it has met the objectives of Community policy: see Cogliandro, *supra*, n. 21.

[34] Article 40 CR.

[35] Treaty of Brussels 1975, amending the then Articles 206 EC, 180 Euratom, and 78 ECSC.

[36] For instance, its rules provided for it to meet not more than once every two months and membership was effectively part-time.

[37] This analysis is based on a contemporary assessment in DG XIX historical documentation.

Membership of the Court

The Court consists of fifteen members, one from each State.[38] The Treaty requires that the independence of members 'must be beyond doubt' and members 'shall neither seek nor take instructions from any government or from any other body'.[39] On appointment, members give a public undertaking before the Court of Justice that they will act independently.[40] Other than for reasons of retirement, death or resignation, members can be removed from office only by the Court of Justice, acting on an application from the ECA itself.[41]

Members are appointed for a renewable term of six years, by unanimous decision of the Council. Appointments are staggered to ensure continuity; a third of the members are replaced at any one time. The Parliament is consulted about proposed members but has no right of veto and appointments have sometimes gone ahead despite a negative opinion.[42] A Parliamentary resolution outlines the procedures and criteria it uses in giving its opinion.[43] The resolution reflects the view that states have in the past nominated unsuitable candidates and that the Council has made appointments without always having due regard to the professional competence and independence of members that are required by the Treaty. The role of the Council, combined with the convention of one member per state, effectively places the power of appointment in the hands of each state. Members are also dependent on the support of their state to ensure reappointment.

The Court elects its own President for a term of three years. The President distributes portfolios and so the election ensures lively internal Court politics, with members interested in particular portfolios. An extra dimension is added by the fact that the election of the President usually comes either just before, or just after, a change in membership of the Court. In principle, however, members act independently of their government in voting for the President.

The Structure of the Court

The President is the public face of the Court and, internally, a key figure in the organization of its work. The Court is a collegiate body and

---

[38] It is not a Treaty requirement that there should be a member of the Court for each member state, but in practice this has been the case.

[39] Article 247 EC (*Article 188b*).

[40] See House of Lords, Select Committee on the European Communities, *Financial Control and Fraud in the Community*, HL 75, 1993–94, (hereinafter HL 75, 1993–94) evidence from A. J. Wiggins, current British Member of the Court.

[41] Article 247(6) EC (*Article 188b(6)*).

[42] EP 21 Nov. 1989; the Parliament also gave a negative opinion on a candidate in 1993.

[43] PE 202.258/fin A3-0345/92 (OJ C 337/51 1992) and more recently, PE 210.658/fin A4-0001/95.

reports are issued in the name of the Court as a whole.[44] However, each member is responsible for a specific area of Community activity. These 'portfolios' are distributed by the President, who also sets the agenda for plenary meetings and chairs the annual discussion of the Court's work programme, when members put forward plans for their areas of responsibility.

In theory, the fact that the Court as a whole must agree the work programme limits the autonomy of members. In practice, it is difficult for members to know enough about other areas of specialization to challenge a proposed programme, even assuming that they had any incentive to do so. These factors make it difficult to achieve a systematic and consistent approach. To mitigate the problem, members meet in five smaller audit groups to plan and review work in detail before it is agreed by the Court as a whole.[45] A system of *contre-rapporteurs* introduced in the mid-1990s for three of the groups, whereby proposals put forward by one member were the subject of a written opinion by another, operated only for one annual report.[46] It is unclear why this system was not continued.

The structure of the Court is rather top-heavy, with the result that members tend to get involved in work that should be delegated. There are some 500 staff in all. Each of the fifteen members has a five-person *cabinet*. There are some 175 staff to deal with administration, information technology and translation, leaving only 250 or so people to do the business of audit. They are divided relatively evenly between the members of the Court, regardless of the volume of work or the perceived risks to Community funds in different areas of responsibility. Furthermore, the collegiate structure of the Court encourages members to interpret their individual roles in the light of the very different national understandings of the role of audit.[47] As noted above, there is no common European culture of financial control, but rather a number of overlapping and competing national traditions, with correspondingly different interpretations of what the role of an external audit body should be.

Accountability

The Court receives regular feedback from the Commission and the European Parliament. The UK House of Lords Select Committee on the

---

[44] The collegiate structure was inherited from the Court's predecessor, the Audit Board, whose powers were required by the FR to be exercised collectively.

[45] Audit Groups I, II and III have 3–5 members and are organized to deal with different areas of Community activity. The ADAR group administers the work of the Court, coordinating the annual report and other reports as well as dealing with the programme of work. The DAS group deals with the Statement of Assurance.

[46] *Décisions de la Cour relatives aux contre-rapporteurs*, 10.11.94 (DEC 168/94 Final (PV)).

[47] See, for example, HL 75, 1993–94, evidence of Jo Carey, a former Member of the Court.

European Community has also conducted ad hoc inquiries into its work. Since 1995, the NAO has reported on the ECA's annual report and DAS.[48] However, there is no systematic external evaluation of the Court's performance. Guarding the guardians themselves is a perennial problem. Whilst it is clearly desirable that the Court should have its performance scrutinized, its independence demands that it be free to choose its own methods and work programme.[49] The Court itself recognizes the need for transparency and, since 1987, its internal management accounts have been examined by a private auditor.[50] This does not, however, provide any evaluation of the Court's performance.[51] The most fundamental problem of accountability stems from the absence of a consensus about the scope and purpose of the Court's activities. If there is no agreement about what the Court is supposed to do, how can the outcomes of its activity be assessed in any meaningful way?

THE WORK OF THE COURT

The Court's principal mandate under the Treaty is to examine 'whether all revenue has been received and all expenditure incurred in a lawful and regular manner and whether the financial management has been sound'.[52] The second part of this requirement is interpreted to refer broadly to *vfm* considerations. There was some argument as to whether the EC Treaty, before the Maastricht amendments, implied a duty to examine the accuracy of the accounts as a whole. The Court's interpretation was that it did not. However, the Treaty now explicitly requires the Court to provide a statement of assurance as to the reliability of the accounts of the Community and the legality and regularity of the underlying transactions.[53] Not all members of the Court welcomed the 'DAS'[54] provision and the British government claims credit for ensuring that it was included in the TEU.

---

[48] See, for example, NAO Report, HC 332, 1996–97. The C&AG also reported on the Court's 1994 report and DAS in a note to the PAC in February 1996; the PAC subsequently published their own report: see PAC, Tenth Report, 1995–96.

[49] See INTOSAI, *Auditing Standards*, (June 1989), para. 52.

[50] Until 1992, the chairman of the Budgetary Control Committee (see below) was notified of the auditor's reports. Since that date, the reports have been published in the Official Journal: see, for example, OJ No C 299/6 1994.

[51] See also Pollitt, C., and Summa, H., 'Reflective Watchdogs? How Supreme Audit Institutions account for themselves', 75 (1997) *Public Administration* 313.

[52] Article 248(2) EC *(Article 188c(2))*. The Court may also submit observations at any time and deliver opinions at the request of one of the other institutions (Article 248(4) EC *(Article 188c(4))*. It must also be consulted during the legislative process for making Financial Regulations under Article 279 EC *(Article 209)*.

[53] Article 248(1) EC *(Article 188c(1))*.   [54] From the French, *Déclaration d'Assurance*.

Financial Audit

To fulfil its obligations under the pre-DAS provision, the Court relied on a systems-based audit, examining different areas of revenue and expenditure over a four-year cycle.[55] It also carried out relatively detailed audits of complete sections of budgetary management and accounting, either as a financial audit, or as part of a *vfm* study. Coverage was not comprehensive and, in principle, the Court focused its effort on areas that were felt to require special attention.[56]

The first DAS relating to the 1994 accounts, was reported on in November 1995. It was published at the same time as the Court's annual report and was accompanied by a special report explaining the basis for the opinion the Court had reached. In 1997, the DAS was incorporated in the annual report and it seems likely that will be the case in future.[57] The DAS requirement applies to all the Community accounts (for commitments, payments, receipts and the balance sheet) and the underlying transactions on which they are based. Of the various accounts, those for payments are the most problematic, since the Court has decided that it needs to audit expenditure down to the level of the final recipient of the Community spending. The necessary information to enable this to be done is frequently not available in the Commission because, as already noted, most of the budget is finally disbursed by national administrations.

The Court has decided to fulfil the DAS requirement in relation to underlying transactions (commitments and payments) by using a method known as 'monetary unit sampling'. For the 1994–95 accounts, this involved taking individual units of account as the population and then taking a sample of about 600 so-called 'hits' for payments and another 600 or so hits for commitments. The methodology for DAS sampling is still experimental and the Court has established a panel of experts to advise on the sampling technique. In 1996–97, the sample size was reduced to 400 hits for payments and 300 for commitments. The transactions of which the 'hit' units form part are audited down to the level of the final beneficiary, a judgment is made about the significance of any errors detected and the result from the sample is then extrapolated to the whole budget. The Court's aim is to be able to say with 95 per cent certainty that error in the execution of the total budget is no more than 1 per cent. In theory, when it cannot do this, it qualifies its opinion on the reliability of the accounts and the legality and regularity of the underlying transactions.

---

[55] See further Kok, *supra*, n. 2.

[56] HL 75, 1993–94, evidence of A. J. Wiggins, current Member of the Court and H. Rozema, Head of Division, FEOGA-Garantie.

[57] It would appear that the separate publication for the first two years of the DAS was a result of timing difficulties.

There is an ongoing dialogue between the Commission and Court concerning the methodology and the practicalities of DAS. The Court's explanation of how it has reached its DAS audit opinion takes the form of a report, subject to the contradictory procedure (see below). The substantive audit opinion is not submitted to this procedure by the ECA.

Co-operation with National Audit Institutions

The Treaty does not specify that the Court must itself do all the DAS audit work and it has had discussions with the national audit institutions (NAIs) of the member states about the possibilities of co-operation. This would clearly be desirable given the high proportion of Community expenditure that is managed at a national level. In relation to the Court's own audit work, the Treaty provides for 'on the spot' audits in the states to be conducted in liaison with the NAIs.[58] Each NAI has a liaison officer, responsible for assisting the Court in arranging on the spot audits. The liaison officer's role limits the Court's ability to visit a member state in that a visitation must be arranged through the NAI. This also provides the opportunity for the NAI to participate in the audit, though many choose not to do so.

In the context of DAS, however, the question is whether the Court can make use of audit work done by the NAIs themselves. One problem in doing so is the differences that exist in the status and powers of NAIs. Some do not have the necessary rights of access in their own right; others are constitutionally part of the executive branch of government.[59] Some are unwilling to carry out work outside their normal remit, or at any rate not without payment. More fundamentally, it is hard to see how the DAS could be justified by adding together the results of work based on very different national approaches to the purpose and concepts of audit. In any event, some NAIs regard it as unacceptable that the Court should even try to do so, since this would involve checking the quality of their work. There is also an important difference of perspective in that what the Court views as expenditure, NAIs view as revenue. The Court has acknowledged that collaboration with NAIs is unlikely to be a significant input into the DAS for the next few years. A possible exception is in the cases where the NAI performs the function of 'certifying body', as agent for the Commission, in relation to the clearance of the accounts of paying agencies in relation to EAGGF guarantee expenditure.[60]

[58] Article 188c(3) EC (*Article 248(3)*).

[59] As noted in Ch. 6, in Sweden and Finland, for instance, the main external audit body is constitutionally part of the Ministry of Finance, although they claim to meet the INTOSAI standard for independence.

[60] As part of the Commission's internal controls, 'certifying agencies' are appointed in each member state, to provide an opinion on the different paying agencies accounts and to report on the legality and regularity of the payments. A certifying agency could be a

The Significance of the DAS

The DAS is supposed to be about regularity and legality, rather than *vfm*, but otherwise the Treaty is silent about its form and purpose. As currently put into effect, it is hard to see the DAS as a major step forward in improving the management of Community finances, or the effectiveness of the Court. The requirement to provide an assurance can, of course, do nothing directly to improve the quality of financial control, or the reliability of the Community's accounts (the possible indirect effect is considered below). The proponents of DAS appear to have had a number of objectives in mind, including:

(1) providing a basis for the Parliament to make a global judgment about the work of the Commission in the discharge process;
(2) providing a lever for the Court to use in getting better access to information; and
(3) putting pressure on the Court to adopt a more coherent approach to its work.

The role of the DAS in the discharge procedure (see below) is unclear. It has probably been an important factor in the Court obtaining access to the results of the Commission's internal audit and in a revision of the Commission's rules about access more generally (see below). The DAS process has also put pressure on the Court to reassess its own methods and to devise a corporate approach, but it has not yet led to a more rational allocation of its resources. Unlike the position in the UK or Sweden, for example, there is no formal division of staff at the ECA as financial or *vfm* auditors. The staff who perform the DAS work are assigned to the different divisions of the ECA and do not operate from a central unit. Nor will the DAS help the Court to define the scope and purpose of its own role in relation to the other institutions (see, further, below).

The indirect impact of DAS will depend on how it is received by the various audiences for the Court's work. Here, there is a considerable risk of a gap between what the Court thinks the DAS means and what others may understand it to mean.[61] This is especially so in relation to fraud. The DAS is not intended to detect or measure the extent of fraud. However, there is a danger that it will be misinterpreted. Euro-fraud is big news and politically sensitive. In recent years, the Court has pursued a high-profile strategy, seeking to mobilize public opinion in favour of

private firm of auditors, or part of a ministry of finance, or an NAI, or part thereof. Where an NAI does this work, it is in its capacity as agent for the Commission and not as an NAI per se. In the UK, the NAO won a three-year contract to perform this certifying task. See Council Regulation 1663/95, as amended, and the NAO Annual Reports for 1995 and 1996.

[61] The 'expectations gap' has been extensively analysed in relation to private sector audit, see Power, M., *The Audit Explosion*, (London: Demos, 1994).

the reforms it has advocated. Inevitably, this has been reported in terms of fraud, even where the Court's actual words may not have justified this.[62] Opportunities for fraud are best minimized by careful design of the programmes in question and by appropriate processes of financial control, accounting and internal audit. The primary responsibility for preventing and detecting fraud rests with management. External audit may aid management by advising on weaknesses in processes and identifying risks which might lead to problems and, as such, external audit is a deterrent to fraud. So, although external audit is an effective way of evaluating the capacity of such processes to prevent and detect fraud, it is doubtful whether it is useful in combating fraud directly.

VFM Audit

VFM audit can be unpopular.[63] Assessing 'effectiveness' means asking whether policy objectives are being achieved. Economy and efficiency also depend on the existence of clearly defined and coherent objectives. The less success the auditee has in defining and achieving his objectives, the more difficult it is for the auditor to draw a clear line between questioning the merits of policy objectives and assessing whether *vfm* has been achieved in the pursuit of those objectives.[64] The legitimacy of the public sector auditor is thus likely to be most precarious precisely when his function is most important.

The Court's 'Stuttgart report', produced in 1983 at the request of the Council, identified significant failings in Community policies and legislation.[65] The report was not well received by the Commission, which regarded the Court as trespassing into areas that are not properly its concern. More generally, the Commission has tended to resist the Court's increasing focus on *vfm* issues, claiming that these raise policy questions which are for the Commission and Council. Its view has been that the Court should be concerned primarily with regularity and legality.

The Court's difficulties in pursuing *vfm* audit have two main origins. First, *vfm* audit is not accepted in all states as a legitimate part of the work of an external audit body. The idea that the proper role of the auditor

---

[62] Contrast for example the title and the content of Kok, C., 'The fight against Euro-fraud', December 1994, *European Brief*, 30–1. The Court's Report to the 'Reflection Group' on the operation of the Treaty on European Union in May 1995 also draws attention to the Court's role in the fight against fraud.

[63] See, for example, the ECA's Special Report of the EU Administration in Mostar, OJ C287/1, 1996.

[64] Cf. National Audit Act 1983, s.6; see, further, Ch. 5.

[65] *Report in response to the conclusions of the European Council of 18 June 1983*, OJ C287/1 1983. See also Kok, *supra*, n. 2 and House of Lords, Select Committee on the European Community, *The Court of Auditors*, HL 102, 1986–87.